DOUBLED UP

Published by Princeton University Press
41 William Street, Princeton, New Jersey 08540
99 Banbury Road, Oxford OX2 6JX

press.princeton.edu

Library of Congress Cataloging-in-Publication Data

Names: Harvey, Hope, author.
Title: Doubled up : shared households and the precarious lives of families / Hope Harvey.
Description: Princeton, New Jersey : Princeton University Press, [2025] | Includes bibliographical references and index.
Identifiers: LCCN 2024043558 (print) | LCCN 2024043559 (ebook) | ISBN 9780691247021 (hardback) | ISBN 9780691247045 (ebook)
Subjects: LCSH: Households. | Families. | Social history.
Classification: LCC HB820 .H36 2025 (print) | LCC HB820 (ebook) | DDC 306—dc23/eng/20241207
LC record available at https://lccn.loc.gov/2024043558
LC ebook record available at https://lccn.loc.gov/2024043559

British Library Cataloging-in-Publication Data is available

Editorial: Rachael Levay and Erik Beranek
Production Editorial: Ali Parrington
Jacket Design: Katie Osborne
Production: Erin Suydam
Publicity: Tyler Hubbert and Kathryn Stevens
Copyeditor: Cynthia Buck

Jacket image: Valentyna Yeltsova / iStock

This book has been composed in Arno

Printed in the United States of America

10 9 8 7 6 5 4 3 2 1

Doubled Up

SHARED HOUSEHOLDS
AND THE PRECARIOUS LIVES
OF FAMILIES

HOPE HARVEY

PRINCETON UNIVERSITY PRESS
PRINCETON & OXFORD

CONTENTS

The Rise of Doubled-Up Households

ISA'S FIRST PREGNANCY, at age nineteen, was unplanned.[1] She was still living in her mother's home, but she and her partner of three years planned to find a home of their own and raise their daughter together. This plan never materialized. After a serious accident left her partner injured and depressed, she watched helplessly as he began drinking. Ultimately, he landed in jail when their daughter was just six months old. As a young, newly single parent, Isa felt she "had to step it up." She worked hard to earn her high school degree, then pursued higher education, trying to find a fulfilling career that would provide a stable income for her family.

By the time I met her, Isa was twenty-nine years old and had three daughters, ages nine, five, and one. She was busy finishing cosmetology school, cultivating a clientele for the massage and hair services she provided in her home, and attending hair and makeup shows to build her network in the hopes of landing a position in a salon. Although she was working toward her career goals, her income was extremely limited. She received regular child support payments for just one of her three daughters, and those payments, along with the money she earned from hair and massage clients, brought her income to just under $6,000 that year. She received about $400 a month in food stamps but no other public assistance. Unable to afford housing of her own and without adequate public assistance, Isa relied on the private safety net: she and her daughters lived in her mother's single-family home in Dallas.

A large and growing number of American families like Isa's live "doubled up" in households shared with extended family or friends. As of 2018, more than eleven million children in the United States—that is, over 15 percent—lived with a parent in a household they shared with an adult extended family member or nonrelative.[2] These numbers reflect a cascade of structural forces and changes that have left many families, particularly low- to moderate-income families, in need of private safety net support from extended family and friends. Parents like Isa struggle to raise their children while navigating an increasingly unaffordable housing market, an often precarious labor market with few protections against economic instability, and a severe shortage of affordable quality childcare. In each of these areas, the public safety net falls far short of meeting families' needs, and parents are largely left to cobble to-gether solutions of their own. For families like Isa's, doubling up is one make-shift response to these challenges—though, as this book will show, it is typi-cally an imperfect and insufficient solution to a family's needs.

The housing market has largely left behind lower-income families like Isa's. In the face of rapidly rising housing costs, affordable housing for low-income families is in short supply.[3] For every one hundred renter households with incomes below 30 percent of area median income, there are just thirty-six available and affordable rental units.[4] Moreover, the impacts of rising housing costs extend far beyond very low-income households. The rental market is increasingly focused on high-end renters, leaving even moderate-income fami-lies with fewer rental options and at growing risk of housing unaffordability.[5] In Texas, where Isa and her daughters lived, a family needs an income of $57,980 a year—more than a majority of renter households earn—to afford even a modest two-bedroom rental.[6] Moreover, home prices have contin-ued to climb alongside rents, leaving many would-be homebuyers unable to afford a down payment or to qualify for a loan. As of 2022, 92 percent of renter households were unable to afford the down payment on a median-priced home without help from family or other sources.[7]

An insecure and uncertain labor market poses additional challenges for families like Isa's and amplifies the housing challenges they face. In recent decades, much of the burden of managing economic risk has shifted from the government and employers to individuals and families, and many institutions that traditionally supported economic security and mobility have deterio-rated, leaving families reliant on private safety nets to fill in the gaps.[8] Employ-ment has become more insecure and risky, with rising rates of nonstandard employment, decreasing employment stability, and declines in access to security-enhancing benefits like living wages, pension plans, and employer-subsidized health insurance.[9] Likewise, relative to other wealthy nations, the United States provides little protection to workers who face employment instability, illness, or caretaking needs. Low-wage workers like Isa are particularly disadvantaged in this area.[10]

Compounding these challenges, the childcare that facilitates stable employment, especially for mothers, is increasingly unaffordable and difficult to find.[11] If Isa had not had her mother to help look after her daughters, she would have struggled to afford childcare on the private market; in her home state of Texas, the annual average cost of childcare for just one of her three children was more than she earned in a year.[12] The vast majority of families who are eligible for childcare subsidies do not receive them, and even those families who are lucky enough to receive them face limited provider options and often still find high-quality care unaffordable.[13] Moreover, given high costs and a limited supply of childcare providers, securing affordable, quality childcare is now challenging for parents across the income distribution, not just very low-income parents like Isa.[14]

Two-parent families can share child-rearing responsibilities, and by pooling risk and income, they may be better able to weather the precarity of the modern labor market compared to lone parents.[15] Yet concurrent shifts in family structure have left many parents—like Isa, after her partner was incarcerated—raising children alone. The share of children living with two coresident parents declined from the 1960s before plateauing around 70 percent from the 1990s to today.[16] Many children, like Isa's daughters, will live with an unpartnered parent for some or all of their childhood. Because the United States has a distinctly unsupportive policy environment for single parents compared to other high-income countries, families like Isa's are particularly vulnerable to the challenges of precarious work, unaffordable housing, and insufficient childcare support.[17]

Given the racialized and gendered nature of both the housing market and the labor market, these multiple sources of precarity are further amplified for families of color and for single mothers. Disproportionately concentrated in lower-wage jobs with fewer protections, women and workers of color like Isa are left at greater risk of poverty and economic instability.[18] Historic and ongoing racism has limited homeownership opportunities and left many families of color in lower-quality housing and disadvantaged neighborhoods.[19] Relatedly, families of color are more likely to experience unstable and unaffordable housing than their White counterparts.[20] Unmarried mothers likewise continue to have low rates of homeownership and face a heightened risk of eviction and housing unaffordability.[21]

The public safety net in the United States provides meager support to families facing housing and economic needs. Housing assistance for lower-income households can lower rent costs and provide a lifeline for families.[22] Yet rental assistance is not an entitlement program, and Isa's was just one of the 14.2 million households eligible for such assistance that do not receive it.[23] Moreover, the number of households in need of federal housing assistance is growing far more quickly than the number of households receiving this assistance.[24] Assistance with utility bills, another important housing cost, is limited as well; just 20 percent of households eligible for the Low Income Home Energy Assistance Program (LIHEAP) receive this assistance each year.[25]

The United States also provides little cash aid that families could use to help pay for housing, utilities, and other necessities. Today's cash assistance safety net is targeted primarily at working poor families, leaving little cash support for parents who lack regular formal employment.[26] Working poor families have access to the Earned Income Tax Credit (EITC), the largest means-tested cash assistance program today. Families receive the EITC annually as a tax refund, and many families use some of this payment to pay rent for the month and to pay off debt, such as to landlords and utility companies. Yet the annual payment is not well designed to cover regular monthly expenses, like housing costs, throughout the year.[27]

The precarity of modern life, especially in a context of limited public supports, has left families highly reliant on private safety nets like doubling up.[28] In this way, private safety nets serve as a substitute—though an imperfect one, as this book will demonstrate—for a robust welfare state. Doubling up is now a standard childhood experience; over two in five children live in a doubled-up household at some point during childhood.[29] What does it mean that so many families with children, like Isa's, now rely on others and provide support themselves by sharing a household? To answer this question, I spoke with parents to gain an in-depth understanding of their experiences doubling up. I interviewed parents like Isa who doubled up as "guests" in someone else's home, as well as "host" parents who had a home of their own that they shared with an additional adult or family.[30] With these data, this book answers three questions that are central to understanding what doubling up means for families with children: What circumstances and motivations lead parents to form doubled-up households? How does living in a doubled-up household shape their daily lives? And how do families fare after these arrangements dissolve?

For the parents I met, doubling up provided a vital safety net. Many parents doubled up in the home of an extended family member or a friend in response to a sudden housing crisis—from eviction to housing disrepair to the breakup of a romantic relationship. Other parents, like Isa, had not experienced a housing crisis, but they probably would have if they had not been doubled up. Even some moderate-income families gained support by moving in with friends or family. Although these families were often not in crisis, their aspirations for the future—like owning a home or simply renting an affordable unit in a neighborhood near extended family—were also constricted by high housing costs.

Doubled-up households provided a multifaceted safety net. Isa and her daughters lived comfortably in the large single-family home owned by her mother, Antonia. The home was located in a neighborhood that Isa described as not her ideal, but calm. Rather than paying a set amount in rent and utilities each month, she gave Antonia what she could afford—$600 when she was working full-time as an administrative assistant, but only $200 in recent months, as she was "trying to build myself up again and get on my feet." Her mother also provided reliable childcare for her three daughters, enabling Isa to work and to pursue higher education—first in massage therapy, then court reporting, and finally cosmetology, where she found her passion and an outlet for her artistic instincts.

Although we typically think of families that host additional adults or families in their home as the support *providers* in doubled-up households, many hosts in my sample needed the economic, care, and emotional support that guests could provide. While living with Isa, Antonia benefited from her daughter's monetary rent payments, but also from her companionship and help with day-to-day tasks. In this way, doubling up was a support strategy for vulnerable hosts as well as guests. As Isa described her household, "It's just something temporary, but we're helping each other out, so that's a good thing."

Yet the support that parents both sought and provided by doubling up came at a high cost, as the complicated dynamics of sharing a home could foster conflict, stress, and uncertainty. Doubling up often limited parents' ability to enact their ideals of family life. Compared to nuclear family households, doubled-up households had few taken-for-granted norms that guided household functioning; household members had to resolve basic questions about how the shared household should function and how residents should relate to one another, and they often disagreed about how to do so. For instance,

Isa disliked her mother's seemingly constant surveillance; even a minor change in her usual routine, she said, caused her mother to "check on me like I'm a little girl." Parents like Isa who lived doubled up as guests in someone else's home typically entered such negotiations with less household authority than their host.

Moreover, negotiations over roles and household functioning had far-reaching ramifications for family life. Antonia took an active role in raising her three granddaughters—often too active for Isa's taste (as I show in chapter 6), and Isa worried that her mother was encroaching on her own role as a mother. Living doubled up also influenced Isa's own parenting practices, as she sought to prevent her daughters from doing the tiny everyday things that bothered Antonia, such as leaving their bikes in the driveway. Living in her mother's household even shaped Isa's family structure: when she wanted her younger daughters' father to move in with her, she had to get permission from Antonia, who had never gotten along well with him. Antonia ultimately allowed Isa's partner to move in, but Isa felt that her mother's interference contributed to their eventual breakup. Antonia pressured her to have her partner clean up more, Isa said, and wanted them to eat with her in the dining room rather than taking their food to their room. When her mother and partner disagreed, Isa felt torn about whose side to take. "Stuff like that kind of would put me kind of against the wall. I want to do what my mom was telling me, because we live here, but I knew [I should do] what the father of my kid wants to do because we were actually a family." After Isa's partner moved out, Antonia eventually banned him from even visiting, forcing Isa to leave the house to allow her daughters to see their father.

For many parents, navigating shared physical space and negotiating expectations about household roles and relationships required immense effort. This constant invisible labor absorbed parents' time, energy, and mental bandwidth on a daily basis. In addition to the effort they required, these negotiations had profound consequences for families. They shaped how household members interacted with one another's children and romantic partners; determined how resources and expenses were shared between hosts and guests, many of whom had little disposable income; and threatened household members' deeply held identities as adults and good parents. Hosts and guests also often faced uncertainty about how long they would live together.

Living in a doubled-up household often had social, emotional, and even economic costs, yet many families experienced limited long-term payoff to enduring these challenges. The quick dissolution of most doubled-up households often pushed guest parents into another doubled-up arrangement or unaffordable housing and sometimes left host parents struggling to meet financial and childcare needs. For instance, Simone, a mother featured in chapter 7, lived with her partner and his son in the homes of three different hosts in less than two years as they tried to find a stable arrangement that would enable them to comfortably save up for a home of their own. Household instability introduced new challenges for both parents and children, including residential moves and school changes, economic instability, and the stress of navigating a new household arrangement. In this way, temporary doubled-up households, rather than reducing the precarity that families faced, too often perpetuated it.

Although stable doubled-up households like Isa's were not immune to the challenges of coresidence, they could provide lasting support with day-to-day needs. Yet, as Isa discovered, even years of living doubled up was rarely sufficient to allow guest parents to overcome barriers beyond the home, such as income volatility and the limited availability of desirable and affordable housing. Despite living doubled up in Antonia's home for years, Isa made little progress toward her ultimate goal: renting an affordable two-bedroom home in a neighborhood that she felt would be safe for her daughters. Although she and her daughters could remain in Antonia's home indefinitely, she continued to dream of a home of her own. "I feel that right here I'm just in a little box," she reflected. "I want to do more, I want to reach those goals and those dreams that I have." Parents like Isa hoped that with temporary support from doubling up and enough hard work, everything would eventually fall into place for them to be able to achieve their economic and housing goals. Yet the compounded, systemic challenges parents faced were often too great for the private safety net to overcome.

What Is Doubling Up?

Doubled-up households are those that include any adult besides the householder and the householder's romantic partner. Doubled-up families can be divided into two categories: the host, or householder, who owns or rents the home and is allowing an additional adult(s) to live with them, and the guest, who is living in someone else's home and does not have a home of their own. Scholarly and public attention has typically focused on guests who double up to receive housing support.[31] Yet fully half of children who live in a doubled-up household do so as hosts—that is, their parents have a home of their own that they share with others.[32] As described in this book, doubling up shapes the daily life and well-being of hosts as well as guests.

Because doubled-up households include adults beyond the nuclear family unit of parent, romantic partner, and minor children, they are also known as "shared" households. Of course, cohabiting with a romantic partner also involves sharing household space. Yet coresiding with extended family and non-relatives is conceptually distinct from cohabiting with a romantic partner, both in the research literature and among the parents I spoke with.[33] (See the methods appendix for further details.) The distinction that demographers and parents draw between living with a romantic partner and living with other adults reflects the primacy of the idealized independent nuclear family household, a topic I turn to in the next section.[34]

Although it specifically excludes households formed solely with a romantic partner, the term "doubled up" encompasses a wide range of household relationships. Multigenerational households are the most common type of doubled-up arrangement for families with children. About 10 percent of all children live with a parent in a three-generation household with grandparents, parents, and children coresiding, most commonly in the home of the grandparent.[35] About one-quarter of children will live in a three-generation household at some point during childhood.[36] Additionally, young adults are increasingly likely to remain in or return to their natal home. About 19 percent of children live with a parent and an adult sibling at some point during childhood.[37] Although most doubled-up children live in multigenerational households, a substantial share (about 21 percent) live with only non-grandparent extended family members. In these arrangements, parents are most often the host. Additionally, about 14 percent of doubled-up children live with nonrelatives only—again, most commonly with their parent hosting.[38]

Residence in doubled-up households is not distributed randomly across the population. Probably in part reflecting the support functions that doubled-up households can serve, these arrangements are particularly common for Black, Hispanic, and Asian families, families headed by an unmarried parent, and families with lower socioeconomic status.[39] Over 20 percent of Black, Hispanic, and Asian children live with a parent in a doubled-up household, roughly twice the share of White children who do (11 percent). Children with a never-married mother live doubled up at about three times the rate of children with a married mother (33 percent versus 11 percent; children with a previously married mother fall in between at 22 percent). And 22 percent of children whose mother completed a high school degree or less live doubled up, more than twice the share of doubled-up children whose mother has a college degree or higher (9 percent; children whose mother completed some college are in between, at 16 percent).[40]

This book asks how doubling up shapes the lives of the families with children who live in these households. I show that fully answering this question requires attention to the housing aspects of doubling up, as well as to the impact of this housing arrangement on social relations. Doubling up is inherently a housing arrangement, one in which adults who would be expected to live independently under the normative nuclear family household model share a single physical home. Academic and popular attention to doubling up has often focused on its emergency housing role.[41] In this book, I attend closely to the housing aspects of doubling up, showing how families come to move in and out of others' homes, the reasons families share the home they own or rent, and how doubling up shapes families' residential trajectories.

The role of doubling up as a housing arrangement is important, but as Isa's story demonstrates, doubling up involves far more than just the roof over one's head. Those who double up share not only housing but a *household*, and they navigate day-to-day life with coresident adults beyond the nuclear family. By attending closely to the social dimensions of doubling up, in addition to the physical housing dimensions, this book bridges scholarship on housing and on family complexity. This approach provides a more comprehensive view of the myriad ways in which doubling up shapes families' lives, impacting parents' autonomy, material well-being, romantic relationships, and child-rearing, as well as their residential outcomes and stability.

Beyond the Nuclear Family

Understanding the social dynamics of doubled-up households first requires us to consider the household form they are defined in contrast to: the nuclear family household. In the United States, the independent nuclear family—comprising just a householder, their romantic partner, and their minor children—is the archetypal household unit. As of the mid-twentieth century, canonical sociologists theorizing about urban and family issues viewed the isolated nuclear family as the ideal family type and "an essential underpinning of the American way of life."[42] In the years since, social scientists and historians have consistently countered these claims by documenting the involvement of extended family and fictive kin support networks and highlighting their importance for survival and mobility.[43] Other scholars have highlighted that, historically, assumptions about the independence of nuclear family units are relatively new and that they poorly reflect the lived realities of many low-income families and families of color.[44]

Despite challenges to the scholarly dominance of the nuclear family ideal, it remains ubiquitous in sociological and popular conceptions of families. Sociologist Karen Hansen calls this assumption that families operate within an insular and independent nuclear family household unit the "ideology of the nuclear family."[45] This ideology pervades understandings of home life. It influences the personal understandings that shape how families seek to arrange their lives, as well as the institutional understandings built into policy and popular discourse. Because the nuclear family unit and the household are assumed to be coterminous, the home serves as a physical and symbolic boundary around the nuclear family unit. It is a marker of privacy that sets the private affairs of a nuclear family unit apart from the outside world. Inside the household, the family is assumed to be a "solidarity unit" that shares economic resources and collective interests.[46] Outside these boundaries, the American values of independence and self-sufficiency dominate.[47]

Parents like Isa echoed this ideology of the independent nuclear family. Her desire to move out of her mother's home, despite the practical benefits of coresiding, reflected her belief that she and her daughters were "our own little family"—separate from Antonia—and that as an adult and as a mother, she needed to be "taking care of my kids and myself" rather than relying on her mother for help. "I have to do it on my own," she explained.

Despite this ideal, the independent nuclear family household is often insufficient to meet many of the challenges of modern life. Particularly in the US context of limited public support, expectations of self-sufficiency stand in stark contrast to families' need for support. In his 2020 *Atlantic* article titled "The Nuclear Family Was a Mistake," commentator David Brooks declared, "The family structure we've held up as the cultural ideal for the past half century has been a catastrophe for many."[48] Sociologists have consistently noted that families' proclaimed desire for independence and nuclear family insularity contrasts with the support they need and seek from extended family and fictive kin across a variety of arenas, from economic support to childcare.[49] To borrow a phrase from sociologists Natalia Sarkisian and Naomi Gerstel, American society is characterized by "nuclear family values, extended family lives."[50]

Of course, the independent nuclear family is not the universal family model worldwide. Individuals in Africa, Latin America and the Caribbean, and Asia and Oceania spend a much lower proportion of their lives, on average, in nuclear family households compared to individuals in North America and Europe.[51] Indeed, in many African countries, most of residents' lives are spent in households that extend beyond the nuclear family unit.[52] Even within North America and Europe, regions where nuclear family households are more common, there is substantial variation; for instance, shared households are relatively common in eastern Europe, in contrast to other parts of the continent.[53] North American and northern European countries are also characterized by high levels of individualistic (rather than familistic) values, which may shape how parents interpret doubling up.[54]

Even though the independent nuclear family household is often considered the archetypal household arrangement in the United States, the share of families who actually *live* in nuclear family households has declined in recent decades. Families are increasingly sharing space with extended family members or nonrelatives. Between 1996 and 2018, the percentage of children living with a parent and an adult extended family member or nonrelative increased by more than 40 percent, from 10.7 percent to 15.4 percent.[55] Moreover, there is little evidence to suggest that rates of doubling up will decline anytime soon. During the economic uncertainty and childcare concerns of the Covid-19 pandemic, the upward trend in rates of doubling up accelerated, particularly among Black and Hispanic families, lower-socioeconomic-status families, and unmarried-parent families.[56]

Today's high rates of doubling up among families with children are far from unprecedented. Recent increases are best understood as a return to historic levels of household sharing. The best evidence of historic trends comes from analyses of the most common type of shared household for families with children: the three-generation household with a parent, grandparent, and minor child. Rates of residence in three-generation households increased slightly from 1880 to 1950 before declining sharply from 1950 to 1980 to a historic low (near 5 percent)—a decline that is all the more notable given increases in the availability of grandparents over this period. Rates of residence in three-generation households increased again after 1980, and the share of children who live in three-generation households today is approaching the peak from 1950 (around 10 percent).[57] Thus, in many ways, today's rates of shared households are not the historical anomaly—the prominence of nuclear family households around 1980 was. Yet it is the nuclear family household that structures modern ideals of family life.

An Incomplete Portrait of Family Life

The shift toward doubled-up households after 1980 is one of a host of changes in American families since the mid-twentieth century. During this period, rates of divorce, nonmarital childbearing, and cohabitation also increased. These changes prompted a growing academic literature on "family complexity," defined as "when roles and relationships diverge from the simple nuclear family scheme" of a coresident mother and father raising their children within marriage as a stable and exclusive family unit.[58] This literature documents how the complex household and family arrangements introduced by modern patterns of partnering and childbearing can subject families to social instability and economic insecurity, particularly within the US context of limited public supports for families with children. It highlights how these forces may contribute to inequality and reproduce disadvantage across generations.[59]

The family complexity literature focuses primarily on complexity in the nuclear family unit: parents, their romantic partners, and minor children. This subfield is not unique in its focus; contemporary family research more broadly also tends to focus on the nuclear family, giving less attention to household members beyond the nuclear family unit.[60] This approach fails to capture the full household experience of many families—disproportionately Black, Hispanic, and Asian families, families with lower socioeconomic status, and unmarried parent families—whose households extend beyond the bounds of the nuclear family unit. Today over 15 percent of children live with a parent in a doubled-up household, far more than the approximately 8 percent of children who live with cohabiting parents (either two biological or one stepparent) or the 7 percent of children who live in a married stepparent family.[61] Yet our knowledge of doubled-up households lags far behind research on these complex family forms—a limitation this book helps remedy.

Likewise, policies across a wide range of domains are built around assumptions of nuclear family households. Countless forms sent home with children ask for information about the child's mother and father, ignoring other potential caretakers in the child's household.[62] After Hurricane Katrina, the Federal Emergency Management Agency (FEMA) provided rental assistance to only one person from each pre-Katrina address, leaving many families who were doubled-up prior to Katrina ineligible for assistance.[63] Doubling up complicates eligibility for the Earned Income Tax Credit because the Internal Revenue Service (IRS) allows only one tax filer in a household to claim a child on their taxes, even though other tax filers in the household might be eligible to do so.

Having multiple filers claim the same child can trigger an IRS investigation, which can dissuade families from claiming EITC benefits in the future.[64]

Many other policies seem poorly suited to the realities of living doubled up. Child protective services investigations often involve talking to and even running background checks on everyone in a household, a requirement that may feel invasive to mothers who live with—and may rely on housing from—adults outside the child's nuclear family.[65] Head Start programs encourage parents to create "engaging, predictable environments" and establish a consistent routine for children, but such parenting advice may be difficult to follow when sharing household space with other adults who are not working toward the same goal.[66]

In sum, policies that are designed with nuclear family households in mind can make interacting with the state and other institutions more challenging for families who deviate from this household form—with disproportionate impacts by race and ethnicity, socioeconomic status, and marital status. Better understanding the dynamics of doubled-up households is an essential step toward crafting policies that better reflect and serve these households. Moreover, by uncovering these dynamics and their impacts on families, this book deepens our understanding of the consequences of the policy decisions that leave so many families reliant on the private safety net.

Toward a Study of Household Complexity

This book extends the study of *family* complexity to *household* complexity. A focus on the household, and not just the nuclear family unit, gives us a more comprehensive understanding of family life for the millions of families like Isa's. Traditional family research would focus on her status as a single mother, her repartnering and multipartner fertility, and the involvement, coresidence, and economic contributions of her daughters' fathers. The central role of Antonia in the family life of Isa and her daughters, however, would be missed by focusing solely on the nuclear family unit. Living with Antonia shaped Isa's and her daughters' material well-being, family structure, and home environment, and it circumscribed Isa's autonomy, household authority, and parenting decisions. By showing the profound ways in which living in a shared household reshapes family life, a look at the lives of families like Isa's demonstrates the importance of extending our focus beyond the nuclear family.

Family complexity research has not typically included doubled-up household arrangements, but sharing intimate household space with adults beyond the nuclear family certainly introduces complex roles and relationships that diverge from the simple nuclear family model.[67] Conceptualizing doubled-up households as household complexity underscores two important aspects of these arrangements. First, compared to simple nuclear families, complex family forms are less *institutionalized*; that is, there are fewer taken-for-granted scripts to guide household roles and relationships.[68] Sociologist Andrew Cherlin first described the "incompletely institutionalized" status of remarriage in 1978, and in the years since, this framework has been extended to consider cohabiting couples as well as the changing dynamics of marriage.[69] The incomplete institutionalization framework posits that because incompletely institutionalized family forms lack laws and clear social norms that would set shared expectations for relationships, family members face greater ambiguity in how they organize their family life. As family members seek to establish among themselves how their household and relationships will function, there is substantial risk of disagreement and conflict.

Many of the challenges I highlight in this book stemmed from the incompletely institutionalized nature of doubled-up households, which prompted complex questions about how doubled-up households should function and how household members should interact. How much autonomy are adults entitled to when living in someone else's home? Which resources and expenses should be shared with coresident adults outside the nuclear family, and how should these be divided? What are appropriate boundaries around romantic relationships when living with other adults? What role should nonparent household members play in the lives of coresident children? Different household members had different answers to these questions. This book examines how parents navigated their incompletely institutionalized household arrangements, highlighting the complexity that relationship ambiguity and disagreement produced for parents and children. I also show how parents' ideals of family life—ideals based on a nuclear family household—made negotiations over these questions even more challenging.

Second, family complexity scholars highlight the detrimental impacts of the instability that often produces complex family arrangements. For instance, parental separation and repartnering bring adults in and out of children's lives and households. Theories of family instability and change posit that the loss or addition of family members like this elicits stress by changing relationships and household routines and expectations.[70] Changes in family composition are also often accompanied by changes in family income and by residential moves, other forms of instability that can be detrimental for children and parents.[71]

Like parents' romantic partners, extended family members and nonrelatives introduce instability to children's household composition—instability that is missed by the traditional focus on the nuclear family unit. Indeed, children experience even *more* household composition changes involving extended family members or nonrelatives than changes involving parents and parents' romantic partners.[72] This book builds on these demographic insights to shed new light on how families understand and experience doubled-up household instability. I show how household instability complicates the lives of doubled-up families with children as they navigate changing social and physical environments. At the same time, parents often expect doubling up to be a short-term solution, and household *stability* carries challenges of its own.

Learning from Doubled-Up Parents

This book draws on data from sixty doubled-up parents to provide a firsthand look at how families experience doubled-up households. These parents participated in over 170 narrative interviews over a three-year period. In these interviews, parents were asked to "tell me the story of your life," focusing particularly on the details of their family life and their residential history and aspirations. Parents described how they came to live doubled up and what alternatives they considered, their day-to-day life in the home, and what they saw as the benefits and challenges of living doubled up. Over the course of the fieldwork, I often met other household members before or after interviews, and most parents provided a tour of their home, pointing out things that they liked or disliked about the household and how they shared the space. Through these repeated interviews, parents detailed their experiences that led to becoming doubled up and shared how they navigated their shared households and, as happened to many of them, what happened when their doubled-up arrangement dissolved.

These sixty families are a subsample from How Parents House Kids (HPHK), a large-scale interview study about residential decision-making. This book draws on HPHK data, as well as data from independent fieldwork I conducted with families from the HPHK sample who reported living doubled up. HPHK was a collaborative effort, led by sociologists Kathryn Edin and Stefanie DeLuca, with twenty-six fieldworkers including myself. The study was funded by the Annie E. Casey Foundation and John D. and Catherine T. MacArthur Foundation, and the MacArthur Foundation also funded my independent fieldwork focused on doubling up. The HPHK research team interviewed parents about their residential decision-making in the summer of 2013, with follow-up interviews in the summer of 2014. We collected data in Dallas County, Texas, and Cuyahoga County, Ohio, which encompass the cities and inner suburbs of Dallas and Cleveland, respectively. Cuyahoga County, Ohio, has experienced population declines in recent decades and had about 1.3 million residents in 2013.[73] This midwestern county was predominantly White and Black. Dallas County was larger and growing, with roughly 2.5 million residents in 2013.[74] Dallas County had sizable White, Black, and Hispanic populations.

These two metropolitan areas were in some ways relatively hospitable environments for lower-income families looking for housing. The median rent in the Cleveland metropolitan area, $712, was well below the national median of $871 in 2011, and the median in the Dallas metropolitan area, $863, was similar to the national median.[75] The share of renters spending 35 percent or more of their income on rent was slightly below the national average in both metro areas.[76] Because Cuyahoga and Dallas Counties did not represent especially challenging housing markets, the families in my sample were likely to have had, if anything, more housing options available to them than families in tighter housing markets. Doubled-up households may endure even greater challenges in higher-cost housing markets, where families have fewer housing alternatives.

HPHK drew on a random sample of census block groups in the Dallas and Cleveland metro areas, stratified by racial composition and median income. The research team visited randomly selected addresses from these block groups to identify whether the household included at least one child between the ages of three and eight. For households that did, we invited the primary caregiver of the child(ren) to participate in the study. The two-year response rate was an impressive 80 percent. The primary caregivers we interviewed were almost always parents (typically mothers), so I use the term "parents" throughout the book, but I specify when a specific caregiver was a grandparent. All names given in this book are pseudonyms, typically chosen by the parent. Further details about data collection and analysis can be found in the methods appendix.

This book centers the experiences of families with young children, and particularly the parents in these households. Although many families in my sample shared a household with an adult without minor children (for example, a grandparent or a young adult nephew), my analysis focuses on the perspectives of families with minor children. Sampling in this way undoubtedly shaped my findings; the parents in my sample probably felt the pressures of the independent nuclear family ideal more acutely than other groups who were not well represented in my sample. For instance, for unpartnered young adults without children who are still in school or early in their careers, sharing a home as roommates may be a more normative experience, and their motivations and experiences around this household form are likely to differ from those of the doubled-up families with young children I studied. Likewise, reduced control over the home environment and questions about appropriate roles and relationships between household members take on added significance for parents of young children.

From the HPHK sample, I identified all English-speaking respondents who doubled up (their household included any adult besides the householder and the householder's romantic partner) at some point during the two HPHK fieldwork years, 2013 and 2014. For seven respondents, I also included a coresident adult from their household in my sample. As a member of the HPHK interviewing team, I interviewed doubled-up parents myself when possible. Building on the HPHK data, I also conducted supplemental fieldwork with the parents who doubled up, focusing specifically on their experiences with this arrangement. In sum, data collection spanned from the summer of 2013 through the summer of 2015, and the parents in my sample participated in over 170 narrative interviews over this three-year period. Interviewing families longitudinally generated data about how households formed, dissolved, and changed; over the three years, the sixty families lived in over 130 different doubled-up arrangements.[77]

Of the sixty parents in my sample, twenty-seven doubled up as hosts, twenty-two doubled up as guests, and eleven doubled up as both hosts and guests at different points during the fieldwork. Consistent with national trends for families with children, multigenerational homes were the most common type of doubled-up household in my sample; a majority of both hosts and guests lived in a multigenerational household at some point during the fieldwork years. Households formed with other extended family members were the next most common household form. Households formed with non-kin—often long-term friends or, in a couple of instances, relatively new acquaintances—were also well represented; roughly one-quarter of parents spent some time in this household type.[78]

This unique sample, drawn from the HPHK stratified random sample in two metropolitan areas, provides a novel qualitative view of the range of doubled-up families and their households. The book builds on and extends prior research on doubled-up households that sampled deeply disadvantaged groups, such as formerly homeless adults or very low-income adults on subsidized housing wait-lists. The parents in my sample lived in housing ranging from small apartments in public housing complexes to larger single-family homes in more affluent suburbs. Appendix table 1 in the methods appendix describes the characteristics of my sample, divided between parents who doubled up as guests, those who doubled up as hosts, and those who doubled up as both guests and hosts at different points during the fieldwork. Additionally, to help readers recall parents featured across multiple chapters, appendix table 2 lists the individual characteristics of each parent quoted in the text, along with the doubled-up household(s) described.

Although diverse compared to other studies of doubled-up households, my sample was relatively disadvantaged, reflecting trends in the broader doubled-up population as well as the two metropolitan areas I sampled from (see the methods appendix). Some parents in my sample bounced between low-paying service jobs, while others had long-term employment with a steady paycheck. Both hosts and guests tended to have low income levels, with a median income below the poverty line for a family of three that year. Guests' incomes were slightly lower than hosts' incomes.[79] A majority of parents had an education level of high school or less, though a substantial share had pursued some form of postsecondary education. As of their interview in the summer of 2014, about half of the parents in my sample lived with a spouse or cohabiting partner and half had no coresident romantic partner, though coresident relationship status often shifted during the fieldwork period—sometimes because the parent was doubled up, as I discuss in chapter 5. Guests were especially likely to not have a coresident romantic partner. Over two-thirds of the sample identified as Black or African American, but parents who identified as Latino or Hispanic (about 17 percent of the sample) or as White (about 12 percent of the sample) were also represented. The median age for guests was twenty-nine, while the median for hosts was thirty-six.

Of course, these data do not capture all possible dimensions of variation that are relevant to doubling up, and my sample size limits my ability to analyze differences between subgroups of doubled-up families. The sample was drawn from two distinct metropolitan areas that represent some of the variation seen nationally, but Dallas County, Texas, and Cuyahoga County, Ohio, cannot represent all geographies across the United States; for instance, rural areas and extremely high-cost housing markets are both absent from this study. Asian families are also not well represented in my sample, most likely because of the cities and block groups that HPHK sampled; however, Asian families live doubled up as hosts, particularly of multigenerational households, at high rates.[80]

Likewise, because I limited my sample to parents who completed their interviews in English, my sample does not reflect the experience of families whose primary language is not English, such as recent immigrants, who live doubled up at high rates. Qualitative research on the social support networks of immigrant families suggests that doubled-up arrangements can be a complicated safety net for recent immigrants, who often depend on support from extended kin but whose reliance on that support can drain limited resources or introduce complicated power dynamics to their relationships.[81] In some ways, these findings echo the experiences of parents in my sample. Yet the unique circumstances of recent immigrants shape their experience of doubling up in ways that are not fully captured in this book.[82] For instance, challenges specific to international migration and undocumented status play an important role in the household formation patterns of some immigrant families.[83] These factors do not, however, feature prominently in my sample. The methods appendix provides further details on how my sample characteristics may have influenced my findings.

Housing and poverty scholars have typically focused on guests in doubled-up households, but I examine the perspective of both parents who doubled up as guests and those who doubled up as hosts, as well as some who were both guests and hosts at different points during my fieldwork. This innovative approach shows that doubling up deeply impacts the lives of hosts as well as guests and provides insight into what hosts give up—and what they gain—by doubling up. For most parents, however, I do not have data from hosts and guests living in the same household. Thus, although I present the experiences of both hosts and guests, these experiences should not be understood as parallel experiences of the same households.

Drawing on these data, the book unfolds in three parts. Part 1 examines how families come to live doubled up. Chapter 1 asks what circumstances and motivations lead families with children to live as guests in someone else's home. This chapter tells the story of parents like Lola: when a violent ex-partner made her home no longer safe for her and her children, she could not afford the move-in costs for a new rental, so she moved her family to her mother's house to save money. Another parent, Gabby, moved with her children to her aging stepfather's house so that she could reduce her housing costs and save toward homeownership while more easily providing the live-in care he needed. For some mothers, like Noelle, there was never a point at which she was *not* doubled up; Noelle became a mother while still living in her childhood home, and she had remained there, unable to afford the type of home and neighborhood she wanted to provide for her family. Guest parents had diverse housing needs, but all turned to doubling up for support that they hoped would enable them to pursue their longer-term residential or economic goals.

Chapter 2 turns to host families who give up space and privacy to share their home with family or friends. This chapter introduces JC, a father who struggled to provide for his four children but whose stable housing allowed him to provide a valuable private safety net for his niece and nephew, who were homeless. For parents like JC, sharing housing affirmed their identity as an empathetic helper, though it could also leave them even more financially vulnerable if guests contributed less to the household than they expected. At the same time, doubling up could offer valuable support for hosts. Lauren, a middle-class mother, began hosting her own mother soon after giving birth to her second child and received help with childcare and housework. Even when they received support from guests, hosts like Lauren held authority in the home. For hosts of working-age adults, this authority allowed them to evaluate whether guests were deserving of their housing assistance and to set timelines and conditions for coresidence.

In part 2, I trace how living doubled up shapes families' daily lives, highlighting both the benefits and the unique challenges that this safety net "solution" creates for hosts and guests. This section examines household dynamics across four domains of household life. Chapter 3 shows the centrality of questions of adulthood and authority to host-guest relations and to parents' common dissatisfaction with doubling up as guests. In this chapter, we meet mothers like TaKayla, who lived with her children in her mother's home and under her rules and oversight. TaKayla's subordinate position in the household was inconsistent with her notion of adulthood, which required adults to provide for themselves and to have control over their own decisions. Parents experienced less dissonance between adulthood and living doubled up when they were hosts. For example, Leeann, a mother who shared her home with multiple extended family members and friends, had housing of her own and could set rules and expectations for her guests. Yet, as this chapter shows, attempting to enforce those rules can be stressful, and guests who refuse to follow hosts' rules can raise both the emotional and monetary costs of hosting.

Hosts are often considered support *providers*, but chapter 4 shows that doubling up can provide a safety net for both hosts and guests. Yet this safety net is complex, and doubling up can be a source of both economic support and economic strain—sometimes simultaneously. This chapter features Starr, a struggling homeowner for whom hosting provided a vital lifeline, bringing in income that helped keep her utilities on. But sharing her home also depleted other resources; for example, her children faced food insecurity after guests helped themselves in her kitchen. The complexity of accounting for these costs and benefits—alongside ambiguity around doubled-up household members' obligations to one another—left parents like Starr feeling taken advantage of, rather than supported, by their doubled-up arrangements.

The next two chapters delve into the impacts on intimate family life of living doubled up. Chapter 5 shows how doubling up complicates parents' romantic relationships. Researchers tend to assume that single parents are more likely to double up as guests because they do not have a partner with whom they can pool income and share housing costs. This chapter shows that in fact doubling up itself shapes family structure. Anrisa, a mother of two, was in a stable, long-term romantic relationship, but because her partner Phil did not have a home of his own, coresiding required that they find hosts who were willing to allow them both to move in. Cohabiting thus took great effort and was sometimes impossible. Other doubled-up parents did live with a partner, like Eva, a mother who lived with her partner and two children in the home of her partner's mother. Yet the stress of living doubled up still took a toll on her relationship: sharing the intimate home environment with her partner's siblings and parents complicated her expectations about relationship privacy, intimacy, and boundaries and facilitated interference and oversight of their romantic relationship.

Coresiding with adults beyond the nuclear family also introduces complications to child-rearing, the focus of chapter 6. This chapter returns to Isa to show that doubling up with her mother was a source of both child-rearing support and constraint for her. She benefited from having another adult in the home to help with child-rearing, and the childcare her mother provided supported Isa's school and work efforts. Yet sharing a household also introduced questions about the appropriate level and type of involvement for a nonparent household member. Isa and her mother disagreed about how close her mother should be with her granddaughters and about which child-rearing decisions were hers to make. For parents like Isa, their ideals of parental control over the home environment and child-rearing often conflicted with the realities of living doubled up, which involved sharing space and frequent interactions with household members beyond the nuclear family, and these challenges took a toll. Other parents faced even greater difficulties, however, as they navigated child-rearing within a shared home environment that was unsupportive or even dangerous for their children.

After part 2 describes the implications of living doubled up for families' daily lives, part 3 takes a longer-term perspective by exploring how parents and children experience doubled-up household dissolutions and stability. Doubled-up households are a safety net that catches many families when they experience instability, but these households can also perpetuate instability, as chapter 7 shows. This chapter features parents like Simone, whose frequent and sometimes unexpected doubled-up household dissolutions prompted further economic and residential instability as she, her partner, and his child continually adjusted to new household compositions. Like many guests, Simone had intended to double up temporarily to save money to cover the move-in costs for a rental unit. Yet years of doubling up across different households addressed few of the constraints she and her partner faced in the housing market—including low incomes, a criminal record, and damaged credit—and ultimately left them little better off. Hosts are also negatively impacted by household instability, as we see with hosts like Dana and Zach. After Zach's mother told them she would stay with them long-term, they began counting on her economic contributions to the household. When she unexpectedly moved out, the couple was unable to afford their rent.

Chapter 8 turns to the households of parents who can leverage doubling up as either a long-term source of support—to help them get by on a day-to-day basis—or a stepping-stone to get ahead and make progress toward their ultimate housing or economic goals. We meet Kevin, a father who had lived with his aging mother for seven years, providing financial help and live-in care and receiving low-cost housing and free childcare. Despite the stability of their arrangement, Kevin viewed the household as a temporary stop; he kept his furniture in storage over the years while he searched for employment that paid a living wage and affordable housing in a neighborhood that would be safe for his daughter. But years of living in his mother's home had not brought him meaningfully closer to his residential goals. Parents who are able to achieve their long-term ambitions by doubling up are typically relatively advantaged. Jennifer and her partner were able to purchase a home with her father's help and with the savings and flexibility that doubling up provided. For families like Jennifer's, who already have stable, relatively high incomes and well-off social networks, doubling up can provide time to accumulate resources. Yet, doubling up itself rarely makes dramatic changes to the resources and opportunities available to parents. Thus, it often reinforces existing inequalities, propelling the most advantaged families (like Jennifer's) toward their goals while leaving less advantaged families (like Kevin's) struggling with the same challenges they faced before doubling up.

For the families in my sample, living doubled up was a response to insufficient access to economic resources, housing opportunities, and caregiving support. In the absence of an adequate public safety net, they turned to the private safety net to meet their needs. In turn, doubled-up housing arrangements reshaped family life. Given the millions of families with children who live doubled up, fully understanding American family life and home environments—and crafting policy that responds to these realities—requires attention to these complex household dynamics. This book exposes the processes by which doubled-up households respond to—but also perpetuate—families' needs. More broadly, it advances our understanding of how families respond to precarity by using private safety nets and how these private safety net "solutions" introduce new challenges of their own. Awareness of these processes is increasingly important for understanding economic and social inequality in an environment of limited public supports for socioeconomic security and mobility.

PART I

Becoming Doubled Up

1

Doubling Up as a Guest

WHEN SHAY'S NAME CAME TO the top of the Dallas Housing Authority (DHA) wait-list, she felt ecstatic to have her own place. Shay, a Black mother who was twenty years old at the time, had grown tired of living in the home of her mother, who "kept on trying to tell me what to do and what not to do with my baby," her infant daughter Kyla. She applied for three different subsidized apartments and prepared for a long wait. "And I got it. I didn't think that I was going to get it; I got it within three months after me being on the waiting list. I got my own space. I was so like, 'What, are you kidding me, I have my own smart key? Oh, I rock.'" Shay packed their belongings and moved from her mother's house into the first home of her own, where her partner later joined her.

Over the next four years, Shay's excitement about her subsidized apartment nosedived. First, the apartment complex, which was relatively safe when she moved in, became increasingly violent. "[Things] just started getting bad, and I was ready to go. There was gunshots every night. When me and my kids try to sleep, [we] pull the mattress on the floor because they were constantly shooting." With no refuge from the violence, even inside her apartment, she became increasingly worried about Kyla and later her newborn daughter Nia. Meanwhile, a neighbor began complaining about her music and the sound of four-year-old Kyla running through the unit. After two violations for "disturbing the peace," she was just one violation away from eviction.

Then Shay started a new job. When she reported her work earnings to the apartment management, they notified her that her rent—which was subsidized based on her income level—would be increasing from less than $50 a month to nearly $500 a month. She could not justify paying so much given her dissatisfaction with the apartment. "$25, I'll pay it; I get what I pay for. Why you want me to pay almost $500? . . . The floors were weak. You could fall through the floor. They would never fix nothing. It was so unhealthy, there was mold in the wall, rodents, spiders, all kinds of stuff, and they were never doing a thing about it." She decided not to pay rent that month, or the following month, while she searched for a new place to live. Two months behind on rent, she got into one final disagreement with her neighbor, who again reported her to the apartment managers. They encouraged her to move out immediately, threatening to file an eviction and take her to court if she did not.

Shay wanted to avoid having an eviction on her record—"It's hard to get an apartment after an eviction like that because you haven't paid your rent. And in Dallas it's *hard*"—so she decided to move out before her landlord filed the eviction. She packed the family's belongings and called her "cousin" Shandra. Shandra was not a blood relative (she was her godmother's niece), but they had known each other since childhood when Shandra, who was a few years older than Shay, babysat for Shay. Shandra arrived, ready to help with the move. "She came to get me 'cause she got . . . a truck, so they came to help us move our stuff. And then she was like, 'Where we taking this?' and I was like, 'I don't know, I don't know where I'm taking my stuff,' and I was crying and stuff. And she was like, 'Take it to my house, y'all can come over there. Shoot, I got enough rooms. All the rooms I got, long as I got somewhere to stay, y'all ain't never gonna be hungry.'"

Shay moved with her partner and two daughters into the four-bedroom subsidized rental unit Shandra shared with her teenage daughters. Asked where they would have gone had Shandra not offered to take her in, she shook her head. "I don't know. Really, I really don't know. I'm kinda glad that she did, 'cause there ain't no telling where I would be right now, what I would be getting into. I'd probably be into all kind of stuff . . . 'Cause, excuse my French, but I'm a hood chick. I know how to survive. I have to do what I have to do to survive, and if she would have never taken me in, ain't no telling what I be doing. Just trying to make it."

———

Shay's story of being on the verge of eviction and unable to afford a new unit of her own exemplifies the conventional experience of doubling up. With nowhere to live until Shandra offered up room in her home, she became a member of what some scholars and housing advocates have termed the "hidden homeless population."[1] While living in Shandra's home, she and her family had a roof over their heads but no permanent home of their own. Stories like Shay's appear frequently in research on families living in poverty, stories that vividly reveal doubling up to be a common and vital source of emergency housing.[2] However, much of what we know about why families with children double up as guests in someone else's home comes from studies of families who have experienced housing instability or who are living in deep poverty.[3] The experiences of such families are important, but they may not provide a full picture of the reasons that families double up as guests in someone else's home. Is doubling up as a guest reserved for only the most extreme housing needs? Do all families who double up as guests have such limited housing alternatives that they should be considered effectively homeless? If not, what motivations beyond meeting immediate housing needs lead families to double up? When, if ever, might families choose doubling up over residential independence?

These questions are important for better understanding this increasingly common household type. But they are also central to how we conceptualize and categorize doubling up. To some, the phrase "doubled up" evokes a state akin to homelessness—a housing option of last resort. This understanding hinges on a distinction between doubling up for *economic* reasons and doubling up as a *choice*. For example, the National Alliance to End Homelessness labels doubling up—defined as "sharing the housing of others for economic reasons"—a form of housing hardship.[4] Likewise, federal definitions of doubled-up homelessness focus on those who "are sharing housing of other persons due to loss of housing, economic hardship, or a similar reason."[5] Thus, examining the circumstances and motivations that lead families to form doubled-up households is important for considering what it means for households to be doubled up for economic reasons, as well as for understanding what households this conceptualization may miss.

Answering such questions requires a sample that includes a broad range of households, not just those experiencing housing instability. As described in the introduction, my sample of doubled-up households was part of a diverse sample of families with children across neighborhoods in two metro areas. Parents' stories of becoming doubled up were likewise varied. I asked parents to "tell me the story of how you came to live with this person" and probed for details about exactly when and why the parent had left their previous home and what alternatives they had considered—or not considered. I asked parents who had moved from another doubled-up arrangement how they had first come to live doubled up; that is, what were the circumstances that led to that first move from their own unit into someone else's home? The stories of how parents came to live doubled up, and the variation within these stories, complicate our understanding of doubling up as simply an emergency housing response or an alternative to homelessness.

Instead of simply reflecting a response to crises like eviction, the experiences of doubled-up families demonstrated the breadth of the impacts of rising housing costs. Although very low-income families faced challenges affording any housing at all, rising housing costs limited the ability of families even at higher income levels to pursue their goals for upward mobility. I identified *three* common pathways that took guests into doubled-up households.[6] First, some parents doubled up to save money in pursuit of a goal, like homeownership or higher education. Although many of these parents had moderate incomes that would have allowed them to afford residential independence, they felt unable to pursue their goals with so much of their income devoted to rent. Second, some parents had never lived independently; these parents had remained in their childhood home into adulthood or moved from their childhood home directly into another doubled-up household—or a series of doubled-up households. The difficulty they faced finding affordable housing that met their family's needs delayed their aspirations to form their own household, sometimes indefinitely. Third, many families, like Shay's, doubled up in response to a crisis. However, as this chapter will show, the crises that led families to double up extended far beyond just eviction.

The stories in this chapter highlight the ambiguity in the distinction between doubling up for *economic* reasons and doubling up as a *choice*. For each parent in this chapter, doubling up was preferable to the housing options they could afford; they were all, in some sense, doubled up for economic reasons. Despite the range of pathways that parents took to doubled-up households, they typically did not double up as guests simply because they *wanted* to live in someone else's home. Even parents whose incomes would cover the rent for an independent unit did not describe doubling up as a guest as a desirable choice; rather, it was a preferable alternative to some less desirable housing option, such as living in an affordable but dangerous neighborhood or paying so much in rent that they would be unable to save or, in more severe cases, to afford their other basic needs.[7]

To be sure, the range of alternatives that families had at their disposal varied dramatically. Some parents had no clear housing alternatives and might have turned to emergency shelter or sleeping in a car if not doubled up. Others could afford to rent their own unit or could apply for public housing assistance but chose not to, in the hopes that doubling up would allow them to achieve their mobility goals. Yet, for all these parents, choices about whether to double up as a guest were heavily structured by the unaffordable housing market. As this chapter will show, the challenges posed by the housing market were often compounded by other structural conditions, from the precarious low-wage labor market to the legacy of racial wealth inequality.

Deliberate Decisions to Double Up

A small but notable share of guest parents in my sample—roughly 15 percent—proactively chose to double up to pursue some longer-term aim, like home-ownership or further education. They described doubling up as a temporary tool that would allow them to lower their housing costs and sometimes also obtain support, like childcare, while they pursued their goal. Families who made a deliberate decision to double up while pursuing a goal tended to be more financially secure than other doubled-up guest families in my sample. This relative economic security may help explain why prior studies have paid little attention to parents' deliberate decisions to double up as guests; these families probably would not have made it into the highly disadvantaged samples from which most of our knowledge of doubling up comes.

When I first met Gabby, a Black mother of two, she was renting a three-bedroom apartment in a middle-class neighborhood outside of Dallas, where she had lived with her fifteen-year-old daughter and eight-year-old son for just over three years. About seven months later, she moved "back home" to her stepfather Anthony's house, along with her children. Although Anthony's home was just seven minutes away from her old apartment, the move caused a dramatic change in her housing quality. Compared to her previous apartment complex, which appeared well kept, the homes in Anthony's neighborhood were visibly run down. The older residents who populated the neighborhood seemed unable financially or physically to keep up with repairs, a particularly common condition for Black senior homeowners, given inequality in income and wealth and predatory real estate and lending practices.[8] As I passed through an overgrown lawn to reach Anthony's house, I saw that his residence was no different. One of the front windows was shattered and partially covered by a piece of plywood. Inside, the house smelled musty, and insect carcasses lined the baseboards of some rooms.

Surprisingly, it was an *increase* in Gabby's income that pushed her to move from her own well-maintained apartment and double up in her stepfather's semi-dilapidated home. That year she had received another promotion at the cosmetics factory where she had worked her way up over the last five years from a temporary worker on the production floor to a line coordinator. Her sister's best friend was a realtor who had long tried to convince her that she should purchase a home. In the United States, aspirations for homeownership are ubiquitous.[9] Despite persistent inequalities in homeownership rates, reinforced by historic and present-day discrimination in the housing and mortgage markets, Black and Hispanic householders are no less optimistic about homeownership on average than White householders.[10] Gabby believed that moving from her apartment into a home of her own would improve her children's lives, especially her young son's. "He was like, 'I get tired of being in the house,' you know, and I understand. He's a kid. He want to go outside, play. . . . He need a yard, and so I was like, well yeah, it's time to get a house." In addition to providing a yard where her son could safely play, homeownership represented a source of stability for her and her children. Gabby, who was thirty-eight years old when she moved in with Anthony, explained, "The positive is just knowing that I am building something that is ours. I would have something to leave to my kids, when I get old and they get older."

Although Gabby had long wanted to be a homeowner, the daunting task of repairing her damaged credit record had dissuaded her from pursuing it in the past. Years of allowing her needy extended family members to put bills in her name had left her with a long line of unpaid utility, cell phone, and cable bills. Her damaged credit reflected yet another structural force that contributes to inequality in homeownership rates. Compared to White adults, Black adults like Gabby are less likely to have wealthy extended family members who can facilitate their transition into homeownership, and they are more likely to have impoverished extended family members who may need help themselves.[11] For Gabby, helping disadvantaged extended family members made the transition to homeownership more challenging. However, with a raise and the prospect of more overtime hours after her promotion, she finally felt ready to repair her credit and pursue her dream of homeownership.

When Gabby decided to begin saving for a house, she talked to Anthony because "you always go to your parents when you decide to make big changes." He offered to let her move in with him so she could focus on fixing her credit and saving for a home. He lived alone in a large four-bedroom home, with more than enough space for Gabby and her children to join him. She hesitated at first, telling him that she was "so used to being by myself now." He gave her time to think about it, saying, "Well, it's up to you, whatever you decide to do." Unlike parents who moved in response to a crisis, Gabby could take time to weigh her options and decide whether to double up. Her dream of homeownership—and the impossibility of achieving this dream while paying for her apartment—ultimately overcame her trepidation over living in someone else's home. She took over one bedroom in Anthony's home, and her children shared another.

Today housing costs are the largest expense many families face. In the last decade, rental vacancy rates have dropped to their lowest level since the mid-1980s, with particularly steep declines in the availability of low- and moderate-cost rentals. The tight rental market has pushed rental prices higher, at a rate far outpacing income growth.[12] As the availability of low-cost rental units has declined, the proportion of families' incomes that are taken up by housing costs has increased. The widely accepted standard of affordability holds that families should pay no more than 30 percent of their income in housing costs.[13] Yet, half of all renter households devote more than 30 percent of their income to rent, and a majority of these households spend more than *half* of their income on housing.[14]

Gabby felt like she paid too much in rent, but compared to other parents she was lucky; when renting, she paid approximately 30 percent of her income on housing. However, even with her $35,000-a-year income and comparatively affordable rent, there simply was not enough left at the end of the month—after paying rent and utilities and providing for her two children—to pay off her debt and build her savings. Although her income placed her solidly above the poverty threshold, paying her rent inhibited her plans for upward mobility.

Doubling up in someone else's home often reduced, or even eliminated, families' housing costs. Parents like Gabby hoped that these savings would allow them to quickly advance their long-term financial goals. When she moved in, she and Anthony agreed that she would pay for the utilities and cable, which ran approximately $400 a month, and he would continue paying the $700 mortgage. This arrangement benefited Anthony, but it provided even more substantial savings for Gabby, who had been paying roughly $900 a month for rent and utilities for her apartment. Reducing her housing costs gave her the flexibility to start fixing her credit with the help of a credit repair company recommended by her realtor friend. The last time I spoke to her, she estimated that she was about halfway through repairing her credit, and her realtor was helping her look into down payment assistance programs.

Unlike Shay, who was facing an imminent eviction and understood doubling up to be her only housing option, parents like Gabby could have lived independently. Because she did not face an immediate need, Gabby was able to reject other potential strategies to reduce her housing costs. For example, she greatly valued neighborhood safety and thus would not consider moving to less expensive housing. Housing assistance was also not an option she considered because "I wouldn't want my kids thinking, 'Oh yeah, it's okay to be on government assistance and all that.' . . . Nah, I want them to work and what's theirs is something that they had earned." Because she doubled up to pursue a goal and could afford residential independence, the living arrangement felt like more of a choice than it did for parents like Shay, who doubled up to fill an immediate housing need.

Still, doubling up in Anthony's home was a sacrifice for Gabby. His four-bedroom home was large enough for her and her children to have their own space, but frequent visits from family made the house—and even the room she occupied—feel hectic. "If I'm laid up in the bed and [my nieces and nephews] walked through the door, they might come jump up in the bed with me." In the months immediately after moving in, she frequently debated moving back to her apartment, wondering, "Am I making the right decision?" She described how doubling up meant "just giving up your own stuff. I think I was just struggling with just that idea . . . like I come home, this is mine. And I think it was just that: not being in charge of everything." Despite the loss of control that came with living in someone else's home, she remained at her stepfather's house over the next two years, preferring to live doubled up temporarily rather than continue renting indefinitely, with the hope that this sacrifice and the moderate income level that she had worked toward for years would allow her to achieve homeownership and leave her children with something of lasting value. The last time I spoke with her, she said that her employer had announced plans to build a new factory in the coming years, and she would begin looking for a house once the new location was announced.

Gabby doubled up because her income increased, leading her to pursue homeownership. In contrast, other parents made a deliberate decision to double up because they wanted a housing option that would allow them to live on a reduced income while pursuing a mobility goal. Teresa, a twenty-nine-year-old Hispanic mother in Dallas, decided to move with her two sons, ages four and six, into her parents' home while her husband Miguel, an undocumented immigrant, traveled to Mexico to obtain legal status in the United States. Obtaining legal status for Miguel was the first step in their dreams, she said, "and then from there that would really help us to reach the goals that we made for ourselves, which is going to school, both of us, and hopefully owning a home. Those are our hopes."

After a year of working with Catholic Charities to get the paperwork processed, Miguel needed to attend an appointment and wait for approval in Mexico. He and Teresa were optimistic that he would eventually be approved for legal residency, but they did not know whether it would take weeks, months, or even longer for the approval to come through. He typically worked seven days a week at a car repair shop, bringing in a little over $20,000 a year, while she stayed home with their two young sons. The couple had a couple of thousand dollars saved. However, with Miguel not working, the $700 in rent and $200 in utilities they paid each month for their two-bedroom apartment would have quickly depleted their savings. They worried that she would have to carefully monitor spending—even on necessities like food—to ensure that their savings were enough to cover their housing costs while he was away. Moreover, if he was delayed in Mexico, they might run out of money altogether.

Teresa's parents offered to allow her family to take over the large spare bedroom in their three-bedroom home while Miguel pursued legal residency in Mexico. Doubling up in her parents' home offered Teresa a chance to reduce her housing costs so that she could avoid depleting their savings, which she hoped to use to complete a one-year degree for a medical office assistant certificate. Once he returned, she imagined, living doubled up might even allow them to start saving toward eventual homeownership. They weighed these financial considerations heavily in their decision-making, but they also considered the benefits of the move for their two young sons. In contrast to Teresa and Miguel's small apartment by the highway, Teresa's parents' home was spacious with a large backyard. "I have seen [my sons] at her house, and they're just happier. They're running around," Teresa said, noting that the school around the block from her parents' home was also an improvement over the school zoned to the apartment complex. A few years earlier, they had lived with her parents when Miguel lost his job, so she knew that living with her mother made childcare easier as well. "It was easy in the way that I had my mom there, so if I ever wanted to go out, I could just leave the kids with her."

Despite the economic and child-rearing benefits that doubling up with her parents could provide, Teresa took months to make her decision. She weighed the benefits against the negative implications of doubling up: "That I won't have a place anymore. Everything that I do I would have to consider my parents' decision as well." She imagined how difficult it would be to keep her children quiet and well behaved in her mother's home and how she would have to again "put up with my mom telling me what to do and how to do it with them." Despite her dread of having less control over the household, Teresa, at

Miguel's urging, ultimately decided that the financial risk of retaining residential independence was not worth it. The family moved their belongings into Teresa's parents' attic, stuffed their clothing into a broom closet, and "crowded ourselves" into the spare bedroom.

Natural Progression from Childhood

Parents who doubled up in response to a crisis or as a deliberate decision moved from independent housing into someone else's home. In contrast, over one-fourth of guest parents had never lived independently. These parents never had a moment when they "became" doubled up; the arrangement was simply a natural progression from childhood. Most of these parents had moved from their natal home at some point (or, in some cases, never had a stable natal home) and spent their adult lives living in the homes of extended family members, friends, and acquaintances, always relying on others for housing. Others had remained in their natal home consistently since childhood. Nationally representative data suggest that nearly one-third of mothers who are doubled up as guests have lived in their natal home since childhood.[15]

Noelle, a twenty-five-year-old Black mother, lived with her two daughters in her mother Donna's two-bedroom home, situated in a working-class neighborhood on the outskirts of Dallas. Unlike the parents previously described in this chapter, there was no specific event that precipitated doubling up for Noelle. She had her children young, while still living in her childhood home, and she never moved out. Living with Donna, a cafeteria supervisor for the local school district, allowed her to finish school and stay home with her children while they were young. At the beginning of the study, her daughters were eight and nine, and she had been working at an insurance company for a couple of years. She made around $22,000 a year, enough to put her just above the poverty threshold for a family of three. With this income, it seems likely that she could have moved out on her own, but she remained in her mother's home, not feeling financially ready to find her own home yet, "'cause I just wanted to make sure with my job and with myself, that I myself was ready for this. Because, of course, I have always stayed with my mom, so it is something that someone has to be ready for before they do it."

Noelle was engaged, and her fiancé Damien lived doubled up with his own parents, along with his young daughter. Although he came over often, he always returned to his own mother's home around 8:30 or 9:00 PM to sleep. "Because it is such a houseful, my mom just prefers that he stays at his own house," Noelle explained. "Me as an adult, my mom as an adult, the two children, so there is really nowhere to spend the night. So . . . (*laughs*)." Looking around the tiny living room, which already felt somewhat crowded with the overstuffed sofa and loveseat, it was difficult to disagree. Because there were only two bedrooms, she and her two daughters shared a room and slept in the same bed.

Noelle was more satisfied with her doubled-up living arrangement than many other parents, in large part because of her close relationship with her mother. Yet she was emphatic that she did not plan to stay in Donna's home long-term: "Oh, I'm definitely gonna move, 'cause I'm getting married." She tied residential independence to her ideals of family life, a theme further explored in chapter 5. Though she imagined that her mother would allow Damien to join the household if it became necessary, she described living doubled up as inappropriate for a couple, saying that they "wanted privacy outside of my mom's. And the fact that we're [getting] married, I think it's best that we're under our own roof."

Noelle was one of the countless young people whose efforts to achieve traditional markers of adulthood, like financial independence and marriage, have been stymied by declining job security and stability—and the lack of sufficient public supports to weather such employment challenges.[16] Asked what would make her ready to move out, she emphasized that stable employment for both her and Damien was a requirement before they formed an independent household. "Because you are not just going to pay the minimum that you are paying at your mom's house. All of this is going to be you and I. Like, this is a step we really want to take. The whole job factor. So we had to really be ready for it." Although she wanted to live independently with her soon-to-be-husband and their children, fear of employment instability prevented her from moving out to form an independent household.

In each of her interviews, Noelle was confident that she would soon be moving into her own home but unsure of the timeline. In the first summer, she anticipated moving in September, but she and Damien had not yet begun a housing search and were still deciding between searching for an apartment or a house to rent. The following summer, she was still living in her mother's home after economic uncertainty had sidetracked her plans to move the previous year. Her job working with denied insurance claims had been so stressful that she had been unsure of how long she could continue in it, and she and Damien had decided that "we didn't want to make any decisions like [moving] until I really found somewhere else to work."

Her concerns about economic uncertainty and setbacks were well founded. Over the next year, she grew tired of the stress and quit her job at the insurance company, taking a new position in a hospital billing department, a job that was less stressful but also that paid slightly less. The last time I spoke to her, she was still dreaming of residential independence. For the first time, she was taking active steps toward her housing goals, looking at online listings and inquiring about places advertised with "For Rent" signs that she and Damien saw when they drove by on their way to work. The search was still in the very early stages as they continued to debate whether they should move into a house or an apartment and remained undecided on their price range. Yet she felt sure that by fall they would be living in their own home. "I know we are going to stick to our guns on that," she said.

The security of Noelle's life with her mother allowed her to be cautious in her approach to residential independence. She knew she and her daughters had stable housing in Donna's home until she chose to form a household of her own. Asked whether her mother might ever ask her to leave, she laughed, "That hasn't crossed my mind at all. That is the least of my worries, and I am thankful for it. Because I can see having to think that. Not I!" Even if she had to move, she knew her father's house was always available for her as well.

For parents like Noelle, who felt relatively secure and satisfied with their living arrangements, doubling up was far from a last resort. Noelle described herself as picky in her housing search, though her list of requirements seemed far from excessive. She wanted a two- to three-bedroom home for her family and emphasized the importance of "curb appeal" in deciding which apartment complexes she would be willing to live in. She also limited her housing search to two neighborhoods—one near her mother and one near Damien's family— that she was familiar with and that were not too far from her job. She could impose these modest constraints on her housing search because she was able to remain in her mother's home until she found a good match.

Despite her relative comfort in her mother's home, Noelle's decision to live doubled up was still heavily constrained by the current housing market. She worked full-time, yet finding housing that met her standards and was affordable for her was challenging. In recent decades, median rents have increased by 21 percent adjusting for inflation, far outpacing the 2 percent increase in median renter household incomes over this period.[17] Assuming that Noelle budgeted a full 30 percent of her income for housing costs—which is typically considered the threshold for affordability—she could afford only about $600 a month in rent by herself, well under the roughly $700 median rent in Cleveland.[18]

Yet Noelle would not consider lowering her standards for a neighborhood. "Ah, if I had to make that decision, I would rather just stay home [at my mother's house]." She preferred to remain doubled up with her mother while she saved rather than entering the private rental market, where her near-poverty income would price her out of the neighborhoods and units she wanted and where even a short bout of unemployment would put her at risk of losing her housing. Likewise, although her income hovered near the poverty line, she had never applied for housing assistance, deeming it unnecessary, "because I can [live] here with my mom and be comfortable doing it." Until she could afford a desirable home for her family on the private market, allowing her mother "to see how their own child is going to do on their own two feet," Noelle would remain doubled up. In this way, high housing costs stalled her move to residential independence and her ability to form her own household with her fiancé and children.

Responding to Crises by Doubling Up

So far, this chapter has highlighted two pathways to doubling up that depart from the popular understanding of doubling up as a response to emergency housing needs. Nevertheless, slightly more than half of the guest parents in my sample doubled up after some sort of crisis that made their previous independent housing untenable. Most commonly, these crises were caused by housing issues, such as the impending eviction that sent Shay's family to her godmother's niece's house. Other parents doubled up when a romantic relationship conflict or breakup left them without a place to live.[19]

Lola, a Hispanic mother, lived in her mother Alicia's house in Cleveland with her three children. She met questions about her living situation with an exaggerated eye roll, explaining that it was "terrible" living doubled up. In addition to Lola and her two toddlers and six-year-old daughter, Alicia's large but full four-bedroom home housed Lola's brother, her brother's girlfriend, and their infant child. Lola and her children joined the household out of necessity after a jealous ex left her feeling that she could no longer live safely in her home. One night, when she arrived home after her closing shift at Chili's Restaurant, she had found her ex hiding in her yard. The cinder block he threw through her window damaged her television and left her fearing for her life. "Probably that cinder block was for my head. I could have been dead." She felt forced to move immediately: "I just didn't want to take the risk of staying in that place where he knew where I was at. And if he went to that extreme to throw a block through my window, not knowing if my kids were home that day—which luckily they weren't—but yeah. I just didn't want to stay there, so it forced me into a position where I had to put my things in storage."

Lola and her children moved in with her mother. If Alicia had not agreed to house them, Lola would have moved with her children to New York to live with one of her siblings, but she felt confident that her mother would always provide a place for her. Although their relationship was strained, Alicia had always been close to Lola's daughter, her first grandchild, and she would not want her to move to another state. Lola described the doubled-up arrangement as "hell," but she tried to look on the bright side: "We have a place to stay and just [try] to be grateful, but I don't like it. You know, I'm thirty years old. I'm used to being on my own."

That doubling up was often precipitated by a housing crisis is unsurprising given how often families, particularly lower-income families, are forced to move. In contrast to higher-income parents, who typically have the luxury of moving because they want to live in a particular home or neighborhood, lower-income parents more often move reactively, because they feel forced out of their previous home.[20] Many such moves are literally forced; every year, there are almost a million documented evictions, and these numbers do not include tenants, like Shay, who move out in anticipation of a formal eviction.[21] The striking prevalence of eviction has gained nationwide attention; however, as Lola's story shows, eviction is just one of many reasons that families feel forced to leave their home. In my sample, families also doubled up because their unit had fallen into unlivable disrepair, because their neighborhood was no longer safe for them, because they could not continue to make ends meet while paying their rent, or for some combination of reasons like these. Other reactive moves were prompted not by housing issues but by a romantic relationship conflict or breakup that required the parent to move from the home they had previously shared with their partner.

Housing crises and romantic relationship crises necessitated quick moves. Many families would have struggled to find a unit within the brief time frame they had available. Yet the more pressing issue, typically, was money. Lola was barely able to support her three young children on her limited income as a restaurant server; she got by through careful planning—for example, that summer she was already putting new winter jackets for her children on layaway so they would be paid off by the time the season changed. She covered the move-in costs of her rental unit using money from her tax refund and help from her children's father, and she had paid the $525 monthly rent inconsistently since then.

Living paycheck to paycheck is common among American families. About one-third of adults would be unable to cover an emergency expense of $500 or more with their savings.[22] This economic precarity makes it impossible for many families to respond to housing crises by moving to another unit. When Lola urgently needed to move to escape her dangerous ex, she could not absorb the financial shock of a deposit and first month's rent for a new home, even if she had been able to find a rental that was immediately available.

Public housing support was also often not a realistic alternative for parents like Lola who faced urgent housing needs. At the time of my fieldwork, the estimated wait time for Cleveland Housing Authority public housing units was six months.[23] This was a relatively short wait-list, as wait times across the United States for public housing units often stretch a year or longer, and wait times for housing choice vouchers are often more than two years.[24] Indeed, the wait time for a housing unit from the Dallas Housing Authority was estimated to be three to five years during my fieldwork.[25] Lola might have received priority on the housing assistance wait-list if she had reported herself as a victim of domestic violence.[26] However, she considered no options besides moving in with family when she needed housing right away.

Moreover, Lola had negative personal experience with the subsidized units in Cleveland. She had lived in a public housing apartment complex briefly a couple years prior, but she moved out (again doubling up with her mother) because the roof began caving in in the nursery she had prepared for her newborn. "There was stuff everywhere, I couldn't breathe, I was having asthma attacks, it was really bad." Her experience reflects the disrepair common to the aging public housing stock in the United States. In 2018, over 8 percent of properties received a failing score in the US Department of Housing and Urban Development's physical inspections of public housing, and an additional 20 percent were near failing.[27]

Lola decided to move with her children to Alicia's house while she prepared to reenter the private rental market. Living in her mother's house provided Lola with time to request her security deposit back from her landlord—she anticipated getting it within a month because she moved out in good standing—and to save for her first month's rent for a new apartment. "Once I get that," she proclaimed, "I'm out of here." She had not decorated the space in Alicia's home that she shared with her three children, and she kept their belongings in a storage facility. "We're only going to be here a month, so it's not like we're kind of living here," she explained during her first interview at her mother's house. She also had not told her children that they were living with Alicia and no longer had a home of their own. "They know that we don't live in the same house [as we did before we moved to my mother's], but they don't know that we don't have anywhere else. And they asked to go home every single day, and I hate it." Although Lola and her children, like many guests in my sample, did not view the doubled-up household as their permanent home, they had to remain there until she could afford another rental.

Parents responding to housing crises often sought temporary shelter by doubling up while they saved for the move-in costs of a new unit—though, as I discuss further in part 3, high housing costs and other barriers often kept parents doubled up for longer than they intended. Lola was sure that she would be able to save enough to move out of Alicia's house within a month, but by the next year she had quit her job at Chili's, unable to balance the last-minute work shifts with her parenting responsibilities, and remained unemployed. She and her children were still living doubled up, now splitting their time between Alicia's home and the home of her children's other grandmother. Their belongings were still in the storage unit, now paid for by her children's father, in anticipation of the day when they could move to a home of their own.

Attending to Hosts' Needs

Guests typically doubled up to meet their own needs or to pursue their own goals. But they did sometimes consider how coresidence might also affect their host. Before moving into Anthony's home to save to purchase a home of her own, Gabby had visited him frequently because her seventy-five-year-old stepfather's health had been in decline since her mother passed away the previous year. "I will bring him food every day to eat, you know when I cook for my kids, I bring him food over. And then I really started bringing the kids over so he wouldn't be by himself there. The kids would be like, 'He was falling, missed a step,' or whatever, so I was like, he needs some round-the-clock attention." Doubling up allowed Gabby to save toward homeownership, but it also made it easier for her and her children to provide the twenty-four-hour care Anthony needed. "I would not have moved at all, period, until he started feeling bad," she said.

Given the increases in both the population of older adults and the level of income inequality within this older population, a growing number of families face situations similar to Anthony and Gabby's.[28] Almost half of older adults either need or are receiving help with routine daily activities, like shopping or meal preparation, and family members provide the vast majority of this informal care.[29] Moreover, the number of older-adult households that are burdened by high housing costs is at an all-time high, and unaffordable housing makes it more difficult for older adults to afford other necessities, including food and health care.[30] Doubled-up households may become increasingly important for meeting the economic and care needs of older adults like Anthony.

Although Gabby was eager to move out of Anthony's home, she worried about his ability to live alone. "That's the only thing that kind of scares me is having somebody who'll watch out for him." She wanted to continue helping Anthony, but she rejected the idea of staying in his home indefinitely. "When you call yourself grown, you want to be on your own. . . . I just want that freedom of my own." Yet she did clarify that she would let him move into her new home after she moved out. She took her mother into her home to care for her when she was sick, and she anticipated needing to do the same for Anthony as he became unable to live independently. "I think I probably would take over most of the health [care] and support," Gabby considered, with the qualification that "I wouldn't want to [stay in his house] because I would still want my own stuff." The willingness to live doubled up as a host long-term but not as a guest was not unique to Gabby. Both hosts and guests sometimes commented that they would never want to live doubled up as a guest permanently, but that they were open to hosting, particularly hosting older relatives, as a longer-term arrangement. As I discuss in chapter 3, householder status conveyed authority and a sense of adulthood, making doubling up as a host more palatable for parents compared to coresidence as a guest.

Conclusion

Various circumstances and motivations lead families with children to double up as guests. Doubling up in response to a crisis was common among the parents in my sample. These crises included moves forced by eviction and housing unaffordability, but also crises that have received less attention as causes of doubling up, such as unit disrepair, unsafe neighborhoods, or romantic relationship breakups. For families with limited incomes and little savings, finding and maintaining a unit in the private rental market can be nearly impossible, especially when making a reactive move during a short time frame. However, housing crises are far from the only pathway into doubling up. For some parents, doubling up offers an opportunity to lower housing costs so that they can pursue mobility goals, such as homeownership or the legal status that will facilitate higher-paying employment. Some doubled-up parents have never lived independently, as the lack of quality, affordable housing has kept them doubled up throughout their adult lives.

Parents' stories of becoming doubled up revealed the broad impacts of the current housing market. High housing costs contributed to housing insecurity for low-income families, but they also stifled aspirations for the future even among families further up the income ladder. For each of the parents in this chapter, living in someone else's home was a response to constraints placed on them by high housing costs relative to income. They described living doubled up as a temporary state and planned to move to their own home as soon as they felt financially ready. In this way, parents often viewed doubling up as a guest as a source of temporary support. In the next chapter, I turn to the families with children who provided housing support to others and describe how they came to live doubled up as hosts.

2

Doubling Up as a Host

LAUREN, A THIRTY-EIGHT-YEAR-OLD MOTHER, lived in a one-bedroom apartment in a well-appointed apartment complex in a suburb of Dallas. The stylishly decorated living room had large black-and-white photographs of downtown Dallas, mementos from her involvement in the local African American arts scene before she became a mother. Upstairs was a small loft filled with toys and books, its walls covered in superhero posters, where her seven-year-old son Luca slept. At her first interview, Lauren's household consisted solely of her and Luca, who also lived half-time with her ex-husband (whom she had divorced about four years before), and she was several months pregnant with her second son, Ezra. Ezra's father did not coreside—he was doubled up as a guest in his mother's home—but the couple was attending marriage coaching at their church in anticipation of getting engaged.

Soon after Lauren gave birth to Ezra, her mother, Debra, moved in to help with the new baby. "It was almost a kind of mutual thing," Lauren explained. "I don't think I said, 'Mama, come stay with me,' but it was probably like, 'Well, I'll come down and help so you're not alone,' and I was like, 'Okay, thank you,' you know? So I think she just kind of volunteered to come down." Debra was originally from North Dallas, but when her income dropped precipitously after retiring from the billing department of a large company, she moved into Lauren's sister's home in Abilene, a smaller city a couple of hours away from Dallas. According to Lauren, Debra preferred Dallas to Abilene, even though she could not afford her own housing there; her friends and the rest of her family lived in Dallas, and she disliked the Abilene weather.

Lauren valued Debra's live-in support, and as she described her life as a lone mother raising Luca and Ezra while working full-time as a teacher, it was easy to understand why. Her work hours kept her busy, especially during the school year. She also stayed involved in Luca's sports and school—in fact, she chose his charter school specifically because it required parental volunteer hours. After moving in, Debra began caring for Ezra all day, so Lauren did not need to send the baby to day care. She was thrilled to have her mother there to be "that motherly, nurturing person" when she was not home with her children.

Additionally, when Lauren was home, Debra was there to support her. For instance, Lauren tried to squeeze Luca's homework time in between school and dinner, before basketball practice. The prior evening, "I told him twice to do [his homework], but I was also trying to cook him dinner, and I guess my mama saw it, and he wasn't moving fast enough, and she was like, 'Didn't she tell you to go do your math? Get your math. She shouldn't have to repeat herself.' That kind of thing, it's helpful, because I'm trying to do this, get this done, and she's right there and bam, she got it." Debra also cleaned the house, did laundry, and prepared dinner when Lauren got home late.

Although Lauren clearly appreciated Debra's support, she emphasized that the financial benefits of the arrangement flowed primarily to her mother. Debra, who was retired and lived on a fixed income, did not pay any of the rent. Lauren financially supported her by providing housing and occasionally covering her groceries and other small expenses. From her perspective, the childcare savings from living with Debra canceled out the additional food and utility cost. "It's not really like I'm saving anything except time," she explained. The financial savings from not having to find childcare for her two children was probably substantial, perhaps higher than Lauren acknowledged; in Texas, the average cost of infant childcare was nearly as high as the average rent.[1] Despite the mutual benefits of the arrangement, however, she saw her mother as the economic beneficiary of their coresidence and herself as the benefactor.

Hosting Debra in a one-bedroom loft apartment required that Lauren sacrifice space and privacy. She described how full the house had been since her mother moved in. "Her clothes are in the closet with Luca's clothes, and Ezra's clothes are in the closet with my clothes. So we're busting out the seams." Debra slept in the apartment's only full bedroom. Lauren recently purchased an air mattress for the living room, but before that she had been sleeping on the eggplant-colored couch across from the TV. She missed sleeping in her own bed and having privacy in her home—"I can't walk around naked or whatever," she laughed.

Likewise, Lauren and her mother had their differences, though she kept them in perspective. Her mother spoiled her children, especially baby Ezra, but Lauren shrugged it off, saying, "That's all grandparents, though." She also laughed off their different approaches to housekeeping: "I really can't complain so much because she's helping us out so much. . . . Even though she folds them [the towels] differently, they are still washed and folded, so I'm just going to put them in the drawer and keep it moving (*laughs*)."

Asked to imagine her future, Lauren was unsure where she would be living, but she was sure she would still be hosting. "Just being one big family. My mom probably will stay with us or [Ezra's father's] mom or I don't [know] what, but we'll all be together. Living under the same roof, the village. Yep. It takes a village." Because of the crowding, she was trying to save to buy a house or move to a larger apartment—three bedrooms at least, so she, Debra, and Luca could each have their own room. "When I can get a bigger place, I'm looking to make sure there's enough room for [my mother] to be there, because I don't anticipate her leaving anytime soon," Lauren explained. Although saving was difficult—she earned $55,000 a year, which was quickly drained by her children's expenses—she was determined to find a home where she could comfortably host a multigenerational household. Debra had mentioned returning to Abilene, but Lauren joked that she was not allowed to move until baby Ezra was in kindergarten.

In theory, Lauren could have received help with childcare and housework equally well as a host or a guest. However, she was unwilling to double up as a guest. If her mother were ever to move out, she thought she might want her future mother-in-law to move in, but she would not consider moving into her mother-in-law's home. "It would be different with moving in with us because she would be moving in if she were unable to kind of support herself anymore. I can't see myself and my sons moving into her house. I mean, I just don't see it. . . . It's her house. It's not my house. My things are not there. So it's like it'd be a temporary situation if I ever had to." For Lauren, the benefits of living doubled up outweighed the costs, but only as long as she held the role of support provider, not beneficiary.

Lauren also valued the authority she associated with being the householder. Her fiancé's mother's spacious, three-bedroom house was much larger than her one-bedroom loft apartment, yet "there wouldn't be any room for us as a family to live there," she said. She felt unable to bring her home furnishings— beds, TVs, and the like—to someone else's home. "I can't go into someone else's house and take their stuff out or move their stuff around. It just doesn't work that way." Likewise, she believed that differences in housekeeping would be manageable only if she retained the authority of the householder. "If she moved in with us, I don't think it would be so much of a problem because I would be keeping house . . . because she has a lot of stuff, coffee cups and squeeze bottles and things. So if I get rid of that stuff because it's just sitting on the counter—I don't like clutter—and if I go in and start decluttering, I don't want to offend somebody because that's her house. But in my house we're not going to have a hundred squeeze bottles on the counter. We're just not."

———

Hosts provided a vital housing safety net that filled needs left by the unafford-able housing market and the lack of adequate public supports. In my sample, most families began hosting when their guest experienced a housing crisis, ended a romantic relationship, or exited another doubled-up household. By providing housing to friends and family, these informal shelter providers served a critical function in their community.[2] This chapter examines the foundation of this private safety net by asking how families came to live doubled up as hosts. What motivated host parents to share their housing with other adults? How did they conceptualize their role as hosts and the support they provided to guests?

Chapter 1 showed that guests had a variety of motivations for doubling up. Hosts, on the other hand, generally perceived themselves in similar ways: as support providers who were helping friends and family by sharing their housing with them. Evidence from nationally representative data supports the framing of hosts as support providers. Parents are most likely to become doubled up as guests at times when they might need additional support, such as after a job loss and when children are young. In contrast, parents are particularly likely to start hosting at times when they may be better equipped to provide support, such as when they begin to work or are working stably and when their children are older.[3]

Hosts like Lauren drew a sharp distinction between doubling up as a host and being a help *provider* versus doubling up as a guest and being a help *recipient*. Being a host—and therefore a help provider—conveyed a moral identity as a compassionate and generous person. As chapter 3 will show, this moral identity contrasted with the dependency and corresponding lack of authority that accompanied being a guest. Hosts often received support—such as economic or childcare assistance—from guests as well. However, this assistance did not typically undermine their identity as primarily a support provider rather than a recipient. For example, Lauren and Debra mutually agreed to double up after Ezra's birth, yet Lauren assumed the moral identity of a support provider because she was the householder.

Although hosts identified as help providers, the support they received from guests could greatly impact their lives. As I discuss further in part 2, doubling up helped fill in gaps in the US welfare state that affected both hosts and guests. Without the childcare provided by their guests, hosts like Lauren would have had to navigate a childcare market that is increasingly expensive and suffering from labor shortages.[4] In Texas, the annual average cost of infant care alone is more than $9,000—that is, childcare for just one of Lauren's two children would probably have cost more than 15 percent of her income.[5] As described in chapter 1, some older adult hosts received valuable assistance with activities of daily living, like cooking and cleaning, that enabled them to continue living safely in their home. Financial contributions from guests also provided additional income to hosts. For economically precarious hosts, this extra income could ease the burden of high housing costs, enable them to pay utility bills, or free up enough money for occasional treats for their children. In sum, doubling up often provided hosts with needed support, yet allowed them to project a self-image as a self-sufficient adult with resources to share.

Lauren hosted her mother, an older adult whose fixed retirement income would not allow her to live independently. Hosts were often comfortable providing longer-term support for older adult guests, but as this chapter will show, working-age guests, perhaps particularly men, faced greater expectations of independence. In this way, hosts adopted cultural classifications of needy individuals into those who were "deserving" of assistance and those who were "undeserving"—and therefore required more paternalistic support.[6] Housing assistance to working-age adults was often contingent and temporary, intended to help guests progress toward goals that the host sanctioned. At times, hosts drew on cultural logics of dependency to justify limiting the support they provided, using language remarkably similar to national conversations around the public safety net.

Despite these restrictions, hosts did provide valuable support for guests by sharing their homes. As chapter 1 highlighted, rising housing costs have made it increasingly difficult for lower-income adults to maintain housing on the private market, yet public housing assistance is in short supply. Hosts provide the private safety net that fills in where the public safety net falls short: in one sample of public housing authorities, about 40 percent of rental assistance applicants lived doubled up with family or friends while waiting to receive rental assistance.[7] Doubling up as a guest has become a critical component of the housing landscape for lower-income adults and families—one that is possible only because of the willingness of hosts to share their homes with extended family and friends.

The informal housing assistance provided by hosts undoubtedly has community-level benefits, but hosts—many of whom are families of color and families of lower socioeconomic status—bear the burden of providing this support.[8] As Lauren's story shows, hosts gave up physical space in what were sometimes already cramped quarters, and they lost much of the privacy they were accustomed to in their home. Moreover, in contrast to Lauren's position of relative economic advantage, hosting often fell to parents who were financially precarious themselves. For parents with limited resources beyond their housing stability, doubling up was one of the few ways that they *could* tangibly support others. As this chapter will show, hosting carried financial risks, especially for economically precarious parents. Yet, because the challenges of poverty often pull adults into intense relationships in which loyalty is expected to translate into providing material assistance, denying assistance to friends and family in need also came at a high cost.[9]

Deciding to Help

Hosts claimed a moral identity as a help provider, but they described a variety of other motivations underlying their help. Some described doubling up as a mutually beneficial arrangement that allowed the guest to secure housing while providing the host with some other form of assistance. For example, Lauren provided Debra with housing while benefiting from the live-in childcare and housekeeping Debra provided.

Beyond the potential mutual benefits, doubling up provided hosts with a meaningful opportunity to help their extended family and friends. Sharing one's housing was a way of showing love and compassion, particularly in a context of scarcity. Moke, a thirty-four-year-old Black mother of three, hosted a twenty-year-old friend, the daughter of her childhood friends, after the young woman was kicked out of her sister's home. Moke's family protested. "My daughter told me, she said, 'Ma, we got this one house . . . stop taking people in, you're not a shelter.'" Nonetheless, her compassion got the best of her. She explained, "I just can't help it. I don't like to see people hurt and be all stressed out and going through stuff." Hosting reinforced her positive self-concept as a caring, kindhearted person.

Some hosts worried about where their guests would end up without their assistance. Papi, a fifty-nine-year-old White grandfather, hosted a rotating cast of household members in his spacious single-family home in Cleveland, including his brother, his adult daughters, his adult granddaughter and her infant, and his granddaughter's friend and her young child. By providing housing, he knew his family was taken care of. For instance, his brother was unemployed and had trouble getting along with other potential housing providers. "I like to know he's not living on the street," Papi said, explaining why he hosted.

Providing housing for others demonstrated compassion as well as familial love and loyalty when parents hosted extended family members, as most of them did. Lauren explained why she hosted her mother and had previously provided a home for her younger sister: "Again, it's that village thing. You have to take care of your family." Papi likewise referred to family ties to explain why he hosted: "But like I said, he's my brother, just like I say these are my grandchildren. I'm not going to tell them you can't come to the house." Talking about his nineteen-year-old granddaughter, he explained, "What can I say? I love her. I'd do anything for her. I don't ask for a lot back. I never was that type of a person."

"You Don't Have to Be Rich": Hosting in a Context of Scarcity

Sharing housing allowed economically disadvantaged adults to help family and friends—and assume an identity as a help provider—even when they otherwise had few resources to share. JC, a forty-seven-year-old Black father, lived in a ranch-style house in Dallas with his four children, who ranged in age from two to six. His nephew Tyler, who was in his late twenties, contacted him when he was about to be released from jail. Because he did not have a home of his own, Tyler asked if he could provide JC's address to his parole officer as his place of residence upon release. The three-bedroom, one-bath home was already crowded, but "family is family," JC said. After he was released, Tyler moved in and began sleeping on one of the two white leather loveseats in the tiny living room.

For many hosts, the housing support they provided was not limited to one guest; households frequently not only doubled up but tripled up or even quadrupled up. Just a couple of months after JC allowed Tyler to move in, his niece Ashley told him she was having trouble living with her mother- and father-in-law. JC let her join his household as well. At first, she occupied the second loveseat in the living room. Soon JC agreed to let her husband, who was still living in his parents' house, join them as well. Wanting to provide the married couple with privacy, but having only so much space to go around, he generously began sharing his bedroom with his six-year-old son and had his three younger children share a bedroom so that Ashley and her husband could have the home's third bedroom to themselves.

Like the guests they housed, doubled-up householders tended to be economically disadvantaged.[10] The prior year, JC had earned about $37,000 working from home for an airline company and had to stretch his budget to provide for his four children. He later took medical leave from his job, and although he was working with friends to open a restaurant, money was even tighter than before. He described a lengthy list of household items he needed to replace, saying, "But I can't afford [it], I just use what we have and things like that. So you learn to survive." JC got by with loans from family and friends, but these carried their own stress. As he put it, "And then you robbing Peter to pay Paul, so you always behind."

JC's precarious financial situation made him an unlikely support provider. However, he had stable housing; he had rented his home for over a year by the time his niece and nephew moved in. By sharing his residence, he was able to help his family and cultivate an identity as a support provider despite his limited resources. He explained, "You don't have to be rich in order to be nice, to help each other. You just have to have whatever and if you're willing to sacrifice, then sometimes you have to sacrifice with grown folks and kids in a two- or three-bedroom home. You know you need five or six [bedrooms], but you don't have it."

JC, like most hosts, emphasized that he doubled up in response to his guests' needs. However, it was clear that he also sorely needed the assistance that his nephew and niece could provide. Ashley and Tyler babysat his four children, who adored their older cousins. "It kind of helps me out too sometime if he or she doesn't have to go to work, they can watch the kids while I work over there. I don't have to call nobody here and look for nobody. That's a plus." Later, JC's health took a turn for the worse, and the childcare assistance provided by Ashley and Tyler became even more vital when he was in and out of the hospital being treated for a blood clot.

JC also asked each of the three adults he hosted to pay about $75 a month, an amount that together would have covered nearly half of his $500 rent. As I discuss further in chapter 4, rent payments from guests to hosts were common. JC framed these contributions as scaffolding to prepare his guests to live independently. "Grown folks needs to be [paying]. You have to pay something.

You can't go out there and live for free. If you had an apartment, you were going to have to pay. So you might as well just pay me. . . . And if you can't pay me, then we need to figure out some more arrangements."

Although JC required financial contributions from his guests, he, like many hosts, was adamant that he did not *need* this help. "I already, when it came into it, I could do whatever I needed to do on my own. They were extra. I didn't never want to put myself in the situation where I had to depend on someone else's money to pay my bills," he declared. "Everything kind of get tight, but I had enough funds to do it. So they just kind of helped me out where it made it a little bit more easier, so I could go in and say, 'All right, let's go shopping.'" Being able to pay his own rent was a mark of pride for JC, one that reinforced his identity as a support provider rather than a recipient. The belief that hosts, as householders, should be able to afford rent without assistance from guests was articulated by both hosts and guests. As scholars Frederick Wherry, Kristin Seefeldt, and Anthony Alvarez write, a request for assistance offers potential helpers an opportunity to "enact a confident self-image of a responsible user of money" and a "morally grounded, caring individual."[11] As a host who provided housing but did not rely on his guests' contributions to pay his housing costs, JC claimed both of these identities.

"When Someone Is Ready": Evaluating Guests

Gail, a fifty-four-year-old Black mother, owned a three-bedroom, two-bath house in a lower-income area of Dallas.[12] When she purchased the house, she planned to live there with her two younger daughters. Her older daughter, Krystal, was attending college. Soon after Gail bought her house, however, Krystal dropped out of school because of an unintended pregnancy and returned home. Five years later, Krystal, age twenty-four, and her son still occupied one of the home's three bedrooms.

Gail later opened her home to her sister Vickie as well. Her sister struggled with addiction, although Gail did not know it until Vickie began her recovery. One day, Vickie asked her to join her recovery classes, and Gail began attending the classes. "Then they tell you that it's more than that [classes], that they need somebody that's gonna give them the support and help them," she explained, describing how she came to provide her sister with a place to live during her continued recovery. Vickie could have lived with friends, but Gail's home allowed her to avoid the social context that had enabled her addiction. "She didn't want to be back around the surroundings, because where she was coming from was a lot of drug activities," Gail said. "So she just thought I was the best route," and Gail agreed.

To Gail, providing housing support to her daughter and sister demonstrated what "type of person" she was. She contrasted her desire to be a "rock" when her daughter needed support to parents who were unwilling to provide housing for an adult child. "You know some parents do that and say, 'You get eighteen, you've got to go.' For instance, some say when she had a baby she should have left." Likewise, she linked the housing support she gave Vickie to her identity as a "server," saying, "I'm the type of person that I like to help, and if I can help you, I will. I can do it even if I have to go without."

Gail's proclaimed willingness to "go without" was not hollow. She did not collect rent from her guests and even rejected her sister's offer to contribute, telling her to save instead for her own apartment. Moreover, she gave up much of her privacy when she hosted her sister. So Vickie could have a bedroom of her own, Gail slept on the pullout couch in the living room. "You kind of want to give somebody privacy when they're trying to get themselves together. . . . I would want somebody to do that to me." She did not regret her decision to share her home, though she did regret not getting a four-bedroom home with more space. "Since I've been living in my house, everybody done had my room," she mused, recounting how, in addition to hosting Vickie and Krystal, she had hosted her other sister's family a few months before.

Hosting was part of Gail's "server" identity, but her willingness to host depended on her evaluation of her guests' deservingness. She initially had doubts about allowing Vickie to join her household, but after careful assessment, she ultimately judged her sister to be ready to make a positive change in her life. "When she cried to me—'cause my sister is not the type to cry—and when she just opened up herself to me, I knew that she was really ready this time to do whatever she needed to do." Gail was not only concerned about what it would be like to live with her sister but also evaluating whether Vickie would use the housing support to make rapid progress toward goals that she approved of: recovery, employment, and independent living. "So when someone is ready, they're just gonna put their feet on the step and just move on," she explained.

Gail likewise evaluated her daughter's character. She explained proudly that Krystal did not *want* to remain in her home long-term and instead "just wants to be independent of me." She detailed Krystal's grueling job search as evidence of her work ethic and predicted, "If she gets a job, she won't be there [in my home] long, 'cause as soon as she gets enough money, she will go. I know she will, because she's just very independent." While Krystal was unemployed, Gail did not charge her rent. Yet she believed that her daughter would insist on paying a bill if she held steady employment, and she would accept this payment out of respect for her independence. "If I was living with somebody, I could feel better if I'm contributing something. You don't want to be totally dependent on a person. Especially when you finally get a job. No."

For both Vickie and Krystal, Gail assessed her guests' character and motivation to use the assistance to make progress toward goals that she endorsed. In this way, she evaluated how worthy her guests were of the assistance she could provide. Hosts like Gail drew on long-familiar moral frames in the history of the American social safety net.[13] The US social safety net is shaped by cultural classifications of individuals into the "deserving" poor, for whom assistance is presumed to be necessary because they are not expected to work, and the "undeserving" poor, who are expected to work and therefore should not need assistance. These moral valuations pervade antipoverty policy, and social safety programs for the "undeserving" poor are often designed to teach and incentivize appropriate social behavior, such as work.[14] In a similar way, Gail's assistance was intended to promote residential independence, and her evaluations of whether her guests would use this support to make progress toward that goal shaped her willingness to help.

Moral frames of deservingness are seemingly ubiquitous in discussions of poverty in the United States. For example, these frames have permeated the outlooks of the private actors who provide much of the contemporary social safety net. Landlords who provide affordable housing think about their tenants in paternalistic moral terms similar to those adopted in public programs and attempt to "train" tenants to conform to traditional notions of responsibility and self-reliance.[15] Likewise, women who receive assistance from nonprofit institutions and churches apply moral frames of deservingness to themselves and other beneficiaries, even when the institution does not reinforce them.[16] Gail's evaluations of her guests' deservingness show the role these frames play in the private safety net as well.

"You Have to Fend for Yourself": Providing Short-Term and Contingent Assistance

Gail described living with her guests as easy. Vickie's long work hours kept her out of the house frequently. Gail appreciated the times when they were home together, because "when you're our age, you don't get to spend a whole lot of time with your sister, so it was a good thing for me." With evident affection, she described how Vickie provided "good support as far as just listening and encouragement" and "says stuff that makes you just crack up—she should have been a comedian really." Vickie also deferred to Gail's authority within the home, adhering to rules like being inside the home only when Gail was also home. She adjusted her behavior as needed, such as when Gail told her she was spending too long in the bathroom while her daughters were waiting. With such deference from her guest, it was easy for Gail to share her home.

Yet, because Gail wanted both Krystal and Vickie to be independent, she, like many hosts, intended for the housing support she provided to be temporary. About three months into Vickie's stay, she encouraged her to move out. "One day I asked her, I said, 'When was the last time that you paid a bill or took care of yourself?'" Her sister struggled to remember—Gail estimated it had been twenty to thirty years since Vickie had a household of her own. "You're fifty-two years old. Do you want somebody to take care of you forever?" she recalled asking her sister. As Vickie cried, Gail assured her, "I'm not trying to hurt you. I just want the best for you." This tough love was necessary, in her mind, to encourage Vickie to "be able to just take care of yourself, not depend on anyone."

Gail even began her sister's housing search herself by inquiring about available units, because "sometimes you need somebody to take a step first." Vickie ultimately took over the search so she could avoid neighborhoods that might impede her recovery. When she moved out, Gail was satisfied that her efforts had prevented her housing support from fostering dependency, saying, "She probably wouldn't have wanted to leave because . . . I'm the cushion. But she needed to do it that way."

The arguments of hosts like Gail about the importance of providing only a *temporary* safety net are reminiscent of public discussion around welfare policy. During the 1980s and 1990s, the idea that public welfare spending was a cause of social problems, rather than simply a response to those problems, became well established in the public discourse around poverty. By providing an alternative and disincentive to work, the argument went, welfare "trapped" families in poverty.[17] Likewise, Gail described providing long-term support as counterproductive to helping her sister achieve greater self-sufficiency; time-limiting her housing support ensured that Vickie did not "fall in that same route as far as being dependent on somebody else to take care of you." These frames enabled hosts like Gail to place limits on the extent of their assistance in a way that was consistent with their identities as altruistic helpers.

Similarly, Gail intended to provide Krystal with temporary support to allow her to progress toward sanctioned goals. Gail, like some other parents hosting young adult children, gave her daughter substantial flexibility in her timeline toward independence. She did not ask Krystal to leave the household during the fieldwork period—in fact, she rejected her daughter's plan to move out as soon as she found a job and instead stressed the importance of first having six months of living expenses saved. However, Gail was eager for her to make progress toward these goals, telling Krystal that it was time to "focus on getting herself together" now that her son was getting ready to attend kindergarten.

As Gail described her plans for her daughter's future, it was clear that she had an active role in shaping and pursuing these goals. After Krystal's prolonged and unsuccessful job search, Gail encouraged her to pursue temporary work to gain experience. "We just come to the agreement of it's time for her to go out and do whatever she needs to do," she explained. She also wanted Krystal to return to college, though the expense stalled this goal. Quantitative analyses show that living with relatives is associated with higher chances that young mothers will enter work and school.[18] The way hosts like Gail framed doubling up—as a temporary support intended to promote eventual independence—and the other encouragement they provided may contribute to this association. As chapter 6 discusses, the childcare that coresident adults provided also freed up time for parents to further their education or enter the workforce.

Gail would miss her daughter's companionship if she moved, as well as her help around the house. For instance, at Gail's urging, Krystal cooked many of the household's meals, since she was not working. Still, Gail saw her daughter's eventual exit as necessary progress, explaining that, as an adult, "she was really ready to be on her own." To parents like Gail, hosting was intended to support progress toward eventual self-sufficiency. She equated her desire to have her daughter move out on her own with wanting her daughter to "succeed."

Framing housing support as temporary and contingent on guests' progress toward approved goals allowed other hosts to justify ending the doubled-up arrangement when guests did not meet their expectations. JC's niece and nephew, Ashley and Tyler, both struggled with addiction and still needed to learn, as JC put it, that "you have to fend for yourself, there's no one else out there that's gonna help you." When he allowed them to move in, he planned to provide temporary assistance to give them "a chance to change." His expectations for coresidence were designed to foster independence. "The rules and regulations I gave them, it wasn't nothing hard . . . help me on the rent, go to work. Y'all save y'all some money so y'all can come up and y'all can get out of here and y'all get your own place and do well. I didn't have hard stipulations at all. I don't believe I have to do grown folks like that. If you grown and you want to make it, I shouldn't have to do that to you."

The next summer, JC was again living alone with his children. He had evicted each of his guests one by one as he grew frustrated with their insufficient rent payments. "It started out real good. They was helping me with groceries, helping me on the little rent, whatever case of it is. Then they got the point they wasn't giving me anything on groceries, they wasn't giving me anything on the rent, and they were just here. . . . I was getting the worst end of the stick." First, he put Tyler out of his home after his nephew was fired from his job. When Tyler argued, JC called 911 and had the responding officers escort him off the property. Just a couple of months later, he put Ashley's husband and later Ashley herself out because they did not reliably pay rent to him, which he attributed to drug use.

JC tried to be understanding about his guests' limited incomes, but he felt unable to host, incurring the additional costs of maintaining a larger household, if his guests were neither adequately contributing nor making progress toward residential independence. "I'm not taking care of grown people no more," he explained, adding that "you can only do that for a while and you have to let everybody go, and you have to throw them in the water and let them swim." Hosts like JC were support providers, but their help was constrained. He was willing to share his tiny three-bedroom home, but not to allow his nephew and niece to stay indefinitely while diverting his limited financial resources away from his children. "But I can't do that. Because I have to think about my kids. My kids come before me."

After he put his nephew and niece out of his home, JC knew they had bounced around from house to house, though he did not know where they were at the time of the interview. He regretted that they had not used his help to get back on their feet, but he felt that he had done all that he could. "Now they get mad at me because they can't advance, and they think it was something that I did. I can only lead you to the water. I can't make you drink it." Hosts like JC believed that they provided the support their guests needed to achieve self-sufficiency, but that it was up to the guests to translate this temporary support into long-term improvement in their circumstances. This understanding allowed JC to see himself as a generous person, even when his generosity was time-limited and conditional.

"You Gotta Be the Provider": How the Age and Gender of Guests Shaped Hosts' Expectations

Hosts' evaluations of guests were age-graded and gendered. Hosts of older adults rarely held the strict expectations of their guests that hosts like Gail and JC held for their working-age adult guests. For instance, Lauren never discussed whether her mother Debra was an independent person, nor did she expect that her retired mother would make progress toward residential independence. Instead, she described multigenerational households as "almost how it should be." It was generally better for older generations to live with younger generations, she explained, and for younger generations to benefit from the older generation's childcare assistance and wisdom. She observed that multigenerational households had fallen out of favor but were better equipped to meet families' needs. "In the African culture, families were set up in villages. So it wasn't like Mom and Dad live across state lines or an hour or two hours away from the grandparents. They were all there together, and so it was a lot easier and that child always had that adult supervision. That guidance, that wisdom, it was always around them. I think we got away from that as a culture. We just want your own little house."

Although Lauren's cultural interpretation of doubling up was rare within my sample, her sense that it was acceptable—even desirable—for older adults to double up as guests long-term was not. Vignette studies show that Americans have more favorable views of multigenerational coresidence in response to the *older* generation's needs than in response to the *younger* generation's needs. Likewise, Americans are more likely to invoke familial obligations when the older generation needs help; when the younger generation needs help, they are more likely to say that coresidence should be a short-term exchange of assistance or one step toward saving up to become independent.[19]

Lauren's acceptance of her mother's need for long-term assistance stood in stark contrast to how she interpreted doubling up by her partner, Ezra's father, who lived in his mother's house. After the couple broke up, she retrospectively saw his lack of residential independence as a red flag, recounting how a friend had told her, "Any forty-five-year-old man who still live with his mama, like the old folks say, he ain't wrapped too tight." Hosts' different expectations for older adults and working-age adults reflect societal norms around deservingness of assistance. Whereas working-age adults are expected to use doubling up as a temporary support and to progress toward self-sufficiency, older adults are seen as vulnerable, being unable to work and therefore in need of, and more deserving of, assistance.[20]

Expectations that guests will work toward independence may be particularly stringent for men compared to women. JC tied his disappointment in his nephew's failure to achieve independence to gendered expectations. "I said, a grown man really got to stand on their own. I can understand a woman going through some, but you're a grown man, and if you can't stand on your own, can't nobody stand for you. You gotta be the provider." Gendered expectations of men providing for their families could make hosting men a less acceptable arrangement, compared to hosting women. Even when hosts did allow men to join the household, some imposed higher financial bars than they did for mothers by themselves. Of course, although men at times faced higher expectations than women, moral evaluations and expectations of progress toward independence were not limited to men, as the examples in this chapter show.

Additionally, some doubled-up parents, both hosts and guests, suggested that concern for a child motivated the host to provide housing assistance. Often the primary caregiver for children, mothers may be better able to benefit from concern for child welfare than men. For instance, when Leeann, a host featured in chapter 3, shared her home with her brother, sister-in-law, and their daughter, she grew frustrated by the mess they created. She demanded that her brother leave, but she allowed her sister-in-law and niece to remain, saying, "I'm not going to put my niece on the streets, but I told my brother someone can leave." Likewise, when her cousin and her cousin's ten-year-old daughter were kicked out of multiple doubled-up households, leaving them with no other housing options, Leeann agreed to host them, "because of her daughter. They had nowhere to go, and I'm not going to let her daughter be put in the streets." Hosts' concern about child well-being sometimes motivated them to host mothers but did not always facilitate fathers' entry into the household, as chapter 5 discusses.

The Costs of Hosting—and of Not Hosting

Throughout the examples in this chapter, we have seen how hosts incurred costs by providing housing to others. Lauren, Gail, and JC each sacrificed space and privacy. For economically constrained hosts, like JC, doubling up drained limited resources. Part 2 further documents the challenges that doubling up introduced to daily life. Yet, despite these challenges, hosts chose to provide housing to others, often describing the decision as an act of compassion that transcended concern about their own well-being. Never was this framing more compelling than for hosts like Ron, a thirty-one-year-old Black father who hosted extended family and friends even though it put him at risk of losing his own housing. Although only a couple of hosts described taking such extreme risks by hosting, Ron serves as an archetype of hosts' approaches to doubling up.

Ron and his wife Sheila lived with their son in a freshly renovated two-bedroom, two-bath townhome-style apartment in a low-income apartment complex in a Dallas suburb. They secured the spacious unit for just $184 a month in rent with the help of a housing voucher from the Dallas Housing Authority and an application fee waiver from the apartment manager. This unit, where they had lived for about a year, was their first subsidized rental since Ron successfully petitioned the DHA to reinstate his voucher. He had lost his voucher three months before that because of repeated violations for hosting an off-lease resident, Jasmine, a woman he described as Sheila's sister before later clarifying that she was "more like a close associate, friend of the family type thing."[21] Ron blamed Jasmine's lack of discretion for the loss of his voucher. "That's because people don't know how to keep their mouth closed. I'm going to help you out and you don't know how to—if someone asked, 'Do you stay at this address?' you're supposed to tell them no, you don't, you're just over there visiting."

Ron received approximately $10,000 a year in disability income, and he made ends meet by keeping careful track of his finances—when asked the income he reported on his last tax return, he replied down to the penny. After losing his housing voucher, he could not afford private market rent, and he, Sheila, and their son doubled up with others. First, they moved in with an acquaintance befriended by Sheila at Bible study, a woman who let them join her household even though they "hardly knew each other." When this host unexpectedly demanded a couple of hundred dollars to cover an electricity bill, Ron and his family moved to his mother's house for the final month before getting their housing voucher reinstated.

Although Ron had had his voucher reinstated just a year prior, he had already received a citation for having unauthorized residents. In his new two-bedroom apartment, he hosted Jasmine, his brother-in-law, and Sheila's best friend and her two daughters. He explained that he was simply a helper. "Everybody you see in this house I have helped. Everybody in this house, and they're clueless, but I have helped everybody get on track to know what they should do with their lives. . . . By letting them stay here, even though I know

I'm not supposed to because I'm on housing." Ron was keenly aware of the risk he took by sharing his housing. His family had doubled up as guests themselves when he lost his housing voucher, and they would have to do so again if they lost their housing voucher. He laid out the stakes bluntly: "If I lose my housing, I ain't got no place to go." For hosts like Ron, doubling up was a liability. By hosting, he risked the very housing stability that he sought to share. As the next chapter discusses, Ron may have had other options that he did not pursue, such as adding his guests to his lease. However, as long as his guests were not authorized to live with him, Ron risked his housing voucher by allowing them to stay.

After Ron received the citation for unauthorized guests, Sheila got into a disagreement with her friend—Ron suggested there was jealousy over him at play ("Let me just say, females don't always get along")—and evicted the friend. He did not want to have to ask his other guests to leave but felt forced to do so by the risk of losing his housing. "They don't understand how much it hurts me to tell them that they got to get out," he lamented. He normally requested $150 monthly in rent from each adult, but that month he told them to use it to secure other housing. Meanwhile, he planned to try to make amends for his violation by taking the citation to the housing authority with an apology.

With the household back to just their nuclear family, Ron and Sheila agreed to stop hosting others, an act of self-preservation that went against their usual nature. "We bend over backwards to help somebody before we think about our own well-being, think about our own marriage. That's what we did last year. This year we're thinking about ourselves first, and then if we can help people, we can help them. If we can't, we can't."

Housing vouchers are a precious commodity for low-income families; many localities' housing voucher wait-lists are closed to new applicants, and the average wait time for those who do make it onto a wait-list is over two years.[22] Rules against unauthorized residents place subsidized renters like Ron and Sheila in a bind when their extended family and friends need a place to stay, forcing them to choose between their social ties and housing.[23] Moreover, by dissuading prospective hosts, the high costs of violating occupancy rules may weaken the private safety net. Perhaps because of these risks, parents who receive housing assistance are less likely to double up as a host.[24]

Whereas deciding to host signaled love and compassion, turning down a request could have grave consequences for hosts' loved ones. The next year Ron was again hosting Jasmine in violation of housing regulations. When she initially asked to stay with them, he said no. An issue with his disability checks left him unsure about when income would be coming into the household, and he felt unable to take the financial risk of hosting. "Because we was down to the last on our lights, we was down to the last on our groceries, so I had to tell her no. I didn't want to, I felt guilty . . . I felt really sick . . . but I had to do what was best, I had to look out for my own family first before bringing somebody else in, because it doesn't help bringing somebody else in when we on our last."

Ron and Shelia later learned that Jasmine had moved into a hotel. When Sheila visited her in the hotel, Jasmine told her that she was being evicted by the hotel manager. With her close friend—her fictive kin sister—living in a hotel and about to be put out, Sheila invited her to stay with her again. Ron pointed out that, unlike the prior year, they were only hosting one person, and he again justified the risk: "Only person that's allowed is my friend, and that's because she has nowhere to go, you know what I mean? And I know her staying here is kind of a violation, but I'm doing it for good, so I know God will watch out for me. . . . I'm doing this out of kindness. 'Cause if I was in the same situation, I would want somebody to do it for me."

Why *do* hosts provide housing support when their own resources are limited, or when hosting comes at such a cost? Although it is difficult to pinpoint exactly how hosts like Ron weigh the costs and benefits of doubling up, the provision of assistance by those with too little to share is well documented. For decades, scholars have detailed the critical role of kin and friends as a poverty survival resource.[25] As Carol Stack discussed in her classic ethnography *All Our Kin*, loyalty to kin (and fictive kin, those nonrelatives with whom the relationship is so close that they are similar to kin) acts as a powerful force. Put simply, "kin expect to help one another out"—and are often expected to do so.[26]

Of course, providing help to others can take a toll on individuals' resources and aspirations.[27] Yet declining to provide assistance came at a cost as well. Ron felt sick when he initially had to decline Jasmine's request to join his household. Refusal to meet social obligations to provide assistance to family and friends in sincere need can prompt feelings of self-consciousness or shame, particularly when the refusal leaves close friends or family at risk of being unable to meet their basic needs.[28] The housing that hosts like Ron provided served as a vital private safety net for their needy friends and family, and refusing this assistance could have profound consequences for their friends' and family's well-being.

Conclusion

This chapter has shown that parents who hosted others in their home, despite variation in their housing and economic circumstances and in what they stood to gain or lose by doubling up, nearly all understood themselves to be help providers, providing housing support to family and friends in need. Hosts described providing housing support to others as an act of empathy, the fulfillment of kinship roles, and a signal of their identities as helpers.

Despite these lofty ideals, hosts did set boundaries around the help they provided, at times drawing on norms of deservingness. Their willingness to help working-age adults was in part shaped by their perceptions of guests' character and progress toward becoming self-reliant. The focus on working-age guests achieving independence reflected the assumption that nuclear family units should be independent.

Although hosts identified as support providers, many of these parents needed the support that guests could provide, including childcare and economic support. Thus, in some households, doubling up was mutually beneficial. Yet hosting also came at a cost, from the loss of privacy and space to the economic risks. Part 2 further highlights the ways in which doubling up shaped hosts' lives by adding complexity to their daily routines and interactions. Pushing these costs onto hosts is a public policy decision. In the United States, the hosts who provide a private housing safety net stand in as a substitute for a robust public safety net. The parents in my sample provided housing for other adults in need of temporary housing after they experienced a housing crisis, the breakup of a romantic relationship, or the need to move out of another doubled-up household. Ron's example also highlights how policy decisions further increased the costs of hosting; housing subsidy regulations against unauthorized residents made hosting particularly risky, forcing parents to choose between providing critical assistance to their family and friends and maintaining their own housing stability.

Although parents distinguished between host and guest status, it is important to note that host and guest were not permanent categories. Many of the hosts in this chapter had doubled up as guests at some point as well. Eleven of the sixty parents in my sample doubled up as both a host and a guest at different points during the three-year fieldwork period. Moreover, of parents who only doubled up as hosts, a substantial majority—more than three-fourths—said that they had doubled up as a guest at some point in their residential history.

Chapter 1 documented the need that led guest parents to double up, and chapter 2 has shown how parents thought about the decision to provide housing support to others. In part 2, I explore how doubled-up households, once formed, shaped the daily lives of both host and guest families. As this chapter has demonstrated, hosts typically understood themselves as support providers and drew sharp distinctions between their role as host and the role of doubled-up guests. In addition to an identity as a help provider rather than a help recipient, householder status conveyed authority within the household. The next chapter expounds on how this authority manifested in daily household life. It also takes up this issue from the perspective of guest parents, describing how they experienced living without a home of their own, under the household authority of their host.

PART II

Living Doubled Up

3

Authority and Autonomy

TAKAYLA WAS A Black mother of two who lived in her childhood home, where she had lived continuously for twenty-three years. The tidy two-story house, located on the border of a lower-income Cleveland neighborhood next to a middle-class suburb, was home base for her large extended family. Her grandmother, whom she affectionately referred to as Granny, originally held the mortgage to the home. Her fifty-seven-year-old mother Rose had returned to Granny's home after a year of college and never moved out again. Rose managed the household finances, and after Granny passed away, she would become the householder. The household also included TaKayla's aunt and her cousin, a woman three years older than her, who had also been raised in Granny's home. She and her cousin felt like sisters. "We look just alike. There's a picture of her over there," she added, pointing to one of the many pictures that lined the mantle and hung on the walls. Granny's other five children regularly visited for barbecues, card games, and movie nights.

The four-bedroom, one-bath home was cozy and, with five adults and two children, felt crowded. The living room, where we sat on leather couches, was full but not cluttered. Granny slept in a hospital bed in the dining room, an arrangement that began after she broke her hip. Rose, TaKayla, and TaKayla's aunt and cousin each had one of the four bedrooms. TaKayla's newborn daughter Mia had a crib in her room, and her three-year-old son Noah decided night by night whether he wanted to sleep with his mother or with Rose. "It gets so cluttered, that he has his toys everywhere, his clothes everywhere, my clothes everywhere, her clothes everywhere," TaKayla complained of her crowded bedroom. "And some of that spills over to down here, and my mom yells at me, 'Get his toys out of here, get his shoes out of here.'" When she needed time alone, TaKayla headed to her "hideout spot," the unfinished basement where Noah could ride his bike while she sat on the washing machine and played games on her phone uninterrupted.

TaKayla had long dreamed of having her own home. Upon turning eighteen, she started looking at apartments, thinking, *Okay, I'm eighteen. I think I'm grown. I can do what I want.* The housing search quickly changed her mind. "Looking at a couple of places and seeing how much it cost . . . I'm like, 'Yeah, I can't do this.'" Since then, she had been saving to rent a home where she could live with her two children and her partner, Brandon, who lived with his own mother. She worked at Applebee's, making just $13,000 the year of her first interview, but she worked her way up to roles with increasing pay over the years. She was dedicated to saving for her eventual home and at one point had an impressive amount—enough to cover a security deposit and several months of rent. However, these savings were soon depleted after a car accident left her with a fractured ankle that kept her out of work for three months.

While living with Granny and Rose, TaKayla received regular reminders that she was not the head of the household and thus had little authority in the home. "My grandma, she tries to run things. She'll tell you that every chance she gets, too. 'This is my house. I pay the cost to be the boss, baby.' (*laughs*) I'm like, 'I know, Granny, I know. You just told me five minutes ago.' So that's her favorite word: 'I pay the cost to be the boss.' And it's like, 'I just asked if I could turn the TV.'" After Granny died, TaKayla's mother adopted the householder role, as well as the phrase "I pay the cost to be the boss." "I'm the captain of the ship now," Rose laughed, pointing to TaKayla. "You just a member of the crew." They joked with obvious affection about the household being a "dictatorship," but despite their close relationship, not being the householder weighed on TaKayla. "I want my own place so I don't have to follow nobody else's rules," she lamented, "[and] I can do what I want."

Living according to Granny's and then Rose's rules restricted TaKayla's daily life. Her guests had to leave the home by 10:00 PM, and her son was not allowed to have more than a friend or two over occasionally to play. "Three or more is kind of pushing it, 'cause then she's like, 'Send them kids home.'" These rules limited TaKayla's options for Noah's birthday parties; the year before, she took him to Chuck E. Cheese, but such outings strained her budget. She looked forward to hosting festive but low-cost birthday gatherings once she had a home of her own.

Granny and Rose also kept strict control over anything that could drive up the utility bills. "My granny and my mom: 'Did you leave that light on upstairs?' I was like, 'Yeah.' 'Well, go turn it off. Electricity is not free.' I'm like,

'Okay, okay. I'm going.'" Noah liked to play in the sprinkler outside in the summer, but because it increased the water bill, TaKayla could allow him to do so only with permission. "Yeah, I can't just go and put it on, because it ain't my house. He'll ask me, and then I'll ask one of them, 'Can I put on the sprinkler for him?' And they'll tell me yes or no." During one interview, Rose chimed in with other rules she instituted to keep the water bill down. "Then, they want to have the water fights. And everybody would wash [clothes] a different day when I say this: two people washing the same day, you will cut down the water."

Rose asked TaKayla to begin contributing toward the household finances when she began working after Noah was born. Now she paid $375 a month, more than half the monthly mortgage payment, but these contributions did not buy her authority within the home.[1] This contradiction bothered her. "It's like, 'Okay, you take my money every month, but then you tell me I can't have a party for my son.'" Yet ultimately she accepted the link between householder status and authority. "My granny always goes, 'My house, I pay the cost to be the boss.' I'm like, 'I pay the cost, too, but I can't argue with you. You're right. It's your house.'"

TaKayla also believed that independence and having a home of her own were central to the transition from childhood to adulthood. "So comes the time, all birds have to leave the nest," she declared. She tied her desire for a home of her own to her identity as a self-reliant adult. "I know there are some people that are in this world that are perfectly content with relying on their parents for their whole life. But that's not me. I'd rather get out and work and earn my own. . . . No, do it yourself, grow up, no more relying on Mom, she can't feed you your whole life. It's time to get up and fly."

TaKayla acknowledged that once she moved out she was likely to struggle financially. She even thought it was possible that she would not be able to sustain residential independence. However, the act of moving out was itself important to her; by forming her own household, she would demonstrate how much she valued independence, even if she was unable to maintain it long-term. "I think it will be worth it. Even if it fails and I do have to come back home, at least I can say I tried, I did it, I didn't just sit here and be content with being with my mom my whole life. I tried. I tried and it failed, but I tried. And that'll be something good to show my kids."

Although there was much that TaKayla looked forward to about having her own home, she was not desperate to leave her doubled-up household. Residential independence was important to her, but "I'm gonna miss here as well," she added. Despite the crowding and the rules, her family was close-knit, and the household was relatively peaceful. "Might be hard to believe, but we don't usually clash heads that often," she explained. Household arguments rarely rose above issues like who should get to shower in the household's single bathroom first each morning. "Find somewhere to put a second bathroom and I'd love it," she said, before quickly clarifying, "But I still want to move, though. There's nothing like having your own space. Then my granny can come over and I can tell her I pay the cost to be the boss." Brandon was more impatient and sometimes encouraged her to relax her standards so they could move out of their mothers' houses more quickly. "I can understand that," she acknowledged. "Wanting a space to call your own. You need to be able to invite people over. You need to be able to make your own rules. You are allowed to say what goes and what doesn't."

———

For parents like TaKayla, doubling up as a guest felt inconsistent with their identity as an adult.[2] TaKayla's reliance on her mother and grandmother for housing stood at odds with the economic and residential independence she associated with adulthood. Moreover, she and her children were subject to Granny's and Rose's rules and expectations. In these ways, doubling up as a guest could feel akin to returning to the household role of a child—or remaining in that role for parents who had never lived independently. For parents like TaKayla, being a householder was key to fulfilling their ideal of adulthood. She was ready to "leave the nest" upon turning eighteen and had been working toward this goal ever since.

This chapter explores how doubled-up parents understood and navigated doubled-up households, expectations of adulthood, and household authority. The traditional, normative pathway to adulthood in the United States requires individuals to meet certain benchmarks, such as finishing school, entering the workforce, obtaining independent housing, marrying, and becoming a parent, in that order and by certain ages.[3] In the 1950s, most people followed this path and were married with children and a home by their early twenties. Since that time, however, young adults have taken longer to achieve traditional markers of adulthood, and deviations from this traditional sequence, particularly among young adults from less advantaged backgrounds, are common.[4] These shifts have provided new freedoms for young adults, but recent decades have also brought new challenges. Economic security—including the steady, well-paid employment that parents need to afford independent housing—has become more elusive for poor and working-class adults like TaKayla.[5]

Moreover, American adults are in many ways responsible for providing their own safety net. Accordingly, before moving out, TaKayla wanted, for both herself and her partner, stable employment and a substantial rainy-day fund to pay rent in case of emergency. Her caution was justified: she was forced to drain her savings multiple times over the years I interviewed her, including when she took maternity leave during a difficult pregnancy for a child she lost and later for her daughter's birth, and when the car accident left her injured and unable to work. The United States is one of the few industrialized countries that lack a broad paid leave policy, and low-wage service-sector workers like TaKayla are among the least likely to have access to paid leave from their jobs.[6]

Although the traditional path to adulthood has become more circuitous and arguably more difficult to navigate, cultural expectations of self-sufficiency in adulthood have shifted surprisingly little. The individualistic values held by most Americans, including lower-income Americans, continue to link adulthood with self-reliance and to disparage help-seeking after childhood.[7] Although doubling up has become more common, a large majority of Americans continue to see financial independence and leaving one's parents' home as key steps to becoming an adult.[8] The perceived link between adulthood and economic self-sufficiency shows no signs of weakening. In her study of working-class young adults, sociologist Jennifer Silva describes how economic neoliberalism has further promoted an ideology of individualism and self-reliance. Young adults in her study "see their struggles to survive on their own as morally right, making a virtue out of not asking for help," and they are hostile toward adults who cannot make it on their own.[9]

Reflecting similar values, receiving housing support stood in contradiction to guest parents' identities as adults. As TaKayla explained, "I love my mom. I want to be with her, but I can't. Not forever. I need to grow up and do my own thing." When describing their ideals of residential independence, parents like TaKayla sometimes transitioned seamlessly between their identities as adults and their identities as parents. "I have a family, my own family now that needs me, so I can't constantly ask my mom, 'Well, can you pay this for me, can you do this for me, I need money, I need that.' I gotta do it myself," she said. Because parents typically view becoming a parent as the most important marker of adulthood for themselves, parenthood and adulthood are linked identities for many parents.[10] Doubling up as a guest can thus threaten two identities that are central to parents' concept of self. "If you thought you were grown enough to have a child," said Paula, a thirty-two-year-old Hispanic mother who hosted her cousin's family, "you should be old enough to take action and just be responsible for them. And having a home is like the first thing that you should think about for your children." Chapter 6 provides more detail on links that parents drew between good parenting and residential independence.

In addition to signaling independence, householder status conveyed household authority. The reliance of parents like TaKayla on others for housing went hand in hand with following their host's household rules, setting up a conflict with their expectations for adulthood. Householders retained authority over the home and its inhabitants, so guests faced reduced control within the home and increased oversight of their behavior. TaKayla's day-to-day decisions—from when she was allowed to do laundry to whether she could host a birthday party for her son—were subject to Granny's and Rose's preferences.[11] Scholar Linda Burton and her colleagues argue that because housing is such a valuable and scarce resource, control over housing conveys power. They found that lower-income women who obtained housing of their own, such as by securing public housing assistance, gained authority within their romantic relationship, even when they were otherwise dependent on their partner's income.[12] Similarly, parents of various income levels in my sample associated household authority with householder status. Guests like TaKayla held subordinate positions in the home, while hosts like Rose and Granny set rules and expectations.

"Too Old" to Be a Guest

Katy, a Black mother raising two teenage sons, lived with her mother, Tiji, and Tiji's other three grandchildren, ages three through seven, who alternated between living with Tiji and living with their mother in another household. The ranch-style house, located in a neighborhood off the freeway in Dallas, had overgrown grass and yellow caution tape across the front entryway. The other houses on the block were similarly in need of upkeep, with the exception of some empty lots and a few new and in-progress homes being built by Habitat for Humanity. The inside of the home was in disarray—full of clutter and the strong odor of stale cigarette smoke, burning incense, and pest control products—but the walls were carefully decorated with family photos and other decor. To Tiji, this was home, and the fifty-nine-year-old grandmother hoped to never move again. She and Katy had moved to this house two years prior, after Katy found the listing online. Katy, on the other hand, was eager to move. "I'm praying between now and the end of this year that I have my own place."[13]

Katy moved in with Tiji after her cohabiting boyfriend spent the money she planned to use for rent. Unable to pay her landlord and wanting to avoid a court-ordered eviction, she moved in with her mother. "Ever since then, but I've been trying to get myself straight out so I can get my own place, 'cause I like being on my own more," Katy declared. However, the meager disability payments she received for herself and her son—totaling about $1,400 a month—made saving difficult. In fact, she frequently ran out of money before she could cover the $450 rent and the water bill that she owed in the home she shared with her mother. During one interview, Tiji returned from the grocery store, carting in several cases of bottled water.

Unlike TaKayla, Katy had lived independently before and, at age thirty-eight, was no longer a young adult. Yet she spoke as passionately as TaKayla did about the link between residential independence and adulthood. "I never like living with my mother since I've been grown. I don't have no business up under the same roof with my mother. I am grown. Shouldn't nobody over twenty-one . . . be living up under the same roof with they mother, they parents, grandparents, nobody. Everybody that's grown should be in they own place. If they're not in no relationship, they need to be in they own place, and I need to be in my own place. I miss being on my own." Katy contrasted this expectation of independence with childhood, when coresidence is expected. "It's different from when you're a kid. You don't have no choice because Mom is the one that have to take care of you. But when you're grown, I'm too old, anybody's too old to be living with they parents."

Katy made two exceptions to her strict rules about adults living alone, exceptions that were widely shared by doubled-up parents. First, she saw coresidence with a romantic partner as acceptable. This exception reflects broader societal assumptions that the nuclear family unit, comprised of romantic partners and their children, should be a resource unit—and that support should be exchanged within, but not outside, this unit.[14]

Coresidence with a romantic partner was also more acceptable than coresidence with other adults because parents believed that cohabiting involved sharing, not giving up, householder status. When living with a romantic partner in a nuclear family household, parents expected to share household authority, make household decisions jointly, or divide up household decisions based on gender roles. Yet there seemed to be no established model for sharing household authority within doubled-up households. For instance, consider Lauren, the mother from chapter 2 who preferred multigenerational households so long as she could be the host. Asked to explain why she would not move into her future mother-in-law's home, she contrasted such a move, which would involve giving up household authority, with living with a romantic partner, which would involve sharing household authority. "It's my house. . . . Unless it's me and my boyfriend, it would be our house. But still . . . I'm the lady of the house." Asked what "being the lady of the house" meant, she replied, "I mean what I say and it goes. I mean, we [my boyfriend and I] would have our discussions about what we need or what goes on at the house, but it wouldn't be somebody else coming in and saying, 'Well, that doesn't need to go there. It needs to go there.' If I want it there, it's going to go there." Nuclear family household roles, with one "lady of the house" and one "man of the house," offered a model of shared household authority. In contrast, Lauren assumed that doubling up in her mother-in-law's home would involve giving up, rather than sharing, household authority.

Second, Katy suggested that if the household was formed to support an older adult, coresidence was acceptable. Adults should not share households, she explained, "unless they parent is sick or something like that to where they parent can't move around and just completely do nothing for they selves." This exception did not apply to Katy either. "My mom, she still healthy—she's sick, but she's healthy-wise to where she could still get up and move around and do stuff for herself. She don't really need nobody to come in here and cook or clean or bathe her or nothing like that. So I feel that anybody that got a parent that's older, that's in a situation like that, they too old to be living with they parent." As discussed in chapter 2, working-age adults were expected to be self-sufficient, while receiving help as an older adult was more acceptable. This logic, echoed by Katy, implied that multigenerational households should allow the younger generation to provide support for the older generation, rather than the other way around.

Although Katy firmly linked residential independence to her ideals of adulthood, she was unable to form her own household and relied heavily on Tiji's support. Before her final interview, she stopped receiving her Social Security benefits. With no income, she was unable to pay rent or the water bill for about nine months, until she found a job. Tiji described this difficult period: "So everything was on me. And I had to pay the light bill. I had to pay the water bill. Tried to pay rent, but it was by the grace of God, they kept me here for a whole year." The landlord was threatening to evict them when Tiji's friend Bennie, with whom she had doubled up previously, called her "out of the blue . . . and told me he needed somewhere to stay." He had also fallen behind on rent and was facing an eviction from his apartment, so he called to ask if he could move in with her. She told him he could take one of the bedrooms and pay $450 of the rent. Although Katy appeared far from ready to form her own household, having Bennie there to help with the rent was a relief. Knowing that her mother had help would make it easier for her to leave eventually, she said.[15]

The Symbolic Value of Householder Status

Householders drew symbolic boundaries that sharply distinguished between their status as hosts, with a home of their own, and guests, who lacked a home of their own and instead relied on others for housing.[16] Characterizing guests as needy supplicants justified hosts' authority as householders, and characterizing themselves as relatively stable providers bolstered their self-concept. These *symbolic* boundaries took on particular importance for some disadvantaged hosts because there was little *economic* distinction between them and the adults they hosted. Symbolic boundaries distinguished hosts from the guests they housed, even when they were needy themselves or had been guests themselves in the past.

Leeann was a twenty-six-year-old Black mother who rented a three-bedroom, single-family home on a quiet street in a racially diverse, lower-income neighborhood in Cleveland. When she moved into the home six months earlier, she had known it needed many repairs. She chose it because the landlord was willing to postpone some of the move-in costs, letting her pay her first rent payment in increments so that she could afford Christmas presents for her four children, who ranged in age from four to nine. After moving in, she grew frustrated at the landlord's unresponsiveness to her repair requests. During an interview, she pointed out the sagging gutter over the front porch, the broken front-door lock, and the water marks on the ceiling. Sitting at the dining room table, she apologized for the state of the house, saying, "This is kind of embarrassing for my house to be like [this]; this is why I don't care about cleaning this house, because it don't feel like a home." Despite her dissatisfaction with her residence, the home did not feel dirty—the laundry basket sitting next to us was filled with clean clothes, and when the younger children spilled juice in the kitchen, Leeann instructed her older daughter to clean it up with the mop bucket that sat in the corner of the room.

Leeann's rent was technically $625 a month, but she never consistently paid in full. She often simply could not afford that amount while raising four children with an income of roughly $13,000 a year from disability payments and child support. She described her financial situation: "I'm lucky my grandma keeps me in cigarettes, but I stay broke. All of my money goes towards them [the kids]." Sometimes she made a partial payment and promised to pay her landlord the rest later. Other months she justified a lower rent amount because the landlord would not repair the home.

One day Leeann received a notice in the mail that the house was in foreclosure. Several months behind on rent at the time, she decided then that she would no longer strive to make even partial payments to her landlord. "This month he ain't getting nothing from me because the house is in foreclosure. Why am I giving money for if you're not paying the mortgage? I'm not going to give you money and the next month I could be homeless. I'd rather just save my money." When her mother was injured on the home's damaged front porch, Leeann grew even more confident that if her landlord took her to court for an eviction, she would be able to justify her nonpayment of rent. She did not hear from him after her mother's accident, and she continued living in the home rent-free.

To Leeann, having a home of her own—even one that she felt was dilapidated and did not pay rent for—was a point of pride. She remained in her house, despite its disrepair, because it was her own. "If I want to, I can go live with my mom or I can live with my dad, but I choose to stay here," she declared. "I don't want anybody's help, I don't need it, I don't desire it, I'm going to do it on my own."

Leeann also helped others by sharing her housing. The two-story home had three bedrooms upstairs; her two sons slept in one room, and her two daughters slept in another. Leeann fashioned the downstairs sunroom into a bedroom for herself, covering the door from the dining room with bedsheets so she would have a spare bedroom available upstairs. With this spare bedroom, sometimes supplemented by other free space in the home, she hosted several family members and friends over the next three years: her father and his girlfriend; the young adult daughter of a man she was briefly involved with five years prior, whom she called her stepdaughter; her brother, sister-in-law, and niece; and her cousin and her cousin's boyfriend and ten-year-old daughter.

The flip side of Leeann's pride about her residential independence was her disdain for living doubled up as a guest. When her cousin moved from Leeann's home into her boyfriend's mother's home after a fight, Leeann criticized the boyfriend because he did not have his own home. "I'm like, 'Dude, he's still a kid living with his mom. He don't work, he don't have shit. What makes him a man? Please tell me. Because he has a penis? Who cares? If he can't provide for you and your child . . .'" Like many parents, Leeann saw multigenerational coresidence as acceptable only to support the older generation. "If his mom was sick, that would be a different story, but she's not sick, so they're going to live with a boy and his mom."

Asked if doubling up was more appropriate for a woman, Leeann countered that residential independence was an equally important aspect of being an adult for women like her cousin. "No. It's the same way—unless you're helping your mom out. Unless you're helping with her bills because she can't afford them on her own or she's sick. If you're just living with your mom because you don't want to take care of yourself, then you're still a little ass kid and you need to grow up to be a woman." Leeann contrasted her cousin's experience with her own. "She's always going in and out of somebody's house. She's never stable. I'm not saying I'm particularly stable, but I got my own place." Leeann described proudly how, at age eighteen, she was "living a very adult life" and "had my own place and I had my own family."

Leeann's criticisms of her cousin belied the many times that she had doubled up as a guest herself. At her most difficult moment, about four years earlier, she had spent a couple of months "bouncing from my friend's house to my mom's house from my friend's—so I wasn't stable." Her younger children were too little to understand, but she sent her oldest daughter to live with her aunt to protect her from seeing how much she was struggling. Though Leeann had felt more stable in the past few years—she rented an apartment for two years before moving into her current rental house—she had doubled up again more recently because her home lost power, leaving her and her children without heat or lights in the middle of the winter. While waiting for her landlord to sort out the situation with the utility company over the next month, she and her children slept on a large sectional couch in her brother's home. Despite these past instances of doubling up, being a householder was key to Leeann's identity.

"I Can't Be Superwoman": The Pressure of Living under Householder Authority

June, a twenty-three-year-old Black mother, lived in her Aunt Ruby's two-story suburban home near Cleveland. The home's exterior paint was peeling, but the inside was bright and neat, with big windows. An array of glass decorations was arranged on the coffee table next to the living room couch where we sat. A single toy left on the floor was the only sign that children, June's three-year-old son Carter and nine-month-old daughter Aniyah, lived in the home. However, I learned that the pristine white walls were often sullied by the children, a point of contention with Aunt Ruby. June shrugged it off, though, asking rhetorically, "What kid don't put their feet on the wall? What kid don't mysteriously find something to draw on the wall with, whether it's a crayon, a pencil, or a marker?"

Aunt Ruby, June's father's sister, worked as a bank teller in downtown Cleveland. June said that she was "pretty much the closest person I'm to besides my grandmother and my mother, sometimes even more so." She described several benefits to living with her aunt. In addition to providing housing, Aunt Ruby, who never had children, adored Carter and Aniyah and frequently babysat for them. "She loves them like they're her own," June said. Living with her aunt also pushed her to start "getting myself together more."

At the same time, June and Aunt Ruby had frequent arguments. For instance, around her first interview, June was nine months pregnant with Aniyah and being especially cautious because of her history of miscarriage. Although she cleaned around the house as well as she could, she often failed to meet Aunt Ruby's lofty expectations for cleanliness. When she was fired from her job at Goodwill because she was unable to do the manual labor she was assigned, Aunt Ruby grew furious that June was neither satisfactorily cleaning the home nor working outside of it. "She was complaining, 'Oh, my God, you're always here,'" June said. "'What do you do when I'm not here?'"

After being fired from Goodwill, June began working toward a nursing degree, but as the busy sole parent for two young children, she continued to fall behind on Aunt Ruby's housekeeping expectations. She had to drop Carter and Aniyah off at daycare before taking the bus to the local community college, and in the morning rush she sometimes forgot to move Aniyah's dirty diapers to the outside trash can. "I'm getting up early in the morning. It's going to be sometimes that I'm going to forget stuff," she explained exasperatedly. "I can't be superwoman all the time. Just sometimes, not all the time." June sometimes felt ready to buckle under the pressure. "Like, I got all this on my plate. And you're trying to tell me I need to do all this other stuff? No, it's impossible. I'm only one person taking care of three people."

Aunt Ruby also regulated June's activity inside and outside the house, which June resented as "a grown woman taking care of two kids." For instance, when someone broke into the home, Aunt Ruby accused June's partner, Cameron. She changed the locks and banned June from having visitors to the home. "Hmm, I'm paying you rent, but I can't have company over here, unless it's my mother or my stepdad or my brothers. Really?" June was annoyed, but she followed the rule. However, having to leave the house to see her friends, June would sometimes keep Carter and Aniyah out after dark, another habit her aunt disapproved of. "So then she would complain, 'Well, you got the kids out too late.'"

To June, living with Aunt Ruby seemed to involve nearly constant oversight and criticism. And although her aunt demanded that June follow her rules, she often disregarded June's wishes. For Aniyah's first birthday, June carefully prepared a small birthday party at home, but Aunt Ruby instead picked the children up from daycare and went out with them for the evening, leaving June at home alone with her balloons and cake. "That was just totally disrespectful, but I'm supposed to give you all your respect, not to cuss in your house, not to have people in your house when you not home." Her aunt set the standards for the home, but June lacked the authority to make requests of her own.

Likewise, when Aunt Ruby's boyfriend moved into the home, he spent time in the common spaces only partially clothed. June felt his lack of modesty was inappropriate, particularly around young Aniyah, and brought it up with her aunt, but her aunt brushed off the complaint. June recalled how her aunt had invoked her authority as householder, "Well, it's my house. I pay the rent. He helps me with the rent. So if he wants to walk around the house naked, then he can." June tried to keep Aniyah out of the house more but otherwise had little power to challenge the boyfriend's behavior.

Eventually, the tension with Aunt Ruby grew to be more than June could stand. It began with a routine argument: June's father had paid to have pictures of his grandchildren taken, and Aunt Ruby wanted the copy of the photos. After arguing about who had the right to the pictures, June relented, deciding she could get another set printed. However, Aunt Ruby continued to complain: "She was like, 'Well, I'm still tired of your fucking attitude.' I'm like, 'And I'm tired of you always disrespecting me, talking down about me to my kids, telling my kids that I will never amount to nothing.'" Later, June overheard her aunt talking about her, telling someone she was ready for June and her children to move out. June had had enough. She was determined to move out of Aunt Ruby's home but saw no other housing options available to her. She had lived with her partner, Cameron, in his sister's home before moving to Aunt Ruby's, but a fight had pushed her to move to her aunt's. Now, unwilling to continue living at Aunt Ruby's, June spent two weeks at a homeless shelter with her children.

Eventually Cameron, who at that point was renting a home of his own and hosting his brother's family, moved his brother's family to his basement to make room for June and the children to stay with him. Almost as soon as June moved in, the couple continued fighting. The stress of trying to get the children in daycare, find a job or go to school, take Aniyah to doctor's appointments and Carter to speech therapy—all with little help from Cameron—left her complaining that she could not keep up. "I have to do everything. I don't have the time to take a break for myself. I'm just going, going, going, going."

Worried about the children and about June and Cameron's frequent arguments, Aunt Ruby asked June to return to her home. To assuage June's fear that living together would work out no better than it had before, Aunt Ruby assured her they would sit down and negotiate terms, from what June would be expected to contribute financially to her housework responsibilities. "She was like, 'Well, if you can at least try and do vacuuming the whole house at least three times a week, that's something.' I was like, 'All right. If not three times, I'll at least try and do it twice, Tuesdays and Fridays.'" With the details of their coresidence negotiated, June returned with her children to her aunt's home.

This arrangement was again short-lived. "I give it approximately two weeks. She starts nitpicking," June complained. She again moved with her children to Cameron's house, despite their conflictual relationship. The family spent the months before her final interview alternating between living as hosts and guests with Cameron's siblings and their families: "So it was like, we lose our place, they gain a place. So we ended up going to they place and then they lose they place, and it was like we all just kept making this cycle, going back and forth to each other's place."

June experienced Aunt Ruby's rules and expectations as repressive, but hosts' rule-setting was not always so explicitly felt. Katy, the thirty-eight-year-old Black mother introduced earlier in this chapter, was adamant that "I'm grown, can't nobody tell me to do nothing," and said her mother did not impose any rules in their shared home. At the same time, "it's nothing like having your own place and just totally being free," she said. "I'm used to having my own privacy. I'm used to having company when I wanna have company. I'm used to doing whatever I wanna do, and like I said, staying in the same house with my mom and you grown, you gotta look at the point in the face, 'Oh, you grown, you gotta stop some of the stuff that you doing,' you know what I'm saying?"

As an example, Katy said that she did not have male visitors overnight. Tiji's home was large but narrow, with a long hallway that ran through the house with the five bedrooms and two bathrooms off each side. Although Tiji did not set explicit rules about visitors, Katy felt that having overnight guests was inappropriate given the house's thin walls and the location of her mother's room right next to her own. "She didn't have to ask me. Common sense would tell me: it's my mama, it's respect."

Moreover, Tiji was clearly in charge of the household. For instance, because she worried about pests, she had strict expectations about doing dishes promptly. She proudly declared, "I don't want no dirty plates up in here. When I come in here and make my coffee in the morning, she know I throw them plates in the trash [if they are dirty]." Likewise, she decided that Katy, who used to cook, was no longer allowed to prepare their shared meals because she used too much salt. Asked if Katy minded not being allowed to cook, Tiji responded, "She don't have no other choice, 'cause she can't come here and cook. I ain't gonna let her cook, no, no, I ain't gonna let her cook nothing." Katy chimed in that she would let Tiji season the food herself if she allowed her to cook, but Tiji interjected a quick "no, no, no, no."

Katy's disdain for living doubled up was not limited to multigenerational coresidence. "That's why I don't stay with folks long," she noted. She previously lived in the home of her sister, who had tried to change Katy's lifestyle to be more like her own. "People always try to tell me how to live my life, how to run my life, and I'm like, 'I'm grown. You can't tell me what to do.'" She expected that her behavior would be likewise restricted if she lived with friends. "[It] would be no different than staying with my mama, 'cause I still couldn't have male guys coming in and out or just have company coming in and out late at night, no way," she explained. "So I just chose to go where my mama was at."

With her mother, Katy at least knew that she would be allowed to have a key to the home. "Then versus me staying at a place where I wasn't going to have no door key, so if I would have left out I wouldn't have had no door key to get back in the house." She anticipated that other hosts would not give a key to someone who was staying only temporarily, and she did not blame them. "I wouldn't give nobody no key made to my house neither if someone ain't gonna be there permanent," she said, quickly adding, "and nobody ever gonna be at my place permanently." The right to determine who holds a key and how long they can stay is yet another reflection of the authority that householders hold over guests.

"I Just Want My House Back": Challenges
of Enforcing Rules as a Host

Hosts held authority within the home and, accordingly, typically set household rules. As described in chapter 2, hosts' rules were sometimes intended to ensure that guests were making adequate progress toward residential independence. Hosts also set rules to help limit the costs, both financial and personal, of sharing their household space. Despite having the authority to set rules, some hosts found managing a larger household to be challenging, and fights over the household rules they set were draining.

Leeann paid no rent for the home she occupied, but she retained her authority as householder. Although her guests knew that she no longer paid rent, they continued to pay her for allowing them to stay. Asked whether her sister-in-law ever balked at paying $200 a month now that her landlord no longer collected rent, she replied, "No . . . I wish she would because then she'd have to leave."

Leeann set expectations about her guests' contributions to household purchases, which were influenced by her family's needs. She recently mandated that her sister-in-law increase the quality of the supplies she purchased for the household: "But her thing is buying generic stuff. I don't buy generic tissue. I don't buy generic detergent. I don't buy generic soap because my kids have sensitive skin." In contrast, she required her sister-in-law to use her food stamps to purchase family packs of meat at the discount store, which could feed the entire household, rather than shopping at the brand-name grocery store that her sister-in-law preferred.

Many of Leeann's rules were designed to minimize the potential costs of sharing her housing with friends and family. For instance, because her guests did not have the same standards of cleanliness, she strove to impose her own housework expectations. Likewise, she prized the brand-new couches she rented for her home—the camel-colored couches stood out as notably pristine, surrounded by the stained ceilings and spackled but unpainted walls—so she banned her guests from drinking in the living room after she found two large red juice stains on the couches.

Other rules were designed to minimize the risk that hosting posed to Leeann and her children. For instance, she imposed a curfew to ensure that the house stayed quiet and safe at night, and she grew frustrated when her guests would call one another to ask to be let in after Leeann had locked the door for the night. "When I go to bed I want to know who's in my house," she fumed. "It's for my safety and my kids' safety. My cousin, she's like, 'I'm not a kid. I have a fucking curfew.' I'm like, 'In my house you do because I want to be able to feel safe in my house.'" Likewise, Leeann banned all drugs from her home. "I said, 'If you want to smoke weed, I don't care. Don't do it in my house, and don't bring it by my kids. If you do that, we're going to have a problem.'" When she found her cousin smoking on the porch, it caused an argument, "[She said,] 'Well, the kids wasn't home.' I said, 'I don't care. This is a family house. Do not bring drugs to my house. If you want to do it, you can go.'"

As the householder, Leeann set rules but was not required to abide by them herself. She still enjoyed drinks while sitting on her couch. Likewise, although she smoked in the home, she stopped allowing her guests to do so after she found signs that a cigarette had been put out on the bathroom sink. Leeann's guests pushed back against her rules, arguing that they were infantilizing or unfair because she did not abide by them herself. But she claimed a special role as householder: "Because it's my house. If I want to ruin it, I'm going to ruin it, not you guys." To Leeann, getting her guests to adhere to her rules was a constant battle, made even more difficult because she spent long hours out of the home for work. "I just want my house back. I don't want people in my house. I can't keep up with people when I'm not in there right now."

As the householder, Leeann was able to tell her guests to leave if they did not want to follow her rules—and she could evict them if she chose. Asked how long she thought her sister-in-law would stay, she tied continued coresidence to respect for her household rules: "I'd let her stay as long as she wanted to. As long as she wants. As long as she obeys my rules." Although Leeann sometimes overlooked instances of guests breaking her rules, this threat was not empty; "I have kicked them out of my house before," she declared, describing how she evicted her sister-in-law after she complained that Leeann's children were "not disciplined."

Likewise, Leeann had kicked her cousin and cousin's boyfriend out of her house—and allowed them to move in again—several times over the years. She evicted her cousin's boyfriend after he punched her cousin in the face, sparking a police call and upsetting the children. Not wanting to create instability for her cousin's child, Leeann allowed her cousin to stay. This decision benefited Leeann as well because she relied heavily on her cousin for childcare. Eventually, however, a fight over her cousin's unwillingness to help with housework led Leeann to ask her to leave as well. After her cousin and her daughter made a series of moves, Leeann's compassion overcame her anger, and she allowed them to return to her home—so long as the cousin helped with housework and avoided fighting with her boyfriend in front of the children.

"I Can Hold All the Cards": Maintaining
Household Authority

Householder status was highly valued by hosts and guests alike. As discussed in chapter 2, householder status was associated with being a support provider rather than recipient. Additionally, as this chapter demonstrates, householder status conveyed authority within the home. Ron, the married father from chapter 2 who was at risk of losing his housing voucher because he hosted unauthorized residents, provided a particularly vivid example of the value of being the leaseholder. The Housing Choice Voucher Program that he bene-fited from is a federal program, but local public housing authorities (PHAs) decide how to define a family and what types of household sharing are al-lowed.[17] For instance, the PHA that serves Dallas, where Ron lived, defined a family unit as people who are "related by blood, marriage, adoption, guardian-ship or operation of law" as well as those who do not fit this category but "can verify shared income or resources."[18]

Jasmine was a frequent guest in Ron's household; because her status as an unauthorized resident put his housing voucher in jeopardy, I asked if he had ever considered trying to add her to his lease and moving to a larger apart-ment. His answer sidestepped the question of whether such an arrangement would be allowed by the PHA that administered his voucher. Instead, he de-scribed his unwillingness to add others to his lease, telling me how it would reduce his ability to enforce his own rules. "I'm [not] doing it, because with that—adding them to my lease—they got right to . . . bring over whoever they want to bring over." Likewise, he worried that they would end up evicted after a housing inspection if he could not enforce cleanliness in the household. By keeping others off his lease, he risked losing his voucher if the PHA learned about his unauthorized residents, but he also maintained authority within the home. As the leaseholder for his voucher-supported apartment, he said, "It's like, right now I can hold all the cards mainly."

With only his nuclear family on his lease, Ron set the household rules. His interview took place at a rickety round glass-top dining table in the kitchen, where a list of rules, typed in Calibri font on white paper, was posted on the nearby fridge. Another copy of the rules was taped to the closet door near the stairway. These signs instructed household members to do things like turn off the lights when they were not using them, to not assume that other adults would take care of their children, to use the unit's washer and dryer on Satur-day only (or face a $5 fee), and to "BE CLEAN." Ron had written out the list

recently; he said he had decided to be "a man" by taking greater charge in the household. He also formalized his financial arrangements with his guests: "Everybody had to sign the contract: $150 goes towards the rent, gas, and the lights. $100 of food stamps goes into the refrigerator. Keep my house clean at all times, same with the kitchen, that's a rule."

In exchange for the housing assistance he provided his guests, Ron expected strict adherence to his rules. "You try to tell adults to clean up after their own children. They should just be more responsible and to the fact that, okay, this person is helping me, what can I do to get on my feet while this person is helping me." His frustration with his guests over not following the household rules—particularly about cleanliness—mounted. Moreover, he felt that his guests did not sufficiently acknowledge the value of the housing he provided. "It was just becoming a hassle, a struggle, you know? I try to help people, but you know, sometimes it could be a little bit too comfortable. And they start thinking that, they're figuring that me actually living with someone and . . . that person's actually helping you out so it's kind of hard."

Conclusion

Guests in doubled-up households contended with the emotional toll of not meeting expectations around residential independence. Reflecting the centrality of individualism and self-reliance to American understandings of adulthood and parenthood,[19] householder status was key to parents' conceptions of themselves as adults. Having a home of one's own signaled independence and self-sufficiency, while doubling up as a guest signaled reliance on others. The parents in my study, like lower-income parents in other studies, subscribed to cultural ideals of self-reliance, even when their circumstances made independence practically impossible.[20] Subscribing to these mainstream ideals was itself important to parents' sense of self-worth. By aspiring to independence, parents distinguished themselves from people who might be satisfied with remaining in someone else's home.

In part reflecting their status as support recipients, guests typically held a subordinate position in the home and were subject to hosts' expectations and rules. The paternalistic understanding of their role that some hosts adopted (discussed in chapter 2) could reinforce the sense that residential independence was important for adulthood. The paternalism of hosts' attitudes could be difficult for guest parents, who wanted to be treated as independent adults despite their reliance on others for housing. Living under hosts' rules also

added complexity to guests' day-to-day lives. They pushed back against these rules to varying degrees, but such pushback often had little impact, in part because householders held the authority to remove people from the home.

The ability to regulate activity within their home was a valued aspect of being a householder. As the previous and current chapters show, hosting was often a sacrifice for parents with children. By setting rules, hosts attempted to limit the negative impacts of hosting on their finances, their home, and their children's lives, as well as their own. Although guests' arguments about household rules rarely mitigated hosts' oversight, the effort required to enforce rules increased the costs of hosting.

The power dynamics of doubled-up households made being a guest particularly challenging. Yet it is not clear that equalizing household authority is possible or desirable. As this chapter shows, hosts set rules to limit the costs of doubling up and might have been more reluctant to share their home with extended family and friends if they risked giving up part of their household authority in doing so. In chapter 4, I focus on the economic costs of doubling up for these hosts and the guests they housed.

4

Economic Exchange

STARR, A THIRTY-SIX-YEAR-OLD BLACK MOTHER, had purchased her home just six months before her first interview. Her small three-bedroom, two-story house sat on a street lined with similar, box-shaped houses. In front of the houses, "For Sale" signs were more common than garbage cans, and several houses were vacant, with unmown lawns. Although the suburban Cleveland neighborhood showed signs of decline, Starr found it beautiful, saying, "It's a good area to raise your kids if you're a parent. Good schools. It's all about the family out here." In the past, low wages had kept her in urban areas where she and her children, now ages one, eight, eleven, and nineteen, had dealt with more than their share of housing issues, from lead poisoning to dangerous neighborhoods where the children could not safely play outdoors. Her new home was far closer to her ideal, with its patio, basement where the "family can sit down and eat popcorn," and freshly tiled kitchen big enough for all of the family to eat dinner together.

Starr said that she had "come a long way to own my own house." The year before, she was working as a custodian for a large corporation and had a couple of thousand dollars saved, so she began looking for very low-cost homes she could buy in cash and responding to TV and newspaper ads that promised to help her become a homeowner. After several failed attempts, she responded to an ad that promised to make her a homeowner for $575 a month; using all of her life savings, she paid a stranger to help fix her credit and buy a home. "At the end of the day you're going to have a house," he assured her. "It's your house with your name on the lease [sic]." Starr worried that she was being swindled, but miraculously, the plan worked. "Nobody in my family really believed me because we don't have any homeowners in my family," she recalled. "They was like, 'Yeah, right. You own a house?' And I'm like, 'Yeah, I own a house. I'm a homeowner.'"

Starr's housing costs overwhelmed her as soon as she moved in. When she bought her house, she had been making up to $4,000 a month, sometimes even more. Just a couple of months into homeownership, however, a car accident left her unable to work, and she was forced to live off just $15,000 a year from unemployment and child support. Additionally, she had focused on the monthly mortgage payment amount during her housing search, but after she moved in and utility bills began arriving, she was surprised by "all the bills that come with being a homeowner." Upon receiving her first water and sewer bill, she was overwhelmed. "I started crying. I was like, 'I ain't gonna be out here too long.'" Determined not to lose her home, she began making changes. "I don't try to run a lot of electricity. I don't use a lot of gas. I'm a budget woman." She signed up for assistance programs to help with the heat and electricity bills and found a clothes bank for her children. "I use all my community resources," she said. As her circumstances grew more desperate, she began selling blood plasma as well.

Starr's role as the only homeowner in her extended network made her a beacon for family and friends in need of housing. As scholars like Mary Pattillo have long recognized, middle-class Black adults—as Starr was before her car accident—are often connected to more disadvantaged extended family members who depend on better-off relatives for assistance.[1] Even after she fell from the middle class because of her car accident, Starr's privileged status as a homeowner continued to make her a valuable source of housing assistance for family and friends. Over the next two years, a total of six adults stayed temporarily in her modest home.

These arrangements also benefited Starr, as financial contributions from these guests prevented her from falling even further behind on her bills. First, her nineteen-year-old daughter rejoined the household. When Starr purchased the three-bedroom home, she had not expected her oldest daughter—who had moved out five months before—to live with her. However, her return was fortuitous for Starr. Her daughter was working two part-time jobs when she moved in and soon picked up a third through a temp agency. Starr recalled that her daughter told her, "Mom, don't worry about nothing. I'll take care of everything." Her daughter's income paid all the household bills in those first months, and portions of them in the subsequent months. "All the checks from the second job, she cashed the checks and gave me all the money to pay my home mortgage," Starr said. "I couldn't believe it. I was like, oh my God. That was a blessing. She gave me like $1,500."

Soon her best friend decided to move out of her rooming house, and Starr allowed her friend to move into her home. Her friend contributed $200 a month in exchange for the housing, income Starr used to help pay her bills. However, this support was short-lived; the friend decided to return to her rooming house just four months later. Later, when Starr's sister faced an informal eviction after a fight with a neighbor, she asked Starr where she should go. "I said, 'You can go with me. I'm your big sister,'" Starr recounted. She was looking out for her little sister by allowing her, her three-year-old son, and later her partner to move in, but Starr also needed her help; she asked her sister for about $100 a month in exchange for the housing, and because she did not have a car at the time, she relied on her sister's help to get around the city.

Starr's sister received about $700 a month from disability, and her partner was unemployed. This low income was hardly enough to support them and their son, and they regularly ran out of money and asked Starr for help. Starr described her sister's smoking and drinking habits derisively, saying she was "drinking up" all her money. Yet she usually avoided conflict by giving in to her sister's requests for help, giving her $5 for gas here and $5 for a six-pack of beer there. Because of these small-dollar gifts, she estimated that her net gain from hosting her sister might have been no more than $25 many months. Thus, even though her sister contributed income and transportation, Starr felt that doubling up with her was "not worth it." She accused her sister of using the arrangement for her own gain. "She's just trying to take advantage of me, I believe."

Finally, Starr's thirty-year-old nephew, who had been moving between the homes of other extended family members, wanted to join her household. She allowed him to move in—he was later joined by his girlfriend—and asked him to contribute $300 a month to help with the bills. At first, he was full of promises to help. She recalled him saying, "Auntie, I'll do anything you need me to do and I want to be here for you." By the third week, however, he was arguing about how much he should have to pay her. She described the $300 rent as a modest request, given how expensive her mortgage and utilities were. "I need help with the bills and everything, and he was getting like $800 a month. I was like, 'Just give me $300 of it,' and that's something because I'm paying . . . on all this stuff and no help, and really no income." He also began refusing to help around the house. "I couldn't get him to cut the grass, take out the trash, nothing." Ultimately, Starr realized that hosting her nephew would not provide the support she had anticipated, saying, "He hoodwinked me, bamboozled me."

She put him out of her house with help from the local police department, still feeling taken advantage of. "I can't take care of no grown people. He didn't want to help out . . . just try to use everybody."

Starr provided housing for family and friends, but she expected them to pay for this support. Moreover, the promise of financial assistance led her to double up even when she preferred not to. For example, she once called the police to remove her sister from her home—the denouement of repeated disagreements about how much her sister should contribute to the household and how she should interact with Starr's children. Her sister moved to another doubled-up household, but after getting into arguments in that household as well, she wanted to return. She told Starr about a large settlement payment she was supposed to receive for a car accident, warning her, "You can leave me out here in the cold, but you won't get none of my money." Starr agreed to allow her sister and nephew to rejoin the household, saying, "All right, you can come back, 'cause I know I need the help." Her sister did eventually receive her settlement and moved out, but not before fulfilling her promise to help. "She just looked out for me a little bit," said Starr, explaining that her sister paid her late water bill just in time to prevent a shutoff and proudly pointing out the big-screen TV and new furniture she purchased with her sister's help.

———

Hosts provided vital assistance to their doubled-up guests, but as Starr's experience demonstrates, many hosts needed the financial and in-kind benefits that doubling up could provide. Past depictions of doubled-up households have mostly focused on the housing support that hosts provide for guests. By treating guests as the beneficiaries of doubled-up arrangements, discussions of doubled-up households often treat hosts, at least implicitly, as support providers. However, closely examining the flow of resources in doubled-up households from the perspectives of both host *and* guest families reveals that patterns of support within doubled-up households are far more complex. Guests receive housing, but they are also often expected to help their hosts. For many hosts, particularly those who are economically constrained themselves, doubling up can provide an important safety net.

Analyses of survey data show that the economic benefits of living doubled up lift many families, both guests and hosts, out of poverty.[2] Looking at *personal* incomes alone, both hosts and guests in doubled-up households have high rates of poverty, yet, when income is calculated at the *household* level,

doubled-up households are no more likely to be in poverty than households that are not doubled up.[3] Forming a doubled-up household reduces the risk of household-level poverty for both hosts and guests, though guests reap the largest antipoverty benefits.[4] The antipoverty impacts of doubling up are in part due to the greater number of adults—and thus potential incomes—in the household. Doubled-up households also benefit from economies of scale; the financial costs of Starr's shared home were far lower than the costs that would be incurred by each household member if they maintained a separate home. The apparent antipoverty effects of doubling up led one Pew Research Center report, which documented the rise of multigenerational doubled-up households during the Great Recession, to label these households "the American public's self-designed anti-poverty program."[5]

Yet fully understanding how doubled-up households shape economic well-being requires attention not just to the overall level of income in the household but also to how resources are exchanged within the home and how predictable these exchanges are. Calculating poverty at the household level implicitly assumes that doubled-up household members have shared access to household income. The official poverty measure, the primary way of assessing the number of needy American families, adopts a similar but slightly different approach: it assumes that coresident individuals who are related by birth, adoption, or marriage pool their resources, while those who are not remain economically separate.[6]

For the families in my sample, the relationship between doubling up and *individual-level* well-being was far more complicated, and economic arrangements were far less stable, than these straightforward rules suggest. None of the doubled-up households in my sample fully pooled their incomes—an arrangement that has been called a "common pot" approach.[7] Although resources were frequently exchanged in doubled-up households, other household members constituted *potential* sources of support only—support that, in households like Starr's, was far from stable or guaranteed. Thus, total household resources were a flawed measure of the economic well-being of individual nuclear family units, regardless of whether the family was coresiding with extended family or non-kin.

This chapter examines the complicated safety net function of doubled-up households. Although doubling up could confer economic benefits, economic arrangements in these households also—sometimes simultaneously—strained families' limited resources. Moreover, economic relationships in doubled-up households were complex, with often unclear and shifting expectations.

Were hosts providing altruistic assistance or engaging in mutually beneficial exchange with their guests? Was each nuclear family supposed to be fully financially independent, or were families living in the same household supposed to share a similar standard of living? What obligations did household members have to one another in daily life and in times of need? The lack of taken-for-granted answers to questions like these made doubled-up households vulnerable to conflict, and disagreements had particularly high stakes in households with severe resource constraints. The ambiguity around economic expectations, particularly when combined with material hardship, injected stress and precarity into day-to-day life. Thus, despite the tangible assistance provided by doubling up, parents like Starr at times questioned these benefits and felt like other household members were taking advantage of them, rather than helping.

To fully elucidate the complexity of exchange relationships in doubled-up households, this chapter takes an in-depth look at the experiences of just two mothers: Starr, the homeowner living well below the poverty line whose story began this chapter, and LaTonya, a guest whose income was above the poverty line but whose mother's home provided a more comfortable environment and a higher-quality neighborhood than she could afford on her own. These mothers differed in many ways, but both used doubling up as a safety net. Their experiences reflect themes common among the parents in my sample and reveal the economic complexity of doubled-up households.

"Can't Go Anywhere Else for That Amount": Housing Savings for Guests

LaTonya was a Black mother who had moved with her infant son back into her mother Natalie's home about six years before her first interview. After her son's father moved out of their shared apartment when they broke up, she had struggled to afford rent on her own. She tried her best to avoid returning to Natalie's house, "because once you move out on your own you don't want to have to come back home, and it's like, 'Oh no, I had that independence, I had that freedom.'" However, after struggling to afford necessities such as milk, diapers, and rent, while living in an apartment complex riddled with "drug trafficking and prostitution," she decided to "put your pride to the side" and return to her childhood home with her baby. "I just said no, I just need to focus on my son, get back to work, get back on my feet." By the time I met her, LaTonya was

twenty-nine years old and had two sons, ages seven and two, who lived with her in the basement of Natalie's home.

Despite the security bars that covered the doors, Natalie's single-story home in a working-class suburb of Cleveland was inviting, with an abundance of brightly colored flowers in the well-maintained front yard. For her interview, LaTonya walked me down the driveway, through the side door, and downstairs to the finished basement. The main floor upstairs had three bedrooms, including one for Natalie and one for LaTonya's ninety-seven-year-old grandmother. The stairs to the basement led to a large room with a couch and a futon where LaTonya slept. A bedsheet covered the entrance to an adjacent room, where her two sons each had a twin bed. Compared to the upstairs, the basement felt lived-in, with wood-paneled walls covered in family pictures and children's toys scattered across the worn carpet. The space had a fridge and a bathroom, leading LaTonya to liken the basement to "our own little apartment," separate from the rest of her mother's home. However, her sons ignored this symbolic boundary as they wandered back and forth from the basement to the upstairs throughout my visits.

Hair products lined the TV stand in the basement living area, which doubled as LaTonya's salon. She was attending cosmetology school and stayed busy doing hair informally—I had to pause about an hour into an interview when a client arrived. The year I met her, she had a higher income than usual, bringing in about $30,000 from her work as a stylist, the financial assistance she received while attending school, and child support for her two sons. From her income, she paid $350 a month toward Natalie's $700 mortgage, contributed $20 a month to the electricity bill that her grandmother paid each month, and paid the household's $50 internet bill. Her contributions were not limited to cash. When asked whether she paid rent, she first described the nearly $500 a month in food stamp benefits she shared before listing her cash contributions. By working together to scour the circulars, clip coupons, and visit multiple grocery stores to catch the best deals, LaTonya and her mother were able to stretch the food stamps to buy food for the entire household.

Doubling up provided many guests with lower-cost housing than would have been available to them on the private market. As LaTonya explained, "Can't go anywhere else for that amount," and the $350 a month she paid Natalie certainly would not have covered rent for the type of home she wanted for her family: a house like her mother's, with a large yard and in a neighborhood where "you see the kids out and stuff and the older people watering the grass."

She estimated that if she were to rent her own unit, she would pay $600 or more in rent each month. Low-cost units priced under $600 are increasingly rare across the United States; as of 2022, there were 2.1 million fewer units renting for under $600 and 4.0 million fewer units renting for between $600 and $999 (adjusted for inflation) than there were in 2012.[8] Just 16 percent of rental units nationwide have rents below $600 a month, so LaTonya probably would pay more than that living on her own.[9] Rent cost burdens, like those she might have faced if not doubled up, leave families with less money to put toward other necessities, like food and health care.[10]

By providing low-cost housing, doubled-up households offer many guests a private safety net that rivals the impact of large public safety net programs. Using survey data from mothers with young children living in large US cities, scholars Natasha Pilkauskas, Irwin Garfinkel, and Sara McLanahan estimated that mothers' average rental savings from doubling up as a guest, compared to what they would pay if renting, was equal to more than one-fourth of their annual earnings. Based on this estimate, the amount that mothers saved by doubling up as a guest was greater than the average value of either food stamps or public cash transfers.[11] Even assuming LaTonya would have been able to find a low-cost rental for $600 a month, doubling up with Natalie saved her hundreds of dollars in rent alone each month. For guests like LaTonya, doubling up in someone else's home was a pivotal private safety net, one that was equal in importance to—or at times even more important than—the public safety net benefits they received.

Moreover, even a relatively low-cost rental unit would have been affordable to LaTonya only in her higher-income months, and not when her income fell—as it frequently did. Her income fluctuated depending on the state benefits she was able to access, how consistently her child support was paid, and how many hair clients she served. Income volatility, driven in part by fluctuations in employment and instability in family structure, has increased in recent decades, especially for lower-income families.[12] For parents like LaTonya, whose incomes varied from month to month, housing affordability was an ever-moving target.

Living in her mother's house, LaTonya had more flexibility in rent payments than she would have had on the private market. Although she now paid for half the mortgage, her mother lowered her rent expectation to $50 a month when LaTonya's income fell and stopped charging her altogether when she had no income at all for a couple of months. "She does look at it from every angle and try to make it where I can still do something if I want to or take my kids

somewhere if I want, to not leave me completely broke," LaTonya explained. Her mother also loaned her money to ensure that her children's needs were met. For instance, when she needed an unexpected car repair a couple of weeks before her second interview, her mother let her delay her rent payment for a month, and she loaned her money for diapers and wipes.

LaTonya's mother also adjusted her rent based on whether she had a co-resident romantic partner. Until just a couple of months before our first interview, the father of one of LaTonya's sons had lived with her and her sons in Natalie's finished basement. Her partner took up no additional space in the home, but her mother required that he pay $300 a month in addition to the $200 that LaTonya was paying then. Unlike in a private market rental, the family's rent obligation depended on the family composition, not just the space they occupied. LaTonya found the rent increase reasonable, saying that she could not expect a male romantic partner to join the household for free: "Uh-uh, if it's a man, uh-uh." When her partner moved out, she was not responsible for his share of the rent, which insulated her from some of the financial fallout of their breakup that she might have experienced if she had been renting on the private market.

Financial and In-Kind Exchanges

The patterns of exchange in LaTonya's and Starr's households were typical of the households in my sample. Looking at parents' most recent doubled-up arrangement, about three-fifths involved a monetary rent-like payment from guest to host. These contributions were typically paid directly to hosts, but sometimes guests took responsibility for a specific bill, as LaTonya did for the internet bill. In households where monetary payments from guests were expected, the median payment was about $300 a month—a substantial amount considering the low- to moderate-cost housing markets where these families lived.[13] At the time, median market rent was $712 in the Cleveland metropolitan area and $863 in the Dallas metropolitan area, and many hosts paid far less than this for their housing. Moreover, some hosts, like Starr, requested payments from multiple guests at a time. National data reveal that sharing housing expenses in doubled-up households is not unique to Cleveland and Dallas. One study of mothers with young children living in urban areas across the United States found that roughly 70 percent of guest mothers paid rent to their hosts.[14]

Guests' rent payments benefited hosts like Natalie, who was retired and living on a fixed income. In addition to LaTonya's contributions to the mortgage and utilities and the food she brought into the household, she shared the burden of unexpected expenses. For example, when they needed a new $3,000 furnace, LaTonya contributed about $1,000. In this way, living doubled up provided insurance against volatility in consumption for LaTonya, who did not have to worry about being able to afford housing when her income fluctuated, but also for her mother. By increasing the number of potential incomes coming into the household, doubling up could thus increase household income, lessen consumption volatility, and protect household members from material hardship. The financial and insurance benefits of doubling up were imperfect; as I discuss later, LaTonya could be kicked out of her mother's house for nonfinancial reasons, and she and Natalie sometimes disagreed about how much of a safety net they were obligated to provide for each other. However, LaTonya valued knowing that, unlike a landlord, her mother "wants to make it where I'm able to provide for my kids and still provide a roof over their head by my portion of the rent."

Cash payments were just one category of support that guests provided. In-kind goods and services from guests also had a meaningful impact on hosts' well-being. LaTonya gave her mother $500 in food stamps each month, which they used to buy nearly all of the household's food. Living doubled up also made it easier for her and Natalie to share care work. When she needed a break, she spent time with her sister, who lived around the block, while her mother watched her sons. Likewise, when Natalie took weeklong trips out of town, LaTonya stayed home with her grandmother to "make sure she's fed and everything and takes her medicine and stuff." Personal care services like those she provided for her grandmother cost an average of $117 an hour in the Cleveland area, but LaTonya provided this support for free when her mother traveled.[15]

In-kind contributions sometimes stood in for financial contributions, especially for guests with little or no cash income. Toni, a twenty-eight-year-old Black mother who lived with her husband and three children in her adult nephew's home in Dallas, did not pay rent. Instead, she said, "I wash the dishes, I cook, I try to clean. We do things around the house to kinda cover a cost or something like that." Likewise, Gail, the fifty-four-year-old Black mother from chapter 2, had previously lived with her daughters in her father's home after leaving an abusive marriage. Food stamps were her only source of income, she said, "and so to me that was my way of providing. I would get the food stamps and have a meal for him, cook him something, and that was my way of paying."

At times, the nonmonetary benefits of hosting—along with the satisfaction of helping, as described in chapter 2—were sufficient for householders to agree to host. For instance, Starr's friend moved back into a rooming house temporarily before later deciding to return to Starr's home. The friend paid $200 a month in rent the first time she stayed, but the second time she had no income and could not pay rent. Starr worried that without help her friend would end up on the streets, so she allowed her to move in anyway. Her friend provided childcare, cooked, and cleaned, but Starr did not ask for a financial contribution. "She wasn't taking up no space. She stayed downstairs [in the basement]. She came upstairs to help me with the kids or whatever. Sometimes she'll come up and cook, help clean up upstairs, and then she'll go back downstairs. So I didn't have a problem with it."

"Don't Act Like You Don't Need My Help": The Meaning of Guests' Contributions

LaTonya and her mother agreed that she should contribute financially to the household. She began paying rent and sharing her food stamp benefits as soon as she moved back to Natalie's home. "Because, as an adult, I still need to pay something," she asserted. "You can't just live off of people." Many guests expressed a similar willingness, or even desire, to contribute to the household where they lived. LaTonya described careful budgeting, paying her mother and meeting her children's needs first before spending any money on herself. As chapter 3 discussed, parents like LaTonya have internalized norms linking adulthood with self-sufficiency.[16] By prioritizing her monthly rent, she protected her identity as a responsible adult and provider for her children. "I don't believe in handouts," she explained. "The way I was raised, you get out here as a woman and you go to work and you take care of your responsibilities."[17]

Although LaTonya and her mother agreed that she needed to contribute financially, they disagreed about the meaning of these contributions. Reliably contributing to the household allowed her to frame the doubled-up household as a mutually beneficial arrangement and downplay her dependence on her mother. Asked what worked well in the household, she noted that "we kind of help each other out, so that's good." Her mother sometimes undercut this narrative of a symbiotic relationship, suggesting that LaTonya was a dependent rather than a contributing member of the household. LaTonya would retort, "Well, the little bit that I am doing is helping you, so don't act like you don't need my help either. . . . You know you need my help too, just

as well as I need yours, so we in this together." Such disagreements were se-
mantic, but important; how LaTonya's ambiguous position in the household
was characterized—as one of dependency or support—was key to her identity
as a responsible mother.

Moreover, although guests like LaTonya made meaningful contributions,
both economic and in-kind, these contributions rarely purchased them full
membership in the household. Despite the length of her residency and the
importance of the food and monetary payments she provided, she was acutely
aware that she lived in her mother's house, not her own. "Even though we have
access to everything, we can freely use whatever we want or whatever, it still
is not our home—what I consider our home, which means that this is our four
walls, this is where I pay the bills, and all of that," she explained.

LaTonya's contributions also purchased her little household authority. For
instance, the first floor of the house was always pristinely clean, with none of
the clutter of everyday life that I saw downstairs. Knowing that her mother was
a "stickler" for cleanliness, she followed her children around the house cleaning up after them and tried to keep their basement living area up to her
mother's standards. Natalie made regular trips to the basement to inspect for
cleanliness and just the week before had reprimanded LaTonya for leaving the
dresser drawers open in the basement. LaTonya felt that these incursions were
an "invasion of privacy." "But at the same time, it is her house," she conceded.
Despite her contributions to the household, "there's only so much I can say
about that."[18] Other parents echoed the idea that guests' economic contributions did not purchase them equal status with the householder. Keneisha,
another mother living doubled up in her mother's home, put it plainly: "Whoever the head lease owner, you make the rules. I don't care who's paying rent."

"Just Business"? Ambiguous Economic Relationships

Doubled-up household members held dual roles. These arrangements typically involved coresidence by individuals with close social relationships: parents and adult children, other extended family members, or friends. At the
same time, they were analogous to a landlord-tenant relationship in that they
involved the provision of housing, typically in exchange for some payment.
Living doubled up complicated LaTonya's relationship with Natalie, leading
to tension around whether their expectations for one another should be those
appropriate for a mother and daughter or also like those for a landlord and
tenant.

This question became particularly explicit when LaTonya became pregnant with her first son in her early twenties. At that point, she had lived in her mother's home since childhood. Natalie, upset about the pregnancy, told her and her son's father, who was living with them at the time, to move out. LaTonya and her partner had paid her mother rent earlier that same day, so she called the police. "They told me that because I didn't have any proof that I paid rent that I basically had to leave," she recalled.[19] On a wintery December day, LaTonya and her son's father waited outside for her niece to arrive— "she had to come pick us up from off the street"—so they could figure out their next move. They moved in with her partner's mother for a couple of months until they had saved enough to move into their own apartment, where they lived until they broke up. Since returning to her mother's home, LaTonya had required her mother to write receipts for her rent contribution. "I mean, it's just like a landlord. They want their money. If something goes wrong, I let her know . . . 'We got something wrong with the toilet.' I just feel like, if I'm paying her money, then hey, it's business. She writes me a receipt. So it's really just business. We put that family stuff to the side." LaTonya wanted the services and protections of a private market renter in exchange for her monthly financial contributions.

At the same time, after she moved back into her mother's home, the rules regulating LaTonya's tenancy continued to be unlike those of a private market rental in many ways. She appreciated Natalie's flexibility on rent when her income was low, contrasting this familial support with landlords who, in her estimation, were likely to say, "'You need to pay me this money or I'll give you thirty days' notice." She suggested that Natalie hosted her altruistically—"her heart is pure with it"—and described the household as an economic unit in which her mother "is there for me and I'm there for her."

Because there were no clear taken-for-granted norms to guide doubled-up household relationships, household members could shift their interpretation of their relationship to suit their own interests. For instance, when LaTonya had additional income, she suggested that her mother should be *more* like a landlord, with a fixed rent price, and balked at her mother's requests for additional contributions. "But then she set these prices, so if she wanted more money she should have just added that into the rent," LaTonya reasoned, arguing that "anything extra is for me and my kids." The pointed distinction she drew between her and her children's interests and her mother's interests contrasted sharply with the narrative of household unity she espoused at other times. When discussing rent increases, LaTonya also took a less charitable view of her mother's motivations for hosting, suggesting that she was "money-hungry" rather than altruistic and even that she was trying to prevent her daughter from achieving residential independence. "They don't want to put you in a position to move out because they so used to your help," she remarked, accusingly.

LaTonya was similarly inconsistent about whether she considered the household an economic unit or a combination of independent nuclear family units. She received occasional signals from her mother that their household was not an economic unit, despite their mutual reliance on one another. For example, after LaTonya forgot to buy Miracle Whip during a grocery run, Natalie called to ask if she wanted her to pick some up. When she said yes, her mother told her she would owe her $3.59 when she returned with the condiment. "And I'm like, 'I just gave you 400 and something dollars in food stamps . . . and you want me to pay for this Miracle Whip?'" Although her mother adjusted her rent expectations based on LaTonya's income and used her food stamps to feed the full household, in transactions like this, she demonstrated that their finances were *not* fully tied. The household faced resource constraints, and it was LaTonya, not her mother, who was responsible for herself and her children.

Doubled-up parents could rarely provide a full accounting of household income and expenses, which further fostered distrust about hosts' and guests' motivations. LaTonya knew her mother and grandmother were both retired and received Social Security, and she thought her mother might also have a pension, though she was not sure. Some guests did not know exactly how much their hosts paid in housing each month, but LaTonya did—$700 for the second mortgage her mother had taken out on the home. Yet, without a way to verify this information, she sometimes suspected that the home was actually paid off, because she did not see mortgage statements in the mail. "I think she's just telling me that [she still owes money on the house] so I keep paying rent, but I don't have a problem with paying rent," she complained, though she had never brought up her suspicion to her mother. Likewise, LaTonya was not always forthright about her own income. When she had unexpected income, she sometimes hid it to try to avoid increasing her financial obligations to the household.

As LaTonya's efforts to hide income from her mother suggest, the contributions that guests make to hosts sometimes weighed heavily on their constrained budgets. Despite the effort and time she and her mother dedicated to stretching their grocery budget by shopping sales, sharing her food stamps limited LaTonya's ability to buy the foods that she and her children preferred because she had to buy "oxtails and pinto beans and all that kind of stuff" that her mother and grandmother liked to eat. Her feeling that her food stamp benefits were overstretched was not surprising: on average, food stamp recipients spend more than three-fourths of their monthly benefits by the middle of the month.[20] Moreover, LaTonya's benefit amount was set based on herself and her two sons and did not include other household members. She believed that only one household member was allowed to receive food stamps, and "the way county is set up they only base it off of you and your kids, not who all lives in the house." Her accounting of the food stamp program rules was not accurate; in general, individuals who live together and share food are considered a single unit in determining eligibility and benefit levels.[21] However, whether because of misinformation or ineligibility, her mother and grandmother did not have their own food stamp benefits and relied on hers.

A "Self-Designed Antipoverty Program"?
The Unreliable Benefits of Doubling Up

Doubling up undoubtedly held economic benefits for both LaTonya and Starr. For both mothers, the additional household members had income of their own, which raised the overall level of resources in the household. Yet looking only at household income would overstate the benefits of doubling up for these mothers, as both had limited access to the resources that other household members brought into the home. None of the doubled-up households in my sample, regardless of whether the parent was the host or guest, fully pooled everyone's income into a common pot. In contrast to the federal poverty guidelines, which treat coresiding extended family members as a single economic unit, I found no evidence that doubled-up households acted as fully integrated economic units, regardless of whether they were formed with close extended family members or non-kin. Yet neither were doubled-up families fully economically *separate* from other household members. Doubled-up household members shared some resources—at the very least, housing—and typically provided other assistance to one another, as Starr's and LaTonya's examples showed.

The ambiguous middle ground that doubled-up households occupied between fully integrated economic units and economically independent nuclear families made it difficult to quantify the economic impact of doubling up on household members. Often, doubling up seemed to lessen some instances of hardship, while exacerbating others. The ambiguity of economic arrangements likewise was a challenge for the families living in these households. Exactly how much help household members were expected to provide each other and how to interpret these exchanges were open questions, ones that caused considerable strife, especially in households with limited resources.

Like LaTonya's household, Starr's household was neither a single economic unit with shared interests nor a collection of self-interested, independent nuclear family units. Where exactly the household fell on this continuum was unclear and contested. When her sister first moved in, Starr had been making ends meet with assistance from her friends and her daughter, but when this help ran dry, she turned to her sister for more help. Starr had provided a safety net after her sister's near-eviction, and she now expected her to reciprocate by contributing more to the household bills. Moreover, as she fell further and further behind on her mortgage payments, she was at risk of losing the home that housed them all. Yet rather than acting like the *household* was behind on bills, her sister protected her own economic interests, treating Starr like a landlord who had failed to charge enough rent. "I should have sat down and made an agreement with her," Starr lamented. "That's what she said, too . . . I can't just come out of the blue with a [higher] price."

Researchers often treat the household as a risk-pooling entity that insures its members against fluctuations in consumption when an unexpected expense arises or when one individual's income drops.[22] Doubled-up households certainly served this function at times. But Starr's experience demonstrates the limits of this insurance in doubled-up households; household members sometimes provided a safety net, but in many households it was far from something families could count on.

Moreover, as the householder, Starr held primary responsibility for household expenses, despite her economically vulnerable position. She recounted her nephew arguing that he should not have to pay her $300 a month, telling her, "You can pay your own bills or whatever." Likewise, she recalled, her sister argued that Starr's unpaid mortgage and utility bills should not be her concern, saying, "I don't have nothing to do with that. You had bills before I moved here." Several guests, like Starr's sister, argued that because their host would have to maintain the household even if the guest were not living there, anything they contributed should be "extra," not necessary for covering basic expenses. Guests also used hosts' identities as help providers to justify not making contributions to the household. For example, Starr's nephew repeatedly argued that paying rent to her would hinder his progress toward residential independence. "He's like, 'I'm not spending my money this month. I'm going to get me a place.' I'm like, 'Well, you say that every month. You haven't got a place. It's been five months.'" Guests' assumption that hosts were primarily responsible for bills often prevented hosts from realizing the economy-of-scale and risk-pooling benefits of doubling up.

For hosts, complex and contentious economic arrangements often made doubling up *both* a source of support and a drain on their already limited resources. In addition to providing less assistance than Starr expected, coresidence with her sister and nephew raised costs in other ways. She complained about how her home was deteriorating around her. "They messing my carpet up. They messing my furniture up. They mess my refrigerator up. Tear my stove up, tore my kitchen up." Starr had little disposable income she could use to repair such damage.

After doubling up, Starr also experienced greater food insecurity. Her nephew often helped himself to her leftovers. "He be like, 'I only had a few pieces, Auntie. I was a little hungry,'" she recounted. "'No, you ate every damn thing. How are we supposed to eat the rest of the day?'" He received his own food stamps, but Starr said he was reluctant to share his food purchases. Likewise, Starr's sister's family ate food from her kitchen without replenishing it and mostly bought food that Starr's family did not like. Starr's children did like to eat the snacks that her sister kept in her bedroom, which aggravated her sister. As we discussed the hot-button topic of food, her son jumped in, recalling, "She did do that all the time. Talking about, 'Y'all can't have none of our food that we bought,' and then when my mom get her food stamps . . ." His mother agreed: "Mhm, that's how she was. She was real selfish." Food insecurity like Starr and her children experienced worsens parenting stress, and it increases the chances that children will face a range of health and behavioral problems.[23] Doubling up was a complex safety net for Starr, one that alternately saved her family from some forms of material hardship, like utility disconnections, and exposed them to others, like food insecurity.

Mismatched Expectations and the Limits of Doubling Up as a Safety Net

When writing about married couples' distribution of household labor, sociologist Arlie Russell Hochschild argued that marital satisfaction depends in large part on the level of alignment in individual "marital baselines"—that is, what each spouse expects from the other, which is shaped by social norms.[24]

Hochschild applied this idea to housework: a husband who does 20 percent of the housework may expect his wife to be grateful because he does far more than many of his male peers; yet a wife who does 80 percent of the housework may welcome her husband's contributions but not display much gratitude if she compares his efforts to the time she spends on it and how much she wishes he would contribute. There were similar dynamics in economic exchanges in doubled-up households, where the lack of shared, taken-for-granted understandings about resource exchanges left room for mismatched expectations.

Mismatched expectations about economic exchange left both LaTonya and Starr feeling taken advantage of. Doubling up often provided economic benefits to guests and hosts, but without a shared understanding about *how much* benefit doubling up was supposed to provide, parents were sometimes skeptical of these benefits. For example, Starr expected her sister and nephew to help pay her bills, but they saw their contributions as "extra" income and felt that she was asking for too much. The household members' expectations about their economic relationship—particularly, about the extent to which Starr's sister and nephew were supposed to provide a safety net for her—were misaligned. Although they did add to Starr's income and thus felt that they were fulfilling their obligations, their meager contributions fell far short of what she expected and left her describing their help as not "worth the money or anything or problems or the attitudes." Likewise, despite the assistance that LaTonya undeniably received from her mother, disagreements about resources sometimes left her feeling that her mother was trying to limit her opportunities for residential independence rather than trying to help.

When hosts compared guests' contributions against what they felt the guest *should* be paying, it revealed that they implicitly understood the household to be a safety net for themselves, not just for their guests. Yet, when describing doubling up, hosts often emphasized their role as support providers. For example, Starr described doubling up primarily as a way to help her sister and nephew; yet she asked for varying contributions based not only on their income level but also on the household expenses she faced and her own level of need. Although she framed the household as a safety net for her guests, her own need dictated how much of a safety net she felt able to provide—and how much she expected in return. Another host, Tina, featured in chapter 5, charged her sister-in-law $350 a month for a room in her house, "and I'm sorry I couldn't do it any more cheaper, I couldn't afford it." Her sister-in-law's co-residence cost Tina nothing more than the space she took up in the home, as Tina was clear that the $350 was rent only and "didn't include your bills, your food, your transportation . . . air, lights, water." Yet she still set the price based on what she could "afford" to charge based on her own need.

Hosts were more advantaged than guests in terms of housing, but most were not particularly economically advantaged. In my sample, the median income of families who only hosted others in their home (and did not double up as guests) was about $20,000 in 2014 dollars—only a couple of thousand dollars above the median income for families who only doubled up as guests (see the methods appendix). I estimate that roughly two-thirds of host families in my sample faced a level of need that made guests' cash or in-kind contributions an important source of support. That is, whether or not guests contributed as expected could impact the standard of living of these hosts.[25]

Given the mutual need of so many hosts and guests, living doubled up in someone else's home was rarely free, and guests could not count on their hosts to be altruistically motivated. Many hosts, like Starr, simply were not in a position to be purely altruistic.[26] In this way, doubled-up households reflected a broader challenge common to lower-income social networks: although support networks are vital for meeting the day-to-day needs of poor families, these networks are often overburdened and there simply is not enough help to go around.[27] In doubled-up households, the mutual need of hosts and guests introduced tension around reciprocity expectations, as household members held differing opinions about who was supposed to help whom and how to interpret the resource exchanges that did take place.[28]

Economic Disadvantage and the Costs of Doubling Up

Tension over economic exchange was worsened by the material hardship that many doubled-up households faced. Parents like Starr, who were limited in the amount and types of food they could purchase for their family, felt it keenly when another household member ate from their limited supply of food without replenishing it. Some parents, worried that sharing a household with others might reduce their control over their food supply, hid food in their bedroom (as Starr's sister did) or even in their car. Doubled-up children were often jealous when other household members enjoyed special treats that they did not share. Even in households like LaTonya's, in which household members typically had *enough* food, even if not the types they preferred, disagreements were common. These disagreements stemmed in part from the lack of clear norms to guide these exchanges, but they also reflected a more fundamental issue: in many doubled-up households, there simply were not enough resources to go around. In household environments in which every dollar counted, every po-tential exchange—even of a $3.59 bottle of Miracle Whip—was an opportunity for household members to disagree about how much of an economic unit the household was and how resources should flow within it.

LaTonya's household was advantaged compared to many doubled-up households—her income of $30,000 that year put her and her children above the poverty line, and her mother and grandmother both had stable income from Social Security. In more disadvantaged households, understandings of household economic integration had even higher stakes. When Kenya, a thirty-nine-year-old Black mother, lived in her friend's home, her friend would sell her food stamps, leaving Kenya to feed her friend's six children as well as her own five children. Ultimately, she prioritized her own children, feeding them secretly in her bedroom. "The worst time [was] when it wasn't enough to split with everybody, and I just had to make a conscious decision just to give to my kids. . . . And I let her little kids [be] hungry. I did not feed them. Don't have nothing to feed them." Fights with the friend, many of which revolved around her obligation to provide for the friend's children while living with them, pushed Kenya to move out.

Among guests in my sample, LaTonya was also relatively advantaged in another important way: though she lacked perfect knowledge about the household expenses, she could trust her mother to consistently pay the bills. In some households, guests' limited control over household finances left them worried that their contributions might be misspent. Anrisa and Phil, a couple who were unexpectedly evicted when their host failed to pay rent, are an ex-treme example. They and their two children were living with Phil's cousin, paying half of the $600 rent for his unit. However, the cousin was not paying rent, unbeknownst to Anrisa and Phil, who explained, "We weren't able to talk to the people in the office about the apartment because we were not supposed to be there. We were not on the lease." They did not realize the household had fallen behind until the traumatic day when their family's belongings were physically removed from the unit. "So one day we get a knock on the door, and they are coming to move everything. . . . They didn't give us the hint, nothing like that. They just started grabbing everything and start putting it outside the apartment."

Moreover, although doubled-up households provided housing to guests, they often had real economic costs. By living with her mother, LaTonya re-ceived low-cost, flexibly priced housing, but she paid for this assistance, in both cash and in-kind contributions, and she worried that her contributions would slow her exit into residential independence. Similarly, Starr's nephew complained that her rent expectations would prevent him from being able to afford his own unit. As these stories show, receipt of social support could help guests meet their immediate need for housing, but it sometimes came with reciprocity expectations that hindered their longer-term plans. Sociologists have long recognized that the social support that helps lower-income families meet their day-to-day needs is often accompanied by expectations of reciprocity that can impede families' ambitions for upward mobility.[29] The reciprocity expectations for LaTonya, as for many doubled-up parents, were immediate and strict—akin to what sociologist Karen Hansen calls market-based reciprocity.[30] When guests had to pay hosts to be allowed to remain in the household, doubled-up households could seem as much like an extension of the private housing market as a form of social support.

LaTonya's doubled-up household appeared largely supportive, despite its costs. In contrast, other guests described more exploitative arrangements, with hosts who seemed to take advantage of guests' limited housing options. For example, when Shay, the mother from chapter 1, doubled up with a cousin of her children's father, she paid $150 every two weeks in rent from her meager earnings as a part-time hostess, even though the cousin received housing assistance and paid no rent.[31] Shay also contributed other necessities, from food to toilet paper. She described feeling "like they was kind of taking advantage of me because I was the only one in the household that was working," but she paid because she preferred living with the cousin over returning to live with her mother, with whom she had a difficult relationship. The cousin was unwavering in her rent expectation; when Shay missed work due to illness and was not sure she would be able to pay the full $150, the cousin threatened her with eviction. Doubling up provided Shay with housing when she could not pay private market rent or obtain public housing assistance, but otherwise offered an insubstantial safety net.

In the most extreme cases, market-like reciprocity expectations drained family resources as quickly as the private market might have. Anrisa and Phil, the couple described earlier, once paid $40 a day for a room in a friend's home—"like being at a motel," they explained. This amount was far more than a low-cost rental on the private market, but their eviction records, unstable incomes, and limited ability to save for a security deposit kept them reliant on doubled-up households, even exploitative ones, for housing.

As Starr's experience shows, hosting was also risky for economically vulnerable hosts. Guests who moved in with promises to help, like her nephew, did not always keep such promises. Hosting increased Starr's utility costs, and her guests also damaged her home and furniture. Moreover, coresidence with guests who were not adequately providing for their own needs stretched hosts' limited household resources. Starr's meager food budget could barely meet her own and her children's needs, let alone those of her nephew or her sister's family. In this way, providing housing for others could worsen hosts' own financial worries and food insecurity. Although doubling up could carry financial expectations and risk for both hosts and guests, Starr's musing about whether the additional income her sister provided was worth the difficulties of hosting revealed a key difference between hosts and many guests: unlike hosts, guests who had few other housing options were hardly in a position to evaluate whether the benefits of doubling up were worth the difficulties.

Conclusion

From a household-level perspective, doubling up reduces poverty rates.[32] Considering the household as a single unit, doubling up had powerful anti-poverty effects for LaTonya's and Starr's households. In both cases, the other household members brought income and other resources into the household, and these households benefited from economies of scale. Yet, as this chapter has demonstrated, doubled-up households are typically not the fully integrated economic units that household-level measures assume, even when formed with close family.

The level of economic integration varied from household to household, but also within a single household at different moments in time. For example, the contributions of Starr's sister and nephew fluctuated sporadically, leaving her unable to plan around these contributions. The unpredictability of resource flows in doubled-up households presents a challenge to researchers and policymakers seeking to measure the income consistently available to a doubled-up family. How policymakers and analysts should treat such potential sources of support is far from clear. However, it is likely that the official poverty measure, which counts the income of all household members related by blood, marriage, or adoption as a single unit, often overstates the resources that are consistently available to any individual subfamily within doubled-up households formed with extended kin.

The complexity that prevents doubled-up household finances from fitting neatly into policy guidelines also affects the individuals living in these households. Doubled-up households often lack agreed-upon expectations about the extent of support that household members should provide one another. Without taken-for-granted norms to guide them, household members have more flexibility to set their own expectations about household economic unity and to be inconsistent in these expectations. Such inconsistency complicates the economic relationships between household members, raising questions about obligations to one another and the nature of their relationship and at times producing distrust, resentment, and even resource hoarding. These dynamics can leave all household members, even those who seem to be benefiting from doubling up, feeling taken advantage of rather than supported. In this way, one important potential benefit of doubling up—making household members feel more economically secure—is often not fully realized.

Due in part to these dynamics, doubling up has a complicated relationship with families' well-being. The parents in my sample revealed that doubling up could be a source of both economic support and economic strain—sometimes simultaneously. Hosts provided housing for guests, but their requests for payment could stretch guests' meager budgets. Some guests contributed so much to the household that it was not clear whether they should be understood as support *recipients* at all. On the other hand, the payments that host parents received from guests could be inconsistent, and when guests did not sufficiently provide for their own day-to-day needs, coresidence could deplete hosts' limited resources. The costs and benefits of doubling up, which were often variable and unpredictable, made it difficult for household members—and for me—to evaluate the extent of the safety net that doubling up provided.

Although the net costs and benefits are difficult to measure, doubled-up households are undoubtedly sites of exchange, typically with economic costs and benefits for both hosts and guests. When researchers and policymakers think of doubled-up families, we often focus on those who receive housing support as guests.[33] In some ways, this focus makes sense for studying or targeting potentially housing-insecure families, as guests lack a home of their own. On the other hand, as this chapter has demonstrated, understanding the safety net function of doubling up requires that attention be paid to both hosts and guests. Doubling up is often not just a one-way provision of support (in the form of housing) from host to guest, but also a two-way exchange of support. Given the two-way flow of resources between hosts and guests in many households, categorizing hosts as support providers and guests as support recipients does not adequately capture the complexity of the exchange relationships within these households.

5

Romantic Relationships

TAKAYLA, THE TWENTY-THREE-YEAR-OLD black mother described in chapter 3 who lived in her childhood home, and her partner Brandon had been together for six years. They were newly engaged and planned to marry once they were financially stable. Although they were in a committed relationship and had two children together, they lived apart; TaKayla and the children lived doubled up in her grandmother's home, which her mother, Rose, later inherited, while Brandon lived doubled up in his own mother's home in a nearby suburb of Cleveland.

At TaKayla's first interview, Granny was the householder, and she would not allow Brandon to spend the night or even to set foot on the second floor of the home. "Granny is strict. No boys upstairs. No men spending the night. She was saying, 'No shacking up in my house.'" TaKayla wished Brandon could move more freely through the household, but because Granny was the householder, her "old school" rules prevailed. These rules persisted even though Brandon had a good relationship with her family and had been part of their lives for years.

Although not allowed upstairs, Brandon had always been welcome to spend time in the home and came over daily to help care for the children—he was visiting each time I interviewed TaKayla. However, the amount of time he spent in the home, and when, was also regulated by Granny. "If I go get him, she's mad. If I don't go get him, she's mad. Go get him, she's like . . . 'I thought I told you I didn't want to see nobody today.' . . . If I don't go get him, [she says], '[Brandon] ain't going to come over here today? [TaKayla] ain't going to let him see his kids?'" Rather than making decisions themselves about their time together as a couple, Brandon's comings and goings were subject to Granny's preferences and moods. Moreover, because he was only allowed in the downstairs of the crowded home, privacy for the couple was rare. "We're never really alone. There's always somebody in here. Like right before you came, my aunt was sitting here. . . . So if I do go sit by [Brandon] or lean over on him, someone is coming in like, 'Hey, what are you all doing?' 'Nothing, we're not doing anything.'"

When Rose became the householder after Granny passed away, she relaxed the rules and allowed Brandon to stay the night, to TaKayla's relief. He began staying over frequently, but their time together was still subject to oversight and rules. Sitting in the living room with her mother, TaKayla estimated that, "out of seven days, he is here at least four." "When I don't say anything," her mother quickly chimed in. Although overnight visits were now allowed, the couple was still not free to make the final decision about when and how often that could happen.

TaKayla and Brandon planned to move in together and "be together as a family" when they could afford a home of their own. She looked forward to having her children grow up with their mother and father in the same household, and she told me that her son would be especially happy to have his father live with him full-time. For mothers like TaKayla, having an independent household was synonymous with having a family. "I just want to see what it's like to have my own family. . . . I want my kids to be around me, their father, and just do our own thing. Go through our own holiday celebrations together and experience the whole Mommy is getting up, cook dinner and breakfast stuff. See Dad going to work, kiss him when he get back home. 'How was your day?' stuff like that. I want to experience that." Although she and Brandon had children together already, she felt like she would not truly know what it would be like to have her own family until she had a nuclear family household of her own.

It was not just Granny's rules and later Rose's that prevented TaKayla from living with Brandon. She dreamed of having a clearly defined role as the mother in a nuclear family household rather than being both a daughter/ granddaughter and a mother. Explaining why she wanted her own home, she said, "I have my own family now. It's time for me to be Mom and not the other way around." If she ever needed a place to stay in an emergency, she said she would turn to Brandon's mother, and she felt confident that his mother would allow her to join the household if needed. Even though she would be willing to live with his mother if needed, she had never pursued coresidence in his mother's two-bedroom home.

At one point, Brandon's mother moved to the nearby suburb that TaKayla aspired to move to one day. During the three years I met with her, she repeatedly and emphatically declared that this suburb was her ideal residential location because it was "quiet, everyone's nice." She dreamed of her children going to the public schools there and taking advantage of the many extracurricular programs not available in the Cleveland public schools. Despite her desire to live in this neighborhood, moving into Brandon's mother's home was still not an option that TaKayla considered. She considered the idea of living with her future mother-in-law the "same situation [as] here. I just want my own space. I am not going to leave my mama to go live with his mama. I don't want to live with anybody's mama. I want to be the mama." TaKayla's ideal family life involved not only coresidence with her fiancé but also a clearly defined role as the mother-householder in a nuclear family household.

———

Married and cohabiting parents are far less likely to live doubled up, especially as guests, compared to parents who do not live with a coresident romantic partner.[1] Nationally, just 11 percent of children with married mothers live doubled up, compared to 22 percent of children with previously married mothers and over 33 percent of children whose mothers have never married.[2] Previous research on the association between romantic partnership status and living doubled up focuses on how parents' relationship status predicts their likelihood of doubling up.[3] In this chapter, I show how parents in a romantic relationship can have their relationship complicated by doubling up.

Some parents who lived doubled up as guests were deterred from coresiding with their romantic partner. TaKayla looked forward to the day when she, Brandon, and their children would have a household of their own, but this nuclear family household ideal remained out of reach over the following years. Her goal of being "together as a family" was inextricably connected to residential independence, and the couple had not sought coresidence while living doubled up. As the next section of this chapter shows, not all couples were willing to remain in separate households until they could obtain residential independence. Yet even when parents put extraordinary effort into coresiding, finding a host who would allow coresidence could prove challenging. At times, reliance on the private safety net for housing broke up families, separating parents—especially fathers—from their partners and children and contributing to family instability.

Although the parents in my sample were disproportionately single, living doubled up alongside a romantic partner was not uncommon for either hosts or guests. A slight majority of parents in my sample lived in a doubled-up household with a coresident romantic partner at some point during the fieldwork. Yet coresidence did not solve the complexities that doubling up introduced to romantic relationships. Doubling up stressed the romantic relationships of both hosts and guests. Households are inherently intimate environments. In single-family households, the home serves as a boundary between private nuclear family life and the outside world. Coresidence with adults beyond the nuclear family left parents without this clear boundary, and sharing the intimate home environment with additional adults introduced new complications and questions to daily life. Parents' ideals about household life often involved clearly defined, gendered roles for one mother—recall how TaKayla wanted to be "the mama" of the household—and, if present, one father. Living with other adults raised questions about how romantic partners should relate to these other household members and how to navigate shared household life. Moreover, the oversight, interference, and lack of privacy that TaKayla described were common for parents who lived doubled up alongside a romantic partner. Doubling up required daily navigation of layers of relationships, each with its own, often gendered, expectations. How parents navigated these complications was consequential for their romantic relationship, as well as their relationships with other household members.

Parents "Unpartnered" by Doubling Up

Consistent with national trends, most parents in my sample lived doubled up without a coresident romantic partner at some point during the fieldwork.[4] These parents would appear to be "single" or "unpartnered" in surveys that gather data about whether a parent has a cohabiting partner or spouse. However, I learned that many guest parents who did not live with a romantic partner were not actually single; many of these guests *were* in a serious romantic relationship, but their housing status precluded coresidence. In my sample, roughly two-fifths of guest parents who lived doubled up without a coresident romantic partner had a romantic partner who lived doubled up in another household at some point. Researchers often assume that parents double up in part because they do not have a romantic partner with whom they can combine incomes and share housing expenses. In this way, single parenthood is understood to be a cause of doubling up. For many of the parents in my sample, however, the converse was true—they did not have a coresident romantic partner *because* they lived doubled up.

The experience of Anrisa, a twenty-seven-year-old Black mother, and her partner, Phil, illustrates how difficult it could be for couples who depended on others for housing to live together. The couple and their one-year-old son and three-year-old daughter had lived doubled up for over a year before their first interview. When Phil was jailed for nonpayment of child support for a non-resident child, Anrisa could not keep up with rent on their shared home. By the time he was released, she and their two children were doubled up in her mother's spacious four-bedroom house. He had been allowed to live in her mother's house before, but after he was released from jail, he was no longer welcome. Anrisa blamed this change of heart on a sort of jealousy, explaining that her mother picked fights with Phil because she "doesn't have her own man." Regardless of her mother's true motivations, the decision to not allow Phil to coreside pushed Anrisa to move.

Anrisa and Phil began moving from one unstable housing arrangement to another around the Dallas area, struggling to keep their nuclear family together. "We couldn't go to no [homeless] shelter together 'cause [Anrisa's] whole thing is she wanted us to be together . . . as a family. We couldn't do that [at a shelter] because we're not legally married, you know," Phil explained. During a previous spell of homelessness, they found that the family homeless shelters they wanted to use required couples to be married to live together. Anrisa and Phil were a nuclear family unit; they had been together for about a decade, called each other husband and wife, had two children together, and planned to get legally married after they achieved their goal of purchasing a home.[5] In the meantime, however, because of their dependence on others for housing, living together "as a family" required that their hosts acknowledge their relationship and need to coreside.

Because neither Anrisa's extended family nor homeless shelters would accept them as a family unit, they turned to less desirable housing options. The family initially moved in with a friend Phil met in jail. He had inherited a two-bedroom home and rented them the spare bedroom for about $40 a day, as described in chapter 4. The couple regularly sold their food stamps so they could afford this rent. Yet, despite the financial difficulties, she described the payments as "pretty fair stuff for my family to be together."

This home was crowded with other household members and visitors, all of whom used drugs, and the smell of smoke pervaded the household. Anrisa did not approve of the environment but described it as unavoidable, saying, "We doing what we [have] to do to keep our family together." Asked what she meant by "keep your family together," she emphasized coresidence for their nuclear family unit. "For all of us to be together—me, my son, my daughter, and [Phil]—just for all of us to be together. I have my family, but this is my family, so I want all of us to be together." Eventually, however, she grew concerned that the workers she interacted with at food banks would smell smoke on her clothing. "I'm not going to have CPS try to come take my children away," she explained. The family decided to seek alternative housing with Phil's uncle.

Anrisa believed that Phil's uncle was willing to host them because he "believes in family" and enjoyed being around their children. Phil and the children were blood relatives of the uncle, but Anrisa was also welcome in his household, she explained, "me being the mother of [Phil]'s children." Her explanation for why she was allowed to join the household reflected the special rights that householders sometimes accorded mothers but not fathers. Although Phil was the father of Anrisa's children, her extended family refused to host him along with her and their children. As described in chapter 2, the well-being of children could be an important motivator for hosts; some guest parents perceived that their host allowed them to double up out of concern for their children, and some parents who hosted other families with children likewise described being motivated by concern for the guests' children. Mothers—as the assumed primary caregiver of the children—were consistently allowed to double up alongside their children.[6] Hosts were more likely to require fathers to live separately from their children.

When Anrisa and Phil moved in with their children, his uncle was already hosting his brother, Phil's other uncle. Although the household environment was a dramatic improvement over the friend's drug-filled home, their coresidence with the uncle was also short-lived. When Anrisa was hospitalized after being hit by a car, the uncle arrived at the hospital with her belongings—a not-so-subtle hint that she needed to find a new place to live. She assumed that he thought she would be "more of a burden" after being injured and so no longer wanted to host her.

Anrisa's brother lived just down the road from the hospital, so after she was released, she moved with her children into his house. Phil, meanwhile, was only allowed to visit. The couple paid her brother's $25 subsidized monthly rent and bought food to share with his family. Despite the financial contributions, she felt unable to advocate for the family life she wanted. "It used to just get on my nerves [that Phil could not live with us]. I used to want to say something, but it's like I couldn't. I couldn't say nothing 'cause I'm staying here and I need a place to stay."

Eventually, Phil returned to work, and the family briefly checked into a hotel room where they could stay together before looking for a new doubled-up household. In an effort "not to burn bridges," they tried to find new hosts rather than returning to previous hosts. This time they moved in with Phil's cousin. His one-bedroom apartment was far too small for five residents, and Anrisa, Phil, and the children lived out of suitcases in the overcrowded living room. However, they were happy to be able to live together. Because the cousin was planning on moving, they planned to take over his apartment themselves and finally have a home of their own. He moved about six months after they joined the household, but Anrisa and Phil soon learned that he had fallen several months behind on rent. Unable to afford the back rent, they were soon evicted.

While sitting by the apartment complex's dumpster with their belongings, which had been put out of Phil's cousin's apartment, they met their next host. "I never trusted him, but we actually needed him at that point in time because either that or we gonna be sleeping out there by the dumpster," Anrisa explained. Perceiving no other option, they moved in with this near-stranger. This housing arrangement was miserable; the acquaintance "wanted to treat us like children," she remembered, recalling that he would not let them run the AC during the day and required them to ask for a key to use the restroom.

Because Anrisa distrusted their new host, she sent her daughter to stay temporarily with her sister. "I don't know if he probably was a pedophile. I just didn't catch a good vibe from him at all." After just a couple of weeks of living there, she decided to move out with her son as well, even if it meant being separated from Phil. Her sister lived in a large three-bedroom, two-bath public housing unit with her own three daughters and boyfriend. Although she allowed Anrisa and the children to join the household, she not only banned Phil from moving in but also would not allow him inside the home when she was not there. "[Phil] and my sister wasn't getting along at the time. So that [living together] wasn't going to work. And she was like, 'Yeah, you can stay here,' but she didn't want me and my whole family staying in her house." Once again, their reliance on others for housing left their family separated.

The family stress model details how economic pressures, like those Anrisa and Phil faced, can damage relationship quality and stability by increasing emotional distress and exacerbating negative behaviors.[7] Anrisa and Phil faced added challenges from living doubled up. For instance, they found it difficult "having to deal with other people and dealing with other people's energy." They also worried about the effect of instability on their children. "We were trying to do it [move] in a discreet way where the kids wouldn't feel like, hey, I'm just staying from here to here to here to here." Daily stressors like these could undoubtedly undermine healthy relationship interactions for any couple, and Anrisa and Phil often had to navigate these challenges while living on opposite sides of Dallas, which fostered additional distrust. "Us being separated caused so much confusion between us, because he thought I was over at my sister's house cheating with some other guy, I thought he was over at his cousin's house cheating with some other girl. And it was just keeping us at each other's neck," she recalled with a nervous laugh.

Moreover, Anrisa felt that they could only be a "real family" if they were able to coreside together with their children. With Phil living apart from her and the children, "it's like visitation: you come and see your kids for a couple of hours and then you have to go. So there's not really family to me. I don't like that at all." The separation took a toll on her as well as their children, who missed living with their father. Anrisa found herself calling Phil in the middle of the night, waking him up to sing the itsy-bitsy spider song over the phone for their toddler son. Eventually, she concluded that they needed to "get our family back together, because I got tired of my kids waking up in the middle of the night crying for their father." They both found jobs, so they decided to try to rent an apartment of their own and, after substantial searching, found a landlord who would overlook their eviction history. They struggled to pay their rent each month but were adamant that the difficulty was worth it. "Now that we're together with the whole family, everything is great," she concluded.

For some guest parents like Anrisa and TaKayla, living doubled up inhibited them from coresiding with their romantic partner. Nationally, mothers who do not have a coresident romantic partner are particularly likely to live doubled up as a guest, and it would be easy to attribute their high rates of doubling up to the increased need for economic and child-rearing support that often accompanies single parenthood. Yet Anrisa's and TaKayla's stories demonstrate that having the financial and coparenting support of a romantic partner does not ensure residential independence. Both mothers were in committed, stable relationships, but both they and their partners relied on others for housing and had no permanent home of their own. When romantic partners are themselves doubled up or otherwise housing-unstable—as were many of the partners of parents in my sample—cohabitation or marriage is not a viable pathway to long-term residential independence for guests.

Compared to guests like TaKayla and Anrisa, parents who hosted others in their home less frequently described doubling up as constraining their own romantic relationships.[8] Whereas hosts can discourage or even bar their guests' partners from coresiding, guests did not have this authority. This difference may help explain why differences in rates of doubling up by relationship status are larger for doubling up as a guest than for doubling up as a host. Nationally, about 10 percent of never-married and previously married mothers live doubled up as hosts, and the share of married mothers who host is only slightly lower, at 7 percent.[9]

"When We're Having an Intimate Argument, This Is between Us—Not Your Whole Damn Family!": Relationship Interference in Doubled-Up Households

Preventing coresidence was one significant way in which doubling up affected the intimate lives of parents, particularly guests. Yet even for parents who could coreside with a romantic partner, living doubled up with individuals beyond the nuclear family introduced new complications to their relationships. Because doubled-up household members could observe other household members' romantic relationships within the intimate household environment, they had ample opportunity to get involved in the inner workings of each other's romantic relationships.

Eva, a twenty-two-year old mother who identified as White and multiracial, lived with her fiancé Dylan and their children, a two-year-old son and four-year-old daughter, in the home of her fiancé's parents in a working-class neighborhood in Cleveland. The large two-story home with a two-car garage housed Dylan, Eva, and their two children, his parents, his adult sister and her boyfriend, sometimes his adult brother and his girlfriend, and his siblings' children. Each nuclear family was assigned a bedroom, so Eva, Dylan, and the two children had some space to call their own, even if it was only one small bedroom.

However, "being in such close quarters" with other household members left Eva with limited privacy, which stilted her communication with Dylan. "The house, it was so small, and there was people in every room. They would hear," she described. The lack of privacy was especially frustrating during disagreements. "Sometimes you need to have a screaming argument with your partner to get it all out. And I would hold back because they're listening to what I'm saying, so I can't say what I want to say to you right now." Aware that anything she said would likely be overheard, she often held in her feelings, rather than communicating openly.

Coresidence also facilitated household members' direct interference. Despite Eva's efforts to maintain secrecy, Dylan's family members would gossip when they learned that the couple was fighting. These intrusions into her relationship, which she described as an unavoidable effect of living doubled up in a full household, frustrated her: "Like when we're having an intimate argument, this is between us—not your whole damn family!" She grew annoyed at the partial truths and misunderstandings conveyed through this gossip, when other household members "would only see what he was saying, and they would see what I was saying, and they would make their own conclusion." The interloping of other household members made it difficult to keep any disagreement private or contained, which negatively affected the quality of their relationship.

About one year after their first interview, the couple moved into their first independent home together, and she reported that the move dramatically changed their relationship. "Even as partners, we're more freer with each other. We can tell each other more stuff now because we don't have other people switching the story around or giving their opinions and whatever. We just communicate so much better."

Other parents also objected to the interference of other household members in their romantic relationships, but these objections were not universal. For example, LaTonya, the mother from chapter 4, lived with the father of her younger son in her mother's home until just a couple of months before her first interview. While coresiding with her partner in her mother's home, she appreciated the occasions when she was arguing with her partner and her mother "intervened and defused the situation." "I can say it helps on that end to have somebody come in with more experience to say, 'Hey, it's not that serious, you all need to talk about it.'" Of course, as I discuss later in this chapter, interactions appreciated by one partner were not always received the same way by the other partner.

His Family, Her Family: How Gender and Familial Ties Create Different Experiences of a Doubled-Up Household

Romantic couples who lived doubled up together sometimes experienced the same household very differently, prompting disagreement between them. For instance, the expectations that parents faced in doubled-up households were often gendered: women were more often critiqued about cooking, cleaning, and other domestic chores, while men faced greater economic pressure.[10] Additionally, whose family or friends the couple lived with could shape their experience of the household and how comfortable they felt in the doubled-up arrangement. When couples disagreed about how long they should remain in a household, doubling up itself could become a source of conflict.

Eva got along well with her in-laws, and particularly with Dylan's mother, a White woman with spiked blond hair and an authoritative demeanor. Her own mother struggled with drug addiction, which strained their relationship, and Eva—who had her first child at age seventeen—related well to her mother-in-law, who had also been a teenager when she became a mother. "Then for us living together, we got to know each other more and more," Eva recalled, describing long days when they would talk and care for the children while Dylan was at work. "I've heard a lot of her stories. I know a lot about her life. She knows the stuff about mine, so us living together has brought us closer." Co-residence sometimes fostered close relationships between household members, like Eva and her mother-in-law, who saw each other daily and provided one another with emotional support. Her close relationship with her mother-in-law made her a source of support even when she and Dylan were having relationship difficulties.

However, despite feeling emotionally close to her mother-in-law, Eva did not have the same comfort level living with her in-laws as Dylan did living with his parents and siblings. Moreover, she was quick to point out that she and her mother-in-law "don't always see eye to eye," and she tired of spending every day at home with her, rather than in a home of her own. Tension levels were particularly high in the first year after Eva moved in, when she was still figuring out her role in the household. For example, she "felt like it was my obligation to make sure the house was clean and that there was food on the table, because I didn't have anything else better to do, and that was the only thing I could give her for giving us a place to stay." At first, she volunteered this household labor and was eager to use her food stamps to provide food for the household, but "it got to a point where it was expected of me, and then when I wouldn't do it, there was a little bit of gossip." Eva said that her mother-in-law would grumble when she did not cook, complaining about the money she would have to spend to buy dinner for the household. "Or Dylan would come and go, 'Mom, I'm hungry.' She'd be like, 'Well, your woman didn't cook.'"

Dylan, who was at work away from home most days, did not experience the stress of coresidence as acutely. In contrast, Eva, who spent every day, all day, raising her children alongside her mother-in-law, desperately wanted a home of her own. She and her mother-in-law regularly disagreed about rules and discipline for her daughter. At times, her mother-in-law disapproved of Eva's own behavior, such as when she went out to celebrate her twenty-first birthday. For Eva, living doubled up required dealing with "the stress of other people and their drama" on a daily basis. She had to deal with this stress without her normal support system. She avoided having friends visit her at her mother-in-law's home because it "wasn't a comfortable feel, because it was like we are in someone's house. We can't say what we want to say. That did kind of put a little strain on me, because I'm used to having my close friends there."

Compared to Eva, Dylan was more accustomed to living in his parents' home and was in less of a rush to move. He was hesitant to forgo the rent-free housing they received from his parents. Eva, who wanted to move out as soon as possible, recounted, "We were at each other's throats, because I was kind of upset at him because he wasn't trying to move out . . . because it's his parents. He was okay with that." Attributing most of their relationship difficulties to the stress of having to spend each day in the doubled-up household while Dylan was at work, she continued to pressure him. "I just had to keep telling him, 'Okay, do you want to keep staying here with your mom? And me being upset every day you come home from work because I'm stuck here with her? Or would you rather me happy, us happy. More quiet, calm environment.'" Partners like Dylan, who worked during the day and spent less time in the doubled-up household, were sometimes less affected by the stress of coresidence than were mothers who spent longer hours in the home with their children. Eva's and Dylan's different experiences of the household prompted repeated arguments about how urgently they needed a home of their own.

Samantha, a thirty-year-old Black mother, and her husband Benjamin described similar dynamics as hosts of a doubled-up household. Before their first interview, the couple and their young son lived together in a one-bedroom apartment, which they sublet from Benjamin's uncle. In this home, they hosted Benjamin's housing-insecure mother, and they sometimes took in his adult sister and brother as well. "I felt alienated because it was him, his mother, and [his siblings]," Samantha explained.

Just three months later, their roles reversed. Benjamin's uncle ended the sublet agreement and evicted them from the unit, angry that so many people were living in his one-bedroom apartment. Samantha's family moved to her grandmother's home. Samantha felt more comfortable there, even though the house was full with her siblings, aunts, an uncle, cousins, and cousin's children. "It was dysfunctional, to say the least," she remembered, but at the same time, "It was my family, so I knew them. I knew what they were like, I knew what they were going to do, and I knew what they weren't. . . . I was comfortable there, more comfortable than I was at the previous place, where we lived with his mom and his sister. He was not." Less at ease with her large extended family than she was, Benjamin struggled with living in the crowded household.

Her family's gendered assumptions about breadwinning also put pressure on Benjamin that Samantha did not face. She said her family "has a tendency to think of men as supposing to be good providers, so if they think a man is not a good provider, they don't think too highly of him." While mothers often faced greater expectations than fathers that they would provide household labor, fathers like Benjamin faced greater expectations that they would provide economic support. Men and women both faced cultural expectations that they would have a home of their own in adulthood, but hosts were sometimes harsher in their evaluation of men's need for support than women's, as discussed in chapter 2, compounding the emotional costs of doubling up for guests like Benjamin.

After just six months, Benjamin decided that they would move in with his mother, who now had her own apartment. However, Samantha again disliked living with her mother-in-law, particularly given her interference in the couple's relationship. She characterized the household as "mostly a nightmare. It wasn't pleasant. . . . Our marriage suffered because someone was always in the middle of it telling us what we should and should not do, and what should and should not happen, how things should be and judging." Eventually, they found a unit that would accept them despite their poor credit, and they managed to live there stably for nearly a year before they fell behind on rent and again had to move in with Benjamin's mother. They separated soon after.

"I Didn't Want No Other Woman Living Here with Me": Relationship Boundaries and Propriety in Shared Households

Tina, a thirty-six-year-old Hispanic mother, and her husband Carlos had four minor children, three sons ages six, nine, and ten and a seven-year-old daughter. The family rented a house in a working-class neighborhood of Dallas that had a reputation as a high-crime area. The rental was in poor condition. Stained beige carpet ran throughout the home, and large holes in the shower were taped over with plastic bags to cover the insulation. In the kitchen, the cabinets were detaching from the walls and the tiles were cracked, damage Tina attributed to the house shifting on its uneven foundation during rainy weather.

Despite its problems, the one-story single-family home with small yards in the front and the back felt spacious to the family compared to the one-bedroom apartment they had moved from several years earlier. The rental had two bedrooms, one bath, and a den, which they used as a third bedroom. Since moving there, Tina and Carlos had frequently moved the two youngest children into their bedroom so they could host extended family members and friends. In recent years, they had provided housing for Carlos's friend, along with his girlfriend and their infant child, his sister and her three-year-old son, Tina's brother, her young adult nephew, and her young adult daughter from a previous relationship.

Parents like Tina contrasted their doubled-up households with the nuclear family household ideal, which included defined, gendered roles for one man and one woman. She repeatedly characterized herself as territorial because she preferred not to live with other women. When Carlos's friend Eduardo and his young girlfriend Erica needed a place to live with their infant child after being kicked out of their previous doubled-up household, Tina and Carlos hesitantly decided to let them stay in their home. Tina immediately regretted the decision. "That evening and I was already dreading it because I didn't want nobody living here. . . . I didn't [want] no other woman living here with me, okay, because like I said, I'm really territorial about it." She was not alone in her concerns about women coresiding together. The nuclear family household ideal shaped the gender mix that families felt comfortable with, and several parents attributed difficulties they had in doubled-up households to gender, suggesting that having multiple women living in a single household was undesirable.

Erica frequently failed to live up to Tina's gendered expectations of household life. While Carlos and Eduardo were away at work, Tina completed household tasks, but Erica preferred to spend the day watching TV. Tina intervened: "It was like, 'Oh you're cleaning and cooking, bitch. Get up and let's cook for our men.'" To her, the domestic chores that Erica shirked were her duty: "I mean, you're a woman now, you have a baby and you have a husband." Tina saw herself as a mentor to her younger guest, who knew little about cooking and cleaning, and she was willing to show her how to "take advantage of" her new role as a mother and partner. Erica's unwillingness to help with the housework—and thus meet Tina's gendered expectations of her role in the home—ultimately contributed to the household's dissolution. "I was just trying to, I guess, take her under my wing, and she didn't want to accept it, so I was like, 'Well, then, screw her.'"

Tina also carefully guarded the boundaries of Erica's relationship with Carlos. She described how one night, they had been casually drinking together when Erica "walked up to my husband . . . and said, 'Do you have $25 I can borrow? I need to go buy my baby some milk.'" Tina glared at Erica before responding for Carlos, saying, "Lookee here, we don't have money to buy milk for your babies. We barely even have enough to buy for ours." It was not the money that Tina was most concerned about, but the interaction itself: "My thing was, how come [Eduardo] didn't have the balls enough to come to my husband and ask him that? Why did he send that girl to come to my man? Did he think because she was a woman he was going to just go on and hand [her] the money?" Although she had shut down Erica's request for money from her husband, Tina ultimately gave her money for the milk, unwilling to let the baby go hungry.

Tensions escalated over the next couple of weeks, until Tina and Carlos asked their guests to move out. Eduardo blamed the eviction on jealousy. According to Tina, "[Eduardo] went and told his little girl that we were lovers and that I was so jealous, that's why I was treating her like that . . . instead of telling her the truth: 'They want us out because I can't pay rent.' 'Oh, she's wanting us to get out because she's jealous. She used to be my lover'—you little loogie!" Accusations of jealousy were common in doubled-up households, but they were often met with adamant denial. Tina recalled telling Erica, "Your man is very far from the type of man that I want . . . he is not the type, he's never been my type, and no, I have never been his lover, and you are damn wrong if you think I'm jealous over you. I'm not."

In a nuclear family household, the intimate home environment insulates romantic relationships from outsiders, who could interact inappropriately or spark jealousy. As Tina's experience shows, living doubled up with additional adults adds another layer of interactions and relationships to navigate throughout daily life. The line between appropriate and inappropriate behavior is more easily blurred when coresiding. Such complications increase the inconvenience of living doubled up, for both hosts and guests, and provide opportunities for disagreement.

Doubled-up parents also struggled to protect the boundaries of their relationships with romantic partners who were visiting rather than coresiding. When Leeann, the twenty-six-year-old Black mother of four from chapter 3, hosted her cousin and niece, she was romantically involved with a friend who stayed over a couple of nights a week. Her cousin's interactions with the friend were a common source of contention. For instance, her cousin had recently come out of the house, wearing a strapless dress, to where Leeann and her friend were sitting outside. "I'm like, 'Go in the house,' because my dude's sitting right there. . . . That's inappropriate. That's wrong. You do not do that in front of a woman's man. She's all like, I was just being jealous. I'm like, 'I'm not being jealous. That's rude.'"

Coresiding provided her cousin with ample opportunities to interact with Leeann's friend in ways that made Leeann uncomfortable. She said that her cousin began "leaving her thongs on the floor . . . leaving her bras on the floor for my dude to see," behavior that she assumed was meant to entice her friend. She contrasted her cousin's behavior with her own efforts to ensure that she did "not cross no boundaries" when the cousin's romantic partner lived with them: "When I take a shower, I come down in my towel. When they moved into my house, I quit doing that. No matter how cold it is outside, I'm in my T-shirt and pants sleeping. When he came here, I'm fully clothed. I hate wearing bras. When he was here, I kept my bra on, because that's your man and I'm not going to do that to you, I'm going to respect you."

Competing Relationships: Navigating Multiple Types of Relationship Expectations

Parents' ideals of family life often involved a uniquely personal relationship with their coresident romantic partner. Yet sharing a household and interacting daily with someone outside the nuclear family unit could threaten these expected relationship boundaries. Joe, a fifty-two-year-old White father, lived with his wife, Susan, and their three children, ages five, thirteen, and fourteen. He had bought their large, three-bedroom home on a tree-lined street in a middle-class suburb of Cleveland over twenty-three years before and had been living there ever since. The home was showing minor signs of age, and during the interview he self-deprecatingly pointed out the repairs he needed to do, such as painting the chipping paint on the porch.

About two years earlier, Joe's sister-in-law moved in with them after the home she had been renting by herself went into foreclosure. He said his sister-in-law was already "sick of living by herself" before her rental property foreclosed, so Susan proposed that they allow her to move in with them. He thought the arrangement would work well: "It wasn't really a long conversation or anything like that. [My wife] mentioned it to me, and I was like, 'Okay, yeah. That's fine. Sounds good, that will help us financially.'" Joe and Susan were on the higher end of the income distribution in my sample, bringing in over $80,000 a year. However, the family's expenses were often higher than their income, so he looked forward to additional help. By the time I met him, his sister-in-law was living in their finished attic, which was fully furnished— "almost like an apartment," he said—and she was contributing $300 a month toward their $1,300 mortgage.

Although Joe and Susan were more economically advantaged than many doubled-up families, navigating doubled-up household life was still difficult, particularly for him. When I asked him to "tell me about yours and your wife's decision to let [the sister-in-law] move in," he immediately introduced the idea that doubling up could affect romantic relationships, saying, "We didn't really have to discuss it. It wasn't an issue for me at all. I felt like it wouldn't be a problem at all. I certainly don't believe that that was going to hurt our marriage at all or anything like that; having someone, right here, that—no. I didn't see any of that kind of stuff being a problem." In response to follow-up questions about whether having his sister-in-law move in *had* affected his marriage, he revealed that he attributed some of the poor communication between Susan and himself to the presence of an additional household member who provided emotional support to Susan. "It does seem like my wife talks to her more . . . she doesn't talk to me as much as she used to because of it . . . us talking is not the same because she has her sister now here."

Susan enjoyed the emotional support from her sister, and Joe was careful to note that the decreased communication was his perception and that she disagreed. Yet their different feelings highlighted the lack of clear expectations about appropriate relationships and roles in doubled-up households. Even when a guest's involvement was appreciated by one spouse, it was not always interpreted the same way by the other. Joe missed the emotional intimacy that accompanied sharing a household solely with his wife, and he believed that having a third adult in their household threatened his marital relationship by providing an alternative, easily accessible confidant for her.

Intimacy and emotional support are central to modern marriages.[11] Moreover, marital relationships often take primacy over other close relationships, such as relationships with extended family. Marriage has been called a "greedy institution" that monopolizes adults' energy and time, and, compared to unmarried adults, married adults tend to provide less companionship and emotional support to friends and family other than their spouse.[12] Yet, unlike in single-family households, where romantic partners are the only coresident adults, Joe's wife shared a home with both her husband and her sister. Joe believed that the doubled-up household strengthened her bond with her sister to the detriment of their marriage.

Additionally, living with adults outside the nuclear family introduced competing loyalties that made fulfilling relationship expectations more difficult during household disagreements. After Carlos's friend's family moved out from his and Tina's home, his sister moved in with her three-year-old son because she wanted to leave the household where she lived doubled up with friends. Tina had frequent disagreements with her sister-in-law, and she expected her husband to take her side, but Carlos frequently supported his sister instead. For example, his sister would lie in bed late into the morning and open the door for her young son to go into the kitchen, where Tina would be serving her own children breakfast. Tina eventually rejected this added responsibility and told Carlos to get his sister out of bed to feed her child. He told her to just feed the boy at the table with their children, but she refused. "'No. I am not doing that no more. I don't have five kids, I have four. Your sister has one, I'm dealing with my four. Tell her to get up and feed her kid.' . . . And that pissed him off. We did the arguing, the ignoring, fight all day, because he had to go and tell her to get up to feed the baby."

Moreover, Carlos's generosity toward his sister, even at the expense of his nuclear family, caused frequent fights. "It was like every time I turned around, she was wanting him to do something for her," Tina explained. One day they were getting ready to take their children to the park when she noticed that her sister-in-law was preparing to leave without her son. "I said, 'Or is she paying you to watch him because, you know, that could help [financially]. Is she paying you?'" When Carlos responded that he was not charging his sister because she could not afford to pay, she was enraged. "I was like, 'You know what? She makes double what we make in one month and she doesn't have to pay for a babysitter for one kid? No, she's not going to get freebies off of us. You better go tell her,' and I was hollering."

Likewise, Tina and Carlos disagreed about how to divide household expenses. She expected to divide the electricity bill between the three adults, with them paying two-thirds and her sister-in-law paying one-third. Yet he balked at asking his sister to pay more than the $350 a month they charged her for rent. She explained, "He wouldn't want to charge her because he would feel, in his eyes, she was really struggling with that one baby," to which Tina responded by pointing out their own low income and their *four* children. Carlos cared deeply for his sister's well-being, but Tina expected him to prioritize his own nuclear family. Disagreements over competing loyalties to one's nuclear family and extended family undoubtedly occur outside of doubled-up households as well, but sharing a household offered ample opportunities for these disagreements to arise in the course of daily life, as Tina's stories demonstrate.

Conclusion

Doubled-up households are a housing arrangement, but their impacts extend far beyond simply providing a roof over a family's head. This chapter has revealed the restrictions and complexities that doubling up introduced to parents' romantic partnerships and intimate family life. Many parents who were doubled up as guests felt hindered in their desire to live as a "real family" in one household. Even when parents lived doubled up alongside a romantic partner, coresidence with other adults introduced new complexities to daily life in the household. Parents associated the intimacy of coresidence with the nuclear family unit—romantic partners and children—and coresidence with adults outside the nuclear family limited romantic couples' privacy and required special efforts to navigate.

Living doubled up caused stress that some parents believed had worsened their relationship quality. Disadvantaged parents' romantic relationships are notoriously fragile.[13] The relationship challenges described in this chapter may play a role in this fragility for the large and growing share of parents who live doubled up. Given the prevalence of doubling up, understanding these challenges is key to developing effective programming to support lower-income couples' relationships. In her study of a federally funded relationship skills class for low-income unmarried parents, Jennifer Randles shows that policy is frequently unresponsive to the needs of lower-income couples. For example, she observed a relationship skills instructor who encouraged a doubled-up couple to share their feelings with one another at the end of each day, while ignoring the lack of privacy this couple had in their overcrowded household.[14] Understanding the realities of lower-income parents' lives and, as Randles argues, directly addressing the poverty that contributes to their relationship challenges can improve programming targeted at lower-income parents.

The experiences of the parents in this chapter demonstrate the ways in which doubling up challenged relationships and potentially contributed to relationship instability. At the same time, as this chapter makes clear, these parents made extraordinary efforts to maintain their romantic relationships despite these challenges. Parents went to great lengths to keep their families together and housed, to spend time with their children each day despite living in separate households, and to maintain healthy relationships despite the daily stress and interference that accompanied living doubled up. Through these actions, the parents in this chapter demonstrated strong dedication to their relationship, even in the trying circumstances that accompanied living doubled up.

Despite the often-heroic efforts of doubled-up parents to sustain their romantic relationships, however, the differences between parents' doubled-up households and their ideals of family life sparked frustration. Parents often held on to the ideal of a nuclear family household, which they defined as a household with no adults except their romantic partner. Parents' expectations about family life were thus based on the cultural ideal in which the home sets the nuclear family unit apart from the outside world. Sharing this most intimate environment with other adults challenged parents' expectations around relationship privacy, intimacy, and boundaries. Living doubled up facilitated other adults' interference and oversight of parents' romantic relationships. It also allowed for critiques of how they fulfilled other household members' expectations for their roles within the household, expectations that were often highly gendered. As in other domains of household life, guests, who relied on hosts for housing and thus held a subordinate position in the household, often experienced this interference and oversight particularly acutely.

Doubled-up guests faced the additional pressure of not having a home of their own. Relying on others for housing prevented some guests from living with their romantic partner. In their study of cohabiting couples, Sharon Sassler and Amanda Miller find that financial necessity leads some lower-income couples to cohabit soon after beginning a relationship—even when they would prefer to continue living separately—because they cannot afford to maintain two independent households.[15] This chapter has demonstrated that economic need can also prevent couples who *want* to cohabit from being able to do so, since cohabiting requires that the couple either obtain a home of their own or find a host who will allow both of them to join the household.

Other guests saw an independent household as a prerequisite for their ideal family life—including coresidence with their romantic partner and eventual marriage. A long line of research shows that financial stability and assets like a home and car are necessary preconditions for marriage for many couples.[16] When economic goals based on a middle-class ideal become more difficult to achieve, it can halt parents' progress toward their goals for family life. For lower-income guests, the high costs that make it challenging to find housing of their own that is both affordable and desirable push residential independence—and the nuclear family household ideal—out of reach.

6

Raising Children

ISA, THE TWENTY-NINE-YEAR-OLD Hispanic mother we met in the introduction, lived with her three daughters, ages nine, five, and one, in her mother Antonia's house. Antonia's home was located at the southernmost border of the city of Dallas on a narrow road with a gravel and dirt shoulder lined with a dumpster and several parked vehicles. The brick house was tucked behind a lush but tidy front yard filled with trees, rosebushes, and a wrought-iron table and chairs, all surrounded by a decorative metal gate set between brick pillars. Inside, the spacious, open-concept living area had none of the clutter one might expect with three young children living in the home. The decor was elegant, with leather furniture, framed paintings on the walls, and blue-and-white porcelain vases on floor-to-ceiling shelves.

In contrast with the traditional look of the main home, Isa's "little apartment" upstairs—as she called the second floor of the home where she and her daughters lived—was extravagantly decorated with her artistic style. The freshly painted walls were red with gold trim, with a single striped accent wall. To get to her bedroom and her daughters' room, I walked through a tiny sitting area, not much bigger than a hallway, that was crowded with a couch and love seat. Isa had found the ornate furniture—featuring satin with floral designs and rich wood carving—in thrift stores and then lovingly painted and reupholstered each piece. The home's air conditioning did not seem to reach the second floor, which was muggy in the heat of the Texas summer. Yet her three daughters were playing happily in their room, which had a bunk bed and a crib along with a TV and comfy couch.

Isa described her sixty-two-year-old mother Antonia, who worked as a housekeeper, as "very lovable." She explained: "I'm so thankful to have a mother like her. She's always helped me a lot." As described in the introduction, Isa had her first daughter when she was nineteen years old; she was still living in her mother's home at the time, but she was also engaged and planning to establish her own household with her daughter's father. Six months later, her fiancé went to jail, and she was left with the prospect of parenting her first child alone. "I didn't know about how to be a mom, so my mom—she's very protective—she's like, 'Well, I'll help you.'" As a young first-time mother, Isa appreciated having an opportunity to learn from her mother's advice and from her interactions with her granddaughter.

When Isa began working and later going back to school, Antonia took her granddaughter along with her to the church where she worked. Isa relied heavily on her mother's help. "When you're young and you had your kids young, you just want somebody to help you. That was my mom." The childcare assistance continued in the subsequent years; Antonia helped with all three of Isa's daughters when she had school obligations, work, or a hair client. Because of this help, Isa's career plans were not limited by childcare hours or expenses, which left her free to try to find a career that fit her interests. She had only recently completed cosmetology school and was working to build up her reputation as a stylist. At the same time, she was already pondering returning to school to finish her degree in court reporting. Although Antonia thought that Isa should find a job rather than returning to school, Isa was confident that her mother would help with childcare if she chose to continue her studies.

When asked what about the multigenerational household was good for her daughters, Isa immediately highlighted their relationship with Antonia. "I like that they have that bond with my mom, like a grandma. Because I think I met with her mom like twice in my life, and I really never had that grandma in my life, so I like that. I like for them to have a grandmother." Her children, especially her oldest daughter, were extremely close with their grandmother. When Isa was pregnant with her first daughter, her brother had cancer, and she gave birth just a couple of weeks before he passed away. Antonia was heartbroken, but her new granddaughter brought her joy. She often brought the baby to sleep in her bedroom; Isa, feeling "like she probably needs that and that happiness," acquiesced to being separated from her newborn on these nights.

Isa knew that her mother cared about her, but she believed that her children were the primary motivation for her support. "I think she likes the company, for her not to feel alone and my children, I think that's the main part that she loves. I feel that if I really didn't have any children, she really wouldn't show too much interest. But it's my children that she's very attached to." Without her daughters, she conjectured, Antonia "would care, but she wouldn't be too attentive like she is, always trying to help out." With her daughters there, Isa could not think of anything her mother did *not* like about having them living with her. She hoped to move out to a home of her own, but she knew their move would disappoint Antonia. "She always says, 'I don't know what I'm going to do whenever y'all leave. I think I'm going to die.'" Asked whether her mother wanted them to live there forever, she replied, "Yes, she would. I'm thinking maybe if I ever move out, I'll probably have to take her with me."

———

National data show that parents often double up, particularly as a guest, at times when they might benefit from child-rearing assistance.[1] For instance, compared to mothers with older children, mothers with young children more often live doubled up in the home of an extended family member.[2] Likewise, mothers are particularly likely to form a doubled-up household, as either a host or a guest, when a coresident romantic relationship ends.[3] Consistent with these trends, Isa remained in her mother's home while her children were young, a decision driven at least in part by her separation from her fiancé. For parents, like Isa, who would otherwise be parenting alone, a shared household provided an extra set of hands.

Doubling up, especially as a guest, is also more common among mothers who were younger when they had their children.[4] When Isa had her first child as a teenager, living in a multigenerational household provided her with the opportunity to learn to be a mother with the mentorship and support of her own mother. Lorraine, a Black mother in my sample, similarly described her history of doubling up as a guest: "I moved out at sixteen, got pregnant, moved back. Because, first one, I don't know what to do. Who can teach me better than my mom? So I moved back home." For first-time mothers, doubling up with an older female relative facilitated the transfer of generational knowledge about child-rearing.

Antonia also took a direct hand in raising Isa's three daughters, devoting many hours each week to childcare.[5] She was not alone: roughly two-thirds of my sample received childcare assistance from a shared household member at some point during fieldwork, and childcare support was particularly common in multigenerational households. Survey data on three-generation households show that such childcare support can increase the time invested in children and lessen the burden on parents: compared to unpartnered mothers who live alone but have similar characteristics, unpartnered mothers who live with a child's grandparent spend less time on solo caregiving, and their children receive more total caregiving time. Grandparents spend about as much time solo caregiving in multigenerational households as do married biological fathers in two-parent homes.[6] These time investments allow parents in multigenerational households, like Isa, to spend less money on childcare compared to parents who do not live in multigenerational households. These savings are impactful for parents and children: low-income families divert these savings to other child-related investment, such as spending on school and hobbies.[7]

For Isa, who had little income and worked inconsistent hours styling hair, it would have been difficult to obtain sufficient childcare on the private market. Likewise, public childcare support is inaccessible for many families like Isa's; fewer than one in four children who are eligible for federally funded childcare subsidies actually receive them, and even families who receive subsidies face challenges finding affordable, high-quality care.[8] Without her mother's help, Isa would probably have been unable to pursue educational and employment opportunities. Antonia's babysitting allowed Isa to finish cosmetology school and build up her hairstyling clientele, and knowing that she would have childcare support allowed her to consider going back to school to switch careers.

Isa's experience echoes findings from other research linking shared households and economic opportunities. Studies of teen mothers find that grandmother coresidence is associated with both education and employment.[9] Likewise, a study of single mothers found that those who live doubled up as guests with extended family are more likely to enter productive activities, like employment or schooling, than those who do not. This effect is substantial: the estimated effect of living in the home of an extended family member is equivalent to the effect of an 11 percent decrease in the county-level poverty rate.[10]

Isa recognized the value of her mother's child-rearing support and was grateful for it. At the same time, she, like many parents, grew frustrated at times by her mother's involvement. Coresidence created and magnified opportunities for disagreement over child-rearing. On the one hand, doubled-up parents often wanted, or even expected, other adults to be invested in their children when they lived in the same household. They valued child-rearing support from coresident adults and expected that their household would function, to some extent, as a unit dedicated to supporting child well-being. On the other hand, parents typically sought to retain authority over parenting and their children's environments, an ambition that was challenging in shared households. Living with others provided opportunities for oversight and overinvolvement, and it reduced parents' control over their children's home environments.

Moreover, the lack of shared understandings about *how* child-rearing should be shared in a doubled-up household made it ripe for disagreement, with potentially negative implications for parenting and child well-being. Lindsay Chase-Lansdale, Jeanne Brooks-Gunn, and Elise Zamsky posit two potential mechanisms through which multigenerational households may negatively impact parenting: first, high levels of conflict that interfere with parenting, and second, "a diffusion of parenting responsibility" in which different household members assume that another person is caring for the child.[11] This chapter demonstrates that parents experienced each of these challenges in doubled-up households. Additionally, difficulty sharing household space and interference from other household members made it challenging for parents to enact the consistent daily routines that promote child well-being.[12]

Overall, sharing a household with individuals beyond the nuclear family could provide child-rearing support but also constraint. Isa was relatively lucky; her multigenerational home facilitated critical childcare and provided a loving home for her daughters. Other doubled-up parents and their children faced less supportive or even harmful home environments. Even for parents like Isa, however, the child-rearing support gained by doubling up required navigating complicated questions about how parenting rights and responsibilities should be shared.

"They're Not Her Children": Interference and Overinvolvement

Coresidence made it easier for Antonia to provide support and childcare, but it also facilitated unwanted advice and interactions. She sometimes overruled Isa's rules, undercutting her authority as a mother and making it difficult to maintain a regular routine. For example, although Isa's daughters had a bedtime, their grandmother often did not enforce this rule and allowed them to stay up late into the night. Daily disagreements over issues like this were common among the doubled-up households in my sample, and they sent conflicting messages to children about who held authority within the home. For mothers like Isa, such interference was not just an inconvenience but an encroachment on her role as a mother. "They're not her children. She's just the grandmother. I feel that it's the right thing to do that if I'm disciplining them, that's how it should be. If I tell them 'no,' it's supposed to be 'no,'" she explained.

Unlike some mothers in my sample, Isa consciously tried to brush off these smaller issues. Although she conveyed her preferences, she knew her mother would not change ("my mom is a person that she's going to do whatever she wants"), and she had limited recourse while living in her mother's home. Antonia retained authority as the householder, and she dismissed Isa's complaints by reminding her of how much assistance she provided.

Their most fundamental disagreement centered on the children's religious education. Isa was strictly dedicated to the teachings of her nondenominational Christian church, and she wanted to pass along her beliefs to her daughters. Antonia, on the other hand, attended services across a variety of religious denominations, including Catholic and Jehovah's Witness, and she sometimes shared the various teachings from these denominations with the children. For example, she recently taught her granddaughters about saints. "I don't believe in saints," Isa explained. "I just told [my mother], 'Don't be telling her to believe in saints.' She got a little offended, but we talked about it. That's mainly the things that she puts her input in, that stuff." Religious education was an important part of motherhood for Isa, one that was threatened by Antonia's interference. "I want to raise my children in the belief that I believe. And whenever they grow up, I want to feel like I did it. I know they're going to have to see their grandparents, but I'm their mother. . . . So I think it's time for us to put [up] like our wall. I take care of my own kids and I do everything for them, so I want to keep on guiding them in whatever I believe."

Additionally, although Isa loved that her daughters had a strong bond with their grandmother, she felt jealous of the particularly close relationship Antonia had with her oldest daughter, who often co-slept with her grandmother. "I just started seeing that she liked my mom more than she liked me. I felt that. But then, I had my other daughter and she was very close to me." Still, Isa wanted her older daughter to also "love me as her mom," so she put an end to co-sleeping with Antonia, which her older daughter had enjoyed since infancy. Antonia was offended by the change and complained. "If she wants to sleep with me—we're in the same house. Nothing is going to happen to her, and I've been taking care of her all these years. Why are you going to just do that to her?" However, Isa stood firm. For her, requiring her daughter to sleep in her own room was one step in reestablishing herself as the mother and weakening Antonia's relationship with the child so that it would still be close but not maternal. "I want her to see [me as] her mom, and [to see] my mom not like her mom, just like a sister or something."

The sense that Antonia was infringing on her role as a mother was one of the main reasons that Isa wanted to move into a home of her own. When she first became a mother, she recalled, she thought that living in Antonia's home made raising her children easier, but she later came to see it as "a little bit more difficult." In recent years, she had tried to differentiate her nuclear family unit from her mother. Drawing boundaries around her mother's relationship with her oldest daughter was a key part of this effort. Additionally, she was trying to accept less assistance and instead provide for and care for her children more herself. "We're our own little family, so we need to try it and we need to stick together. . . . I have my family, my mom, but they're my daughters, so I'm in charge. I'm held accountable all for them, so I need to teach them. They look up to me . . . we're a family. Because if I would let them, they would look up to my mom, but that's what I don't want. I don't want that. I want them to look up to me and come to me for everything and for me to do everything for them." American families often treat nuclear family independence and self-sufficiency as the ideal, though reliance on support networks is common—and arguably even necessary—for child-rearing.[13] Isa echoed these ideals and disliked how living with her mother hindered her ability to establish strict boundaries around her nuclear family.

Isa saw residential independence as a major step toward separating her nuclear family from her mother. Yet Antonia did not want her to move out; the shared household provided her with valued companionship—both from her coresident daughter and especially from her grandchildren—that she never wanted to give up. Likewise, Isa's brothers and sisters expected her to stay with her mother to keep her company and provide support as she aged.

Receiving care—whether for children or older adults—and giving care were central forms of support exchanged in doubled-up households. As described earlier, most parents in my sample received childcare assistance from a shared household member at some point during fieldwork, as Isa did. Additionally, approximately half of parents described times when they *provided* care support to others in a shared household, typically childcare but sometimes care for an older relative.

Isa's support for her mother was currently limited to providing company, but she was willing to do more as her mother aged. It was important to Isa that she move out of her mother's home—to "get situated and just stable" herself—but "I don't mind taking care of her," she explained. She would prefer to have a separate residence from Antonia and to provide care without coresiding, but she was willing to consider allowing her mother to move in with her—so long

as she was the householder. "Maybe I'll try [living] on my own for a couple of months. If I have a place where she could live with me, yeah, I would do it." She expected that, as the householder, "it would be really different. It would be better." In her own home, she imagined that she could require her mother to respect her authority over child-rearing: "No inputs, no inputs on my religious beliefs, my children's inputs and stuff like that."

Of course, such rules might be difficult to maintain in practice, even as a householder; several hosts in my sample struggled to prevent guests from interfering in their child-rearing. For the moment, however, Isa was confident that she would regain authority if she were the householder. "I feel that it's her house, her rules. And then, if it's my house, my rules. She's my guest, but it's my house." Householder status did provide hosts with at least one recourse that was not available to guests: they could kick them out of their home. Hosts threatened to use this authority in attempts to change behavior and sometimes followed through; hosts' concerns about the impact of the shared household on their children contributed to multiple household dissolutions in my sample.

Parenting Challenges and Contradictions

Shortly after her first interview, Annalise, a twenty-six-year-old White mother, was evicted from her home and moved with her two children to her stepfather's mother's home. "Gram," as she called her, was an older Black woman who worked at a nursing home but hoped to retire soon. She owned a tired-looking two-story home with peeling yellow paint on the far west side of Cleveland. The home was technically a duplex, with separate units upstairs and down, but the downstairs did not have a functional kitchen, and the family treated the whole house as a single home. Annalise's daughters, age two and six, shared one downstairs bedroom, Annalise's adult sister had the other, and Annalise had fashioned a "bedroom" for herself by hanging sheets to divide the downstairs living room. Upstairs, Gram had one bedroom; during fieldwork, the other bedroom was always occupied by some combination of Annalise's stepfather, her stepfather's girlfriend, and her uncle.

Gram provided a critical safety net for Annalise, who moved back into her house twice during the course of fieldwork—first in response to the eviction, and again a year and a half later when she was doubled up in the home of her ex's mother and desperate to find another housing option. Each time Gram let her return, even though Annalise felt that she "didn't really want us to move

back in here." Annalise attributed her grandmother's willingness to provide housing to her concern for her children. Gram was close to her granddaughters, particularly the youngest. "They are each other's world. My kids are her world, and she's my kids' world," Annalise explained, describing how her younger daughter would sprint to the door to greet her grandmother each time she heard her car pull into the driveway. Gram's affection for her granddaughters contrasted with her reluctance to host Annalise, who said, "I'm really not wanted here, but she's not going to tell me to leave because of my kids."

Annalise relied heavily on childcare support from her sister and Gram. She worked the morning shift at a laundromat, and if she were not living with them, she would have needed to wake and dress her daughters in time to make the 5:00 AM bus to drop them off at Gram's house before work. Despite the challenges she would have faced with childcare if she moved out, Annalise was hesitant to characterize her housing situation as convenient: "It's only convenient in a small way. It's more convenient for me to move. If it's not one problem, it's another." Although the household provided ample childcare support, she felt that the constant conflict in the household was not worth it.

Research on young mothers finds some negative associations between multigenerational coresidence and parenting practices.[14] This association seems to be driven at least in part by selection into multigenerational households.[15] However, Chase-Lansdale and her colleagues hypothesize two ways in which multigenerational coresidence may make parenting more difficult, both of which seem plausible in households like Annalise's.[16] First, the high levels of conflict present in many shared households may interfere with parenting. Annalise described multiple arguments that had recently culminated in a family member "cussing and yelling." She had particularly adversarial relationships with her stepfather's girlfriend and her uncle, both of whom tried to set rules that conflicted with her sense of adulthood. She found these rules particularly infuriating coming from these two household members, since neither of them was the householder. As she recently told her stepfather's girlfriend, "Well, this isn't your house. You have no authority here." The stress that these interactions introduced could have been detrimental to both Annalise and her two young daughters.

Annalise also frequently argued with the household members about their roles and responsibilities regarding her children. Although her daughters had their bedrooms on the first floor of the home, they typically spent their days upstairs, where the heat worked better, the TV had cable channels that played *SpongeBob* and *Dora,* and Gram was there to cut up apples and oranges for

snacks. Annalise, on the other hand, did not like being upstairs with the rest of the extended family and preferred to stay downstairs, where she could play games on the TV. She said that the other household members complained that "I'm a bad mom because I'm always down here and my kids are always upstairs."

Other household members expected Annalise to accompany her daughters upstairs, but she expected other household members to take responsibility for her daughters when they were upstairs. "They'll go upstairs and they'll throw stuff all over the house. Well, if somebody was watching them up here, they wouldn't have threw the stuff all the way over the house. If you're not going to watch them, send them back downstairs." Likewise, she expected her family to take responsibility for any messes that resulted when they allowed her daughters to take food into the living room. "They just want me up there with the kids because the kids make messes. . . . If I'm not upstairs and you give the kids chips in the living room—greasy, salty chips and there's chip crumbs all over the floor, there's greasy handprints on the couch, there's chips all over the place—that's not my fault. I did not tell you to give them chips in the living room, so why should I have to clean it up? I understand they're my kids, but I didn't give them the mess to make."

These disagreements echoed the second way that Chase-Lansdale and her colleagues suggest that multigenerational households may harm child-rearing: "a diffusion of parenting responsibility" in which both the mother and the grandmother assume that the other is the child's primary caretaker.[17] As discussed later in the chapter, Annalise vehemently defended her status and authority as primary caregiver. Yet, in day-to-day life, she and other household members disagreed about who should have primary responsibility for her children's behavior and whether this depended on where the children were in their shared home. Likewise, other doubled-up parents expected that the adults they lived with would provide childcare assistance, but these adults were not always eager to help.

Although Annalise assumed that responsibility for her children when they went upstairs would be shared by other coresident adults, she also claimed authority over decisions about how to raise her children and pushed back aggressively against criticism. "They're my kids. The way I choose to raise them is the way I choose to raise them. Everyone's biggest issue is that I'm too nice. My kids run over me and I don't punish them enough. But they're my kids." This type of refrain—"they're my kids"—was common among doubled-up mothers asserting their control over child-rearing in the face of interference or unwanted advice from other household members. Like many mothers, Annalise also limited how much other household members could discipline her children: "They try. I don't [let them]. That's my child, let me deal with it." She often simply brought her daughters downstairs when they misbehaved rather than punishing them. In this way, Annalise maintained strict control over child-rearing. "Everyone kind of knows that they can't tell them what to do or punish them or have any influence in how they're raised, because they're my kids. How I choose to raise them is how I choose to raise them."

Parents like Annalise often wanted, and sometimes even expected, other household members to share in child-rearing when they lived in the same household. At the same time, they reserved certain rights and responsibilities for themselves as parents, such as punishment and rule-setting. These precise, sometimes contradictory expectations—for involvement, but not overinvolvement—were difficult to negotiate within shared households.

"There's Only One Stove": Navigating Shared Household Space

Beyond interpersonal dynamics, sharing physical household space posed practical challenges to parents' efforts to maintain a daily routine with their children. Because her daughters were often upstairs with their grandmother or aunt during the day and Annalise avoided that area of the home, she and her daughters had relatively little interaction on weekdays. As a result, "there can't be any organization here," she said, explaining that she frequently found herself rushing to help her older daughter complete her homework at the last minute.

The time her daughters spent upstairs and away from Annalise made planning difficult, but at the time of her interview, she was pleased that she and her daughters at least had space to sleep downstairs. About a month before, she had finally paid to have the heat turned on in the downstairs unit of Gram's house. Before that, she and her daughters had been sleeping in the living room upstairs on an air mattress that she blew up each night and put away each morning. Annalise did not complain of any sleep loss from this arrangement, but other doubled-up guests described how overcrowded bedrooms, sleeping in common areas, and the presence of household visitors at night negatively impacted their sleep or their children's sleep.

Trying to share the home's single functioning kitchen with multiple family units who each cooked their own meals also made it difficult for Annalise to maintain a regular schedule for her daughters. "Now the issue is with four different people in the house making four different meals, there's only one stove in the house. So, when I go upstairs to cook, if I'm cooking and somebody else is ready, there's an issue and there's an attitude because they're ready to cook. Well, I'm sorry; I'm not going to stop cooking for me and my children to satisfy you. I'll go upstairs at 6:00 to cook and I can't cook until 7:30 because somebody else up there cooking. So me and my kids aren't ready to sit down and eat until 8:30 and their bedtime at 8:00." This experience also highlighted another common source of tension: she believed that her children's needs should be prioritized over those of the adults in the household, yet other household adults did not always meet this expectation. "I think I should be able to cook first because you guys are grown and my kids have to eat first," she explained.

Guests living in someone else's home, like Annalise, also felt pressure—sometimes internally imposed, sometimes reinforced by the householder—to keep their children well behaved. Like most toddlers, Annalise's youngest daughter sometimes got into mischief. "My grandmother had a lamp like this upstairs that she's had for years, since I can remember, and [my daughter] just knocked it off the table, broke the lamp. She took a permanent marker and wrote all over her dining room table." She regretted her daughters' misbehavior but felt unable to prevent it. "This is her house and I understand that, but there's only so much I can do," she said. Furthermore, she was aware that any damage her daughters caused to the home raised the cost for Gram to host them, and this awareness prevented her from asking for any further assistance. "My grandma helps with stuff like diapers and stuff like that for the kids, but I'm already living here rent-free and my kids are tearing up her house. I can't ask her for anything more."

"That's Not Fair": When Children from Different Families Coreside

Many families in my sample, like Isa, doubled up with household members who did not have children of their own. However, when one family with children moved in with another family with children, sharing household space and navigating expectations could be even more complicated. Each time I interviewed Lisa, a forty-year-old White mother, she sat with me on the front porch of her two-story duplex home. The home, located in a lower-income Cleveland neighborhood, looked tired, with its brown peeling paint and warped porch roof. Lisa sat on a worn blue cushion on a bench piled with clothing, while I and the other interviewer sat in two of the camping chairs that lined the porch.

There were two front doors opening onto the porch, one leading to the downstairs unit, where Lisa's aunt lived, and one leading to the upstairs unit. Typically, the upstairs unit housed Lisa, her four-year-old son and ten-year-old daughter, and her seven-year-old niece and five-year-old nephew, whom she was foster parenting. About four months before I met her, she also took in her cousin Danielle, along with her husband and their seven-year-old son. Lisa owned the entire home, having inherited it from her mother, but she allowed her aunt—an older adult with no other housing available—to live in the downstairs unit. Danielle's family joined Lisa and her children in their two-bedroom unit upstairs. Lisa slept in a bed in the foyer, which opened into the living room, where Danielle and her husband slept on the couch and loveseat. The young girls shared a bedroom, where they each had a bed, while the boys slept in bunk beds in the second bedroom. So Danielle's son could have the bottom bunk, Lisa's son and nephew shared the top bunk.

Lisa found the overcrowding challenging, but it was important to her that she provide housing for her cousin, who was moving to Cleveland from Indiana and needed a place to stay. However, when a caseworker for the foster children did her monthly check-in, she told Lisa that the overcrowded conditions were against regulations. "There was a lot of us in the house. . . . She even said this is against fire safety hazard. I said, 'I know, but they're not here for long, they'll be leaving soon,' which thankfully they did. But I mean, what are you going to do? You can't let your family sit out on the street." Lisa was thankful that the caseworker was understanding and did not make her evict her cousin in order to continue fostering her niece and nephew.[18]

When Danielle's family moved in, Lisa sat down with her cousin and her husband to discuss household organization, such as sleeping arrangements and rules for the children. She told them, "Just like what my kids are allowed to do and I can't expect my kids to follow rules if their son isn't going to follow the rules and stuff like that." Although Danielle agreed to have her son follow the same rules, he was not used to living with strict rules. "It probably took about a month, maybe a month and a half, for him to realize that this is the way things were going to go in our house and it was different. Again, I reiterate, it's hard to live with somebody else," Lisa remembered. For example, she told him not to touch the small figurines and other decorations in the home, but the young boy did not listen. Eventually, he broke one. Lisa was annoyed, but luckily it was a knick-knack that held no financial or sentimental value. "Then, after he seen it break and he was all upset and aggravated over it," she remembered, "I said, 'Well see, that's what Aunt Lisa told you, you can't touch.'" Once her cousin's family moved out, she described being happy to be able to have "just a little bit [of] relaxation and you don't have to be on your toes and watching things."

The main source of tension in the household stemmed from different parenting styles. "Everybody parents their kids differently, and her and I both parent different, extremely different," Lisa explained, characterizing Danielle as "more laid-back" and herself as "more on top of it." She warned her cousin that a lax parenting style would make her son "out of control," but she did not try to force her cousin to change, reasoning that, "if she wants to let him go, she's just going to get the negative results." However, she strove to enforce her own rules around the house, partly in fairness to her own children. "I actually am a little bit harder on him [than his mother is], 'cause that's the way I am on my kids. It is hard living with somebody. We're gonna be glad when we have our own space."

Having other children in a doubled-up household raised further questions about household members' obligations to one another's children, as Annalise discovered after moving to another doubled-up household. About one year after moving in with Gram, Annalise used the loans and assistance she received after enrolling in school online to pay the move-in costs for a one-bedroom apartment. She and her partner were able to pay the $650 monthly rent while they were working, but when she experienced a miscarriage, she grew depressed, stopped going to work, and eventually lived through a suicide attempt. During this difficult time, her partner failed to pay the rent, and they were evicted. Annalise broke up with him over the eviction, but she could not return to Gram's house, where there was too much "drama going on with me and everybody in the house" from the last time she had lived there.

For a little over a month, Annalise and her daughters lived in the three-bedroom home her ex's mother shared with his uncle, three sisters, two brothers, cousin, and two-year-old nephew. "We weren't together, but I didn't have anywhere else to go," she explained. The home environment was far from ideal. She and her ex slept in the unfinished basement, but she did not want her daughters to be in the stuffy basement, so she put them to sleep on the couch upstairs or on an air mattress in the dining room. She argued frequently with other household members and had an especially antagonistic relationship with her ex's uncle, who was mean to her children and sometimes got involved in her relationship with her ex. In an effort to avoid confrontation, she spent most of her time in the basement.

Annalise's daughters noticed that she was stressed in this household, and they had complaints of their own as well. Annalise explained, "It was just a problem with my kids. Everybody always did for [my ex's nephew], but they never did for my kids. And I was like, 'That's not fair. I wouldn't ever go out and buy ice cream for my kids and leave him with nothing.' Every time I went out and got them something, I got him something too, even if it was a juice or a bag of chips. He got something too. Because it's not fair." While she believed in treating all children in the household equally, her ex's family prioritized their own blood relative. "But when they cooked, they cooked for just [the nephew]. They didn't cook for my kids. When they went to the store, they bought for just [him]. They didn't buy for my kids. So they were always miserable. And when people would play, they would play with [him], and then my kids would be left out. They would be trying to play, but they were always left out. So that was always a problem. And they knew it." Annalise's daughter interjected at this point in the interview with evidence that she *did* know it: when she and her sister had accompanied the adults to the store, she said, "They buyed [him] something and not us and said they didn't have no money."

Eventually, because of Annalise's daughters' unhappiness, Gram allowed them to return to her home. "She knew I didn't have anywhere else to go, and she knew that my kids weren't happy at someone's house. Because every time we would come over here, they would come with some kind of story about somebody being mean to them, or 'Mommy was fighting with somebody.' They hated it there." As Annalise's daughters' experience shows, children were impacted by tensions between adults in doubled-up households, and households in which adults held different levels of responsibility and attachment to different children could be particularly challenging to navigate.

"You're Not about to Jeopardize My Kids": Protecting Children in Shared Environments

Although Isa and her mother disagreed about some aspects of child-rearing, Isa never doubted that her multigenerational household was a nurturing environment for her daughters. Other mothers were not so lucky. Annalise's uncle lived in Gram's home until he went to jail, then again after he was released. After he was released, she worried about his influence on her daughters' home environment. "He would have his crackhead friends come over here, and I'm like, 'Excuse me! I have children living here. Can you guys leave?' They would catch attitudes with me. I live here. My name's not on the lease, but I live here . . . and I'm not going to have that stuff around my kids." Gram rarely saw these friends firsthand because of her long work hours, and regardless, she would not have interceded on Annalise's behalf in their fights out of loyalty to her son, Annalise explained. With little control over her children's home environment, Annalise tried to avoid the house when her uncle was home.

When Annalise and her uncle were home at the same time, they often argued, including about how he treated her daughters. The last time this happened, he admonished her daughter for going into his bedroom soon after he moved back into Gram's home. "[My daughter] still had toys and stuff like that in his room upstairs, and she went up there one day to get toys, and he yelled at her and he called her a little bitch. I said, 'Whoa! Hold on! You will not talk to my child like that!' I said, 'That's my child; she is not a grown woman. You have a problem, you come to me.' Me and him are standing in the hallway face to face, I was ready to fight him." Gram intervened before the incident could escalate, but Annalise was horrified. "You do not talk to a child like that! You don't yell at her and tell her to get the fuck out of your room and call her names!"

Annalise later received a home visit from a child protective services social worker, who shared concerns about the girls' living arrangement. By this point, the family was staying in the unfinished basement of Gram's home, in an effort to avoid the main part of the house as much as possible. However, the social worker deemed the basement an inadequate environment for the children. To Annalise, the social environment of the main part of the home was also a concern. She explained, "I have to move from here because my dad is selling drugs and his girlfriend is a prostitute and it's not safe for my kids. So we have to find somewhere to move." She looked for an alternative housing arrangement, but she refused to take the social worker's recommendation to move with her daughters to an emergency shelter to try to get priority for housing services.

Some doubled-up parents, like Annalise, described immediate safety concerns about their doubled-up households—including concerns about drug use, unknown visitors in the household, and physical, verbal, and sexual abuse—and took steps to protect their children in these environments. Shay, the mother of two daughters from chapter 1, lived doubled up in the living room of her mother's apartment. Her own history of childhood sexual abuse left her aware of the dangers of sleeping in common areas of a home. "That's probably why I'm two times overprotective of my kids. When we sleep in that living room, I'm not saying that I think my momma's boyfriend would do anything to my kids, it's just that, in my mind I really don't trust nobody with my kids. Me knowing that we sleeping in the living room, they on the couch and I'm on the floor, every time I hear a door open I'm like [watching], because I know he got to pass. If he going to get something to drink I know the path through the living room. I'm up looking like—okay." It is easy to imagine how this kind of constant fear and heightened vigilance could take a toll on parents' well-being.

Likewise, when Moke, the mother from chapter 2, hosted a twenty-year-old friend—the daughter of her childhood friend—she instructed her not to bring strangers to the house. "She was a dancer, so she was more into the club, like inviting guys to my house. She would invite them in, but I told her that was dangerous. 'You're a stripper, you can't meet the guys at the club and then invite him to my house because one day my daughter could be watching. . . . And they could come back to my house and anything could happen.'" During her three-month stay, the friend repeatedly violated the rule about visitors, and Moke eventually kicked her out. "No, she can't stay with me no more, because you're not about to jeopardize my kids inviting people that you don't know, straight strangers from your job." Compared to parents who relied on others for housing, Moke had more control over the home as the householder. She was able to evict her friend, although kicking her out resulted in a physical altercation and a subsequent court appearance.

In their study of deep poverty, Kathryn Edin and H. Luke Shaefer vividly describe serious safety concerns that some doubled-up parents and their children face while relying on others for housing.[19] The fears expressed by Annalise, Shay, and Moke echo these concerns and underscore how severely doubling up can limit parents' control over their children's home and social environment. Moreover, while hosts like Moke were able to evict unwanted household members, guests like Annalise and Shay, who had few other housing options, were particularly vulnerable.

Thankfully, most parents did not voice fears about the immediate physical safety of their children in shared households. However, even parents who did not have concerns about their children's immediate safety were often concerned about how sharing a household shaped their child's daily home environment. When Lisa hosted her cousin Danielle, she did not ask for regular childcare assistance because her children stayed busy with day care and school. The cousins watched one another's children occasionally while the other ran errands, but mostly they cared for all their children together. Lisa was used to organizing activities to fill her children's free time; in recent months she had put on movie nights with popcorn, hosted a "spa afternoon" for her oldest daughter, who liked to paint fingernails, and attended an event at a local park where children could fish from a boat. She appreciated how Danielle joined in these activities. "It was easier as far as we split the responsibilities, yes, because there was somebody else helping out."

Whereas Lisa felt that Danielle "has a positive influence on my kids and is very involved," she found Danielle's husband to be the opposite. "He didn't interact that much with the kids. He didn't even interact with his own kids. He just seemed like [a] very negative influence." Moreover, Danielle and her husband argued often, and although they moved to the porch and away from the children for these arguments, the tension pervaded the household. "You never know what their demeanor's going to be like or what he's going to do or what he's going say."

Hosts like Lisa worried about how guests' moods and influence might affect their children. And when Danielle separated from her husband, his desire for revenge brought even more serious complications to Lisa's home life. "He called children's services and said that my house was unfit. . . . There was three or four caseworkers here. They had to talk to my kids. They had to make them pull their pants down 'cause he said I abused my kids. They would check my kids' bottoms. They'd ask my kids if anybody touches them inappropriately. I was pissed."

Lisa seemed to grow more comfortable opening up to me over time, but despite multiple requests, she never allowed me to tour the upstairs unit where she lived. "My house is a mess," she explained, describing the many repairs that she could not afford to make, the challenges of maintaining cleanliness with so many children, even how her dogs sometimes relieved themselves on the floor (though she did clean it up, she explained). Despite talking frankly about these issues, she was never comfortable showing me this environment. Yet she had no such authority when the child protective services caseworkers arrived. "You have no rights. She told me when she was here the first time— 'cause it was a mess—she said, 'If you don't show me the house, I have to remove the kids.'" After two months, thorough house-cleaning, and a promise to make repairs to the home when she was able, Lisa's case was closed. Even though her case was closed, hosting her cousin's husband—and the ensuing fallout—left a lasting mark on her.

"I Want to Set That Example for Them": The Desire to Provide a Nuclear Family Household for Children

Beyond the practical challenges that doubling up posed for child-rearing, parents perceived living doubled up as a guest as incompatible with their ideals of family life. Guests wanted to provide their child with a home of their own. For instance, Isa saw residential independence as central to fulfilling her role as the provider for her children. "I want to be a good role model to them. For them to see that I'm a single parent and I'm there for them. I want to show them that they can do it without needing a man helping them . . . that experience of us moving out, but that they're going to have their own, like Mom gave us our own home, our own place. That's what I want them to experience." Unlike some doubled-up parents, she was quick to praise her multigenerational household, telling us that her daughters felt that their grandmother's house was their home. She also loved the house and yard, which she described as big and spacious, although she had reservations about the neighborhood. She and her mother had differences of opinion, including about child-rearing and Isa's romantic relationships, but the household was peaceful overall.[20] As she put it, "Everything's good here. I love being here, but it's not something that's I feel in me as a person. I feel that I have to strive for something better."

Similarly, echoing themes from chapter 3, Annelise viewed having a home of her own as an important part of adulthood. "I'm twenty-seven years old. I should have my home. I should be established, and I'm not. I don't want to be thirty, living with my grandmother, not having my own, in a back-and-forth relationship. I want to be stable." Her own childhood was characterized by frequent moves and doubling up—not dissimilar to the experience her daughters were now having. "I grew up in a house where my mom never worked a job. We moved so many different places. We always lived with family members. That's why I'm stuck. I'm stuck in this because I've been stuck in this my whole life, and I don't want them to be stuck," she explained. Annalise wanted to provide her own children with "more opportunities than I had," and she saw being a good role model for them as central to this goal. "I don't want my kids to follow in my footsteps. By the time I'm thirty, they'll be at that age where they're really starting to imagine their future and think about what they want to be, and I want to set that example for them: I have a house, I have a car, I'm stable, I have money."

Isa and Annalise had both internalized the cultural expectation that nuclear families have a home of their own. Fathers are often presumed to be the family breadwinner, the one who bears responsibility for providing a home for the family. Indeed, as discussed in chapter 2, men were sometimes judged against a higher economic bar when they needed to double up, compared to women, who were expected to be primary caregivers for their children. However, as qualitative studies of low-income and working-class mothers have revealed, adequately meeting children's material needs is now a central tenet of motherhood.[21]

Mothers like Isa and Annalise, whose children's fathers' contributions were either inadequate or entirely absent, bore the responsibility of providing for their children with little help. Even in two-parent families, mothers often take on a provider role as well when men's work opportunities are limited.[22] Given the expectation that parents should be able to provide for their children's material needs, doubling up as a guest in response to economic need took a toll on mothers as well as fathers, as Isa's and Annalise's experiences show.

Conclusion

Doubled-up households include adults beyond the nuclear family unit. These additional household adults give child-rearing advice to parents, engage in shared caregiving time, and provide childcare when parents are not home. Of course, family and friends can and often do provide childcare and child-rearing advice when living separately. However, living together facilitates child-rearing support in important ways for parents. For instance, coresiding with an adult who provides childcare eliminates the time and expense of transporting children to and from a childcare provider, an especially important benefit for parents who work late or early morning shifts or who lack reliable transportation. For parents who have stable day care outside the home, having another adult present is less important for meeting daily childcare needs, but it still makes it easier to step out of the house to run errands, and these adults provide an extra set of hands for child-centered activities. In these ways, doubling up supports parents and makes child-rearing easier.

However, sharing child-rearing and household space introduces new challenges for parents. Household members can hold conflicting expectations about whether and how child-rearing rights and responsibilities should be shared. Both the expectation that household adults will work together to raise the children and the expectation that parents hold authority over child-rearing reflect norms based on the independent nuclear family household, and these norms are difficult to maintain in a shared household with multiple nuclear family units. Moreover, when living doubled up, families have to share household space with adults beyond their nuclear family, which decreases parental control over their children's home environment. In some cases, parents even worry that the doubled-up household may be a risky environment for their children, and they take active steps to protect them from harm. The vulnerability of guest parents, who rely on the householder for housing, especially limits their ability to raise their children as they wish.

These challenges are further complicated by dominant cultural ideals that valorize nuclear family independence.[23] Even when doubling up provides a safe environment and support with childcare, parents who have internalized expectations that parents should provide for their children's needs on their own and set a good example of independence see doubling up as incompatible with their ideals of family life. This incompatibility, often compounded by concerns about child-rearing interference, child environments, and household interactions, increases parents' dissatisfaction with living doubled up.

PART III

After Doubling Up

7

The Challenges of Doubled-Up Household Dissolutions

SIMONE, A TWENTY-FOUR-YEAR-OLD woman who identified as Black and multiracial, had lived doubled up for over two years. While pursuing a bachelor's degree in psychology at a university near Cleveland, she ran out of money. Unable to pay her bills, "I had no choice but to drop out, pack up, and go home." She returned to her father's home, where she met and quickly became romantically involved with her neighbor, Darnell, a thirty-two-year-old Black father who lived with his mother in one of the six other houses on their one-way street on the west side of Cleveland. The couple decided to move in together, but neither of their parents was willing to host them both. Determined to live together, they began doubling up with other extended family members and friends, often accompanied by Darnell's three-year-old son.

They first moved in with a friend Simone had known since middle school. The friend, a mother with one young son, lent them one of the bedrooms of her voucher-subsidized apartment. This arrangement did not last long. The friend's son frequently entered their bedroom uninvited, but her friend told them that they were not allowed to reprimand him. She also suspected that her friend was developing a romantic interest in Darnell, and she knew they needed to move before a larger fight erupted. The couple moved in with another friend with a voucher-subsidized apartment. However, when the landlord learned that Simone's family was staying in the apartment, the friend worried that their presence could jeopardize her housing voucher. Simone's family again needed to move.

This time, they "packed up everything necessary and put it in storage, and then we kept one big suitcase for each person full of clothes and necessities." They began bouncing between the homes of "just anybody that had a room or a nice couch to shack up on for a little while." They called friends and family members one by one, saying, "I'm really messed up right now, I haven't much money. I got food stamps, I can help you a little bit. I got a little bit of money. We're trying to save up and get an apartment. Can you let us stay there for [a week]? If we're not off by our feet by then, that's cool, we'll just move somewhere else." Although they knew they would need housing for more than a week, they kept their requests modest, reasoning that a brief stay was more likely to be approved. Eventually, Darnell's mother recognized how desperate they were ("we told her, 'Dude, at this point it's you or shelter,'" Simone recalled) and allowed them to move into a bedroom in her two-story home.

By the time I met them, they had been living there for seven months—a more stable period than they had experienced in years. However, about three weeks prior to our interview, Darnell's mother had told them that her twenty-year-old granddaughter and her baby would be joining the household at the end of the following month and there would no longer be room for them. "At first I was kind of upset because we're not in the financial position to move," Simone recalled. She and Darnell did not plan to live with his mother forever, but they had hoped to stay at least six more months to save up for a rental home of their own. "Now that it's such short notice, it's going to be harder trying to come up with that money quicker."

Still, Simone embraced the idea of moving. "Even though I know it's going to be really hard living on my own, I'm ready to work hard for that because I'm just tired of relying on other people and dealing with all the crap." She asked for additional hours at the Subway restaurant where she worked and began carefully saving. Despite these efforts, the housing search was not going well. "I just have to get a paper and get to looking a little harder because I really don't like the choices that we have where we're going to move." Given the quickly approaching deadline, she was bracing herself to need to move temporarily to an undesirable rental while continuing to search for a better option.

Simone suspected that the household dissolution would be challenging for Darnell's mother as well: "Even though we're here, we're not here for free, so we're more or less helping her." His mother owned her home and received Social Security benefits, but she relied on their help to pay her monthly bills. Simone explained, "Every month when those bills come, depending on how much they cost, she tells me the difference"—that is, the difference between what she had and what she needed. Simone would then "wait until I get paid on Friday and I'll hand it to her." They also provided smaller items, such as cartons of cigarettes, as needed, and they helped with housework and other care. "I hope [her granddaughter] helps take care of her just as good as we did . . . because she's sick, so whoever stays here . . . has to be ready to help take care of her because she needs just as much attention as a child: her medications, her food, things like that. We did her laundry, everything."

That month Simone planned to skip her usual financial contributions so she could save for the upcoming move. "I have to break her the news and tell her I hope whoever gets her money manages it well because I'm not going to be able to help her this month. She doesn't know that yet." The couple also decided to stop providing labor and money for home repairs. "Right now we're not worrying about fixing anything in the house, period. His brother, his daughter, and [his mother] can worry about that now." With only three paychecks before they needed to pay a deposit and first month's rent, they had a strict budget. "Nobody will be able to buy anything for themselves this month. Unless it's just body wash or stuff that we have to get. Besides that, me and him can't spend our money on anything unnecessary—anything, even if it's just cigarettes. We can't mess around this month."

Just a couple of months later, Darnell's mother passed away and his brother took over the home. He planned on fixing the house up and renting it out, so Simone, Darnell, and his son still needed to find another place to live. Before they could move, however, Darnell was sent to jail, so Simone moved into her mother's house and his son moved in with his biological mother. When Darnell was released five months later, he again took custody of his son. The only apartments he and Simone had a chance of affording were efficiency units, so they decided to move in with his other brother so they could save for a larger apartment.

The family moved into the three-bedroom home of Darnell's brother on the east side of Cleveland, where he lived with his girlfriend and her daughter. Simone's family moved into a bedroom so small that their queen-size bed and dresser filled it from wall to wall, leaving them without enough space to even fully open the door. His brother would not allow them to use the larger room, which was his "man cave." Simone grew frustrated at the lack of space, particularly because they were supposed to pay $300 a month—more than half of the $500 rent. "We were like, 'Dude, we need that room, too. We cannot pay you $300 a month and have a room that we can't even put one bed in.'"

Three weeks later, Darnell's sister offered an alternative to their cramped quarters. She would empty out her large downstairs bedroom, which had a closet and space for their queen bed and Darnell's son's child-sized bed. They had not yet paid Darnell's brother rent and decided to save the $300 to pay his sister instead; their first month in his brother's house had been "like a trial" that had not worked out, Simone reasoned. Yet living with Darnell's sister involved putting up with "crazy rules" and "nitpicking"—they were only allowed to do laundry on Sundays, had a limited amount of space to use in the refrigerator, and needed to be out of the house most weekend days. Moreover, his sister's four children, ages seven, eight, ten, and eleven, kept the house perpetually messy. "There is always constant kids, constant moving," Simone complained, describing how the children ran down the stairs each morning at 8:00 AM and argued in the living room adjacent to her bedroom. Ultimately, a disagreement with Darnell's sister over whether Simone broke a can opener pushed her over the edge. Darnell was scheduled to get paid for doing odd jobs the next day, and they decided to use the money to move.

Simone and Darnell had planned to stay with his sister to save up for a better apartment, but less than two months after moving in, they were already ready to leave. "Like the same day that [fight] happened. So we got some money and we went to the store and got a *Plain Dealer* [newspaper] and looked in the classified sections for houses for rent or sale. We found like ten places, circled them all, called them all . . . and this was the first place we had seen that they were like, 'We don't have no one else interested, and if you have the money you can move in tomorrow, I don't care.'" Just two days after beginning their housing search, they moved into a two-bedroom home on the east side of Cleveland. They did not tell his sister they were leaving until they were carrying their belongings out the door, leaving her without the rent money she had expected for the month.[1]

———

The prior four chapters showed how living doubled up complicates families' daily lives and introduces new challenges across multiple domains, from romantic relationships to economic arrangements. This chapter moves beyond life inside doubled-up households and asks how families experience the instability that typically characterizes these households and what role living doubled up played in families' trajectories. Navigating questions of shared space and appropriate roles and relationships is complex on a day-to-day basis, but household composition changes pose particular challenges. Given the high rate of instability that doubled-up households face, understanding the ramifications of these changes is key to understanding how doubling up shapes family life.

The instability that Simone and Darnell experienced was striking, but not anomalous among doubled-up families. Most of the families in my sample experienced at least two different doubled-up households during the fieldwork years. Families who doubled up as guests lived with an average of two to three hosts over that period, while families who doubled up as hosts took in an average of one to two families as guests.[2] Mirroring the instability I found in Cleveland and Dallas, national data show that among children who lived doubled up at some point during a three-year period, just 45 percent of guests and 25 percent of hosts remained doubled up in the same household type (as a host or guest in a household formed with a grandparent, with other extended family members, or with non-kin) over this period. Guests who lived in multiple household types experienced an average of 1.75 changes, and hosts who changed household type experienced an average of 1.65 changes.[3]

As chapter 1 showed, doubling up is often a response to instability, especially for guests—doubling up is a safety net that catches families when they face housing instability, economic instability, and romantic relationship instability. This chapter shows that doubled-up households not only are a *response* to instability but often also *perpetuate* instability. Doubled-up guests like Simone's family frequently moved from one doubled-up household to another, or sometimes to a home of their own. Hosts often had extended family members or nonrelatives moving in and out of their home. This chapter examines how this instability impacted families, highlighting the volatility in families' economic situations and in the social and physical environments in which they lived that often accompanied their household instability.

What happens after families experience household dissolutions? The rest of the chapter shows that parents who experienced household dissolutions, both hosts and guests, were often left little better off than they were before doubling up—and sometimes even worse off. The loss of economic and in-kind support from guests left some hosts with unmet needs. Guest parents typically planned for doubling up to be a temporary stop on the way toward residential independence, but most remained doubled up as guests by the end of my fieldwork period. Even for parents who did move into their own home, the challenges they had experienced prior to doubling up, such as limited incomes and criminal or eviction records, typically continued to severely restrict their housing options. In sum, doubled-up households were characterized by instability that, far from solving the precarity they faced, often only perpetuated it.

Household Instability as Social Environment Instability

When a doubled-up household dissolved, both hosts and guests experienced a change in household composition. Chapters 3 through 6 demonstrated the challenges of navigating doubled-up household life, particularly given the lack of taken-for-granted norms about how these households should function. Parents who transitioned from one doubled-up household composition to another had to start anew with the process of establishing how the household would function—learning the expectations and behaviors of the individuals with whom they now shared a home and negotiating or accepting these expectations when they did not match their own. This process was inherently stressful and disruptive for family routines. Moreover, some parents, quickly convinced by this process that the household was not sustainable, immediately sought another change in household. For example, after just three weeks in the home of Darnell's brother and two months in his sister's, Simone was ready to move from these households.

The movement of adults in and out of the home environment impacted children as well. Scholars have long recognized that family instability—the entry and exit of parents and their romantic partners from households—can disrupt family functioning, and the loss or addition of a parent figure in the household forces children to adapt to new social relationships.[4] Household composition changes in doubled-up households likewise shifted the social relationships that the child had to navigate on a day-to-day basis. As shown in chapter 6, doubled-up household members imposed rules and expectations on children and interfered in parenting; some household members had particularly close relationships with children, while others had very antagonistic relationships. Each change in household composition resulted in a different web of relationships to which both children and parents had to adjust.

Moreover, household composition changes often shifted how children experienced the physical household environment. When households expanded to host extended family members or nonrelatives, children were often shuffled into shared bedrooms to make room for the guests, and areas of the household where the guest resided could suddenly become off-limits. After Anrisa, the mother described in chapter 5, formed her own household with her partner Phil, they began sharing their new home with their siblings and cousins. She described her children's experience of the change in the household: "They feel like they have no freedom. . . . When [our siblings or cousins live] here, they can't go upstairs, they can't go in this room no more, never really knowing why." When families moved into a new home as guests, they had new sleeping arrangements and household rhythms. Household composition changes thus substantially altered children's daily lives, in both host and guest families.

Household Instability as Economic Instability

As chapter 4 showed, forming a doubled-up household—and conversely, dissolving a doubled-up household—often changed the resources available to a family. Household composition instability could be a meaningful source of economic instability for doubled-up families, as changes in doubled-up household composition often coincided with changes in housing support, food sharing, and rent and utility payments. Household composition instability that resulted in a loss of resources put families at risk of material hardships like food insecurity or difficulty paying bills, which are associated with poorer health, increased stress, and reduced positive parenting behaviors for adults and worse child outcomes.[5] Moreover, even in the absence of material hardship, *fluctuations* in resource availability—like the rapid shifts in resources that often accompanied doubled-up household instability—can likewise increase family stress and be harmful to child well-being.[6]

That household composition instability often begets economic instability is not a new concept. Researchers have long recognized the significant role of romantic relationship transitions in shaping access to resources.[7] Household composition changes involving extended family members and nonrelatives are less commonly studied, but this kind of instability also deeply impacted families' economic security. For guests like Simone, a host's decision to dissolve the household could dramatically reshape consumption, forcing the guest family to save urgently for a new home.

Doubled-up household instability likewise injected economic instability into the lives of host families. As Simone secretly prepared to withhold her financial contributions from Darnell's mother so that she could save for a new apartment, she was aware of the economic instability she would create for her host. Likewise, she caused economic instability for Darnell's brother and sister, respectively, when she moved unexpectedly from their homes without paying rent.

Dana and Zach's experience further illustrates the link between doubled-up household instability and economic instability. Dana, a twenty-eight-year-old Black mother, her thirty-two-year-old White partner, Zach, and her eight-year-old daughter and fifteen-month-old son had moved to a new apartment just five days before their first interview. The apartment complex—a series of side-by-side two-story buildings in what they labeled a run-down area of Dallas—was rife with drug use and violence, but with prior felony convictions and poor credit, they had few other housing options. "Anybody can stay here [in this apartment complex] as long as you pay your rent. That's what type of place this is, and that's not the type of place that I really want to be," she explained. The new apartment was at least better than their previous home, where they had lived for just four months before realizing that the management might never address the roach infestation and the broken, backed-up toilet that had plagued their unit since they moved in. "At least we did find a place. At least we do have a roof over our kids' head, and at least we can provide for them."

A couple of months later, Zach's mother, Cathy, showed up at their doorstep. She normally lived with Zach's brother, but his brother required her to remain drug-free while living with him. When she relapsed, she left his household, and then he refused to allow her to return. She instead moved into Zach and Dana's apartment. She had a long history of addiction, and her son was used to providing "last resort" emergency housing, so he was unsurprised when he found her "washing ashore . . . on my porch" after relapses. Zach always agreed to host her. "That's my mom, you know what I mean? You could want to be like, 'No, I can't do it anymore.' But I'm not going to tell her, 'No, I'm not going to put a roof over your head if nobody else will.'"

There was little room for his mother in the tiny apartment; their daughter slept on a child-sized mattress in a small room off the main hallway, and Dana, Zach, and their son slept in a second room accessible through a door in the daughter's bedroom. They moved a plush dark blue leather sofa—left by a previous tenant—from the living room into the entryway leading out from the kitchen. This sofa became Cathy's bed.

Soon after moving in, Cathy told Zach and Dana that she did not want to return to his brother's home, so they agreed to move to a larger, two-story unit with two full bedrooms so she could have her own room. The move increased their rent obligation from about $650 to over $750 a month, but his mother was able to cover half the new rent from her monthly Social Security check. Moreover, when her food stamps and the food she brought back from trips to the food bank were combined with their food stamps, the family no longer had to worry about having enough food. "It helps out [financially] when she's around," they acknowledged.

However, a couple of months after the family moved to the larger unit, Cathy "just up and left," returning to her other son's house on short notice.

Dana had frequent disagreements with Cathy during their three-month co-residence. She described Zach's mother as a difficult guest: she was messy and wanted to stay out at night and sleep during the day. Cathy complained about noise from their toddler son and tried to impose her own rules on the boy. Dana's response was derisive: "When my son is out playing, when he's running through the house, she wants to get mad. You don't have a right to be mad, you know? I'm letting you stay here. This is his house. This is where he resides." Cathy blamed one of these many disagreements for her exit, though the couple could not recall precisely which one. Moreover, they suspected that Cathy had made "a big scene or a problem out of something" just to have an excuse to move out. The couple was used to this behavior: when they hosted her in the past, she had always returned to live with her other son, who was financially better off, as soon as he would allow her back into his home.

Cathy abruptly stopped paying rent when she moved, leaving Dana and Zach with an apartment larger than they could afford. Around the same time, their financial difficulties were compounded when Dana lost her job. The couple urgently spoke to the apartment management and convinced them to allow them to return to their smaller apartment.

Cathy's disregard for the well-being of Zach's family frustrated him, particularly given all the help he had given her—and the help he anticipated needing to give her in the future. "If I let you stay and you still run off and leave me in a tight spot, so the next time you come knock on my door and you're in a bad spot, what should I do? Should I do the same thing that you did to me? Should I close my door in your face and leave you in a bad spot?" He knew he would always share his housing with his mother when she was in need but felt that his generosity was a liability. "It's uncomfortable knowing that if she came over here today and we were to say, 'Yeah, you can stay over here,' we would never be able to determine when she's going to be ready to leave."

Although Cathy's exit damaged the couple's financial stability, Dana and Zach maintained that they were the benefactors of the relationship, not its beneficiaries, and that they did not need Cathy's help. When asked whether they had asked Cathy not to move, Zach responded with incredulity, "No, I never did [ask her to stay], because I'm not going to do that. I'm not going to beg you [to] stay here. You weren't here. You came asking me for help. . . . Because I made it a lot of times without her. I've never needed her per se." With Dana unemployed and Cathy no longer contributing rent money and food, the couple was financially strained, yet they denied wanting her to move back in. Zach said, "I mean, it made things more comfortable and easier to deal with. But I don't mind life being hard."

Eventually, Dana and Zach fell behind on the rent for their one-bedroom apartment and were evicted. They went to court to fight the eviction, but by the following summer they were living in a motel and their children were staying with relatives until the couple was more stable. Eventually, after spending time in a shelter, Dana was able to get a housing voucher and an apartment. Despite the financial hardships that often accompanied living on their own, she and Zach were skeptical about doubling up again, saying, "We are at a point now where we already know what's going to happen. There's been so many chances and so many opportunities to make a good situation out of somebody staying with you or staying with somebody else, and neither situation has ever played out well." Of course, despite similar feelings, many families ultimately turned to doubling up when their needs or the needs of their loved ones left them few other choices.

Household Instability as Residential Instability

Doubled-up household dissolutions prompted changes in household composition as well as economic changes for both hosts and guests. Guests also experienced a third consequential change—a change in residence.[8] Families had to adjust to a new housing unit and often to a new neighborhood, with impacts on their social connections with neighbors, their commutes to work and school, and their proximity to family and friends. Simone and Darnell moved from his mother's home on the west side of Cleveland to live with his siblings on the east side. The Subway restaurant where Simone worked was just around the corner from his mother's home, but when they lived with his siblings, she had to take a bus downtown, then transfer to another bus heading to the west side—a commute that totaled an hour and a half each way on routes that ran only once an hour. "So if I miss it, I'm stuck out there another hour waiting on the next one." The family had to take similarly arduous bus routes from the east side to the west side when they wanted to see their families. "Everything is on the west side, so anytime you want to get up and do something, we have to catch a bus and go over there."

Residential instability could also be detrimental to children's well-being, in part because it could disrupt their social ties.[9] For Shay, the mother of two from chapter 1, moves between doubled-up households prompted multiple school changes for her older daughter, Kyla.[10] Kyla began pre-K in the Dallas suburb where her grandmother lived, a school that Shay loved. "It's Kyla's first year and she already knows a lot," she proclaimed proudly. However, the summer before she entered kindergarten, they were living with Shay's cousin, far from the suburban school where Kyla attended pre-K. "I didn't want to take my baby out of that school. I'm upset about having to take her out of that school, but it's going to be too much gas." Shay did not approve of the Dallas Independent School District elementary school that was zoned to her cousin's apartment, where she perceived that "the teachers don't care." Yet, unable to drive her daughter to school in the suburbs, she saw few other options. As of mid-July, Shay still did not know where her daughter would be attending school the next month. "Well, hopefully we're going to move and all that, and I'm going to find her school," she mused.

Kyla ended up beginning the school year in the Dallas Independent School District. Within months, however, the family returned to Shay's mother's home, and Kyla transferred back to the suburban school district there. Shay was happy about the change. "I like the school that she's in better. They teach her Spanish, they enhancing my baby. I love it so much." Kyla was equally happy, "She said she love it too. She say she don't want to switch schools no more. She said she love her friends, she love her teacher, she love her school." Shay wanted to eventually move out of her mother's home, but she planned to keep Kyla in this school, even if it was far from where she moved. "I'm going to wake up every morning, take her to school."

It had not been easy to enroll Kyla in her suburban school. Shay's mother had a subsidized apartment, and Shay and her daughters were staying in the unit off-lease, in part because she worried that her criminal record might jeopardize her mother's eligibility for the subsidy.[11] "We had already withdrew her out of her school that she was in, and we was trying to enroll her in the school that's over my mom's house. My baby was out of school for almost a whole month before she went to school because the school was tripping about her not being on my mom's lease." To get her daughters on her mother's lease without revealing that she was living in the unit as well, she gave her mother legal custody of her daughters. "I was like, 'Really? Just to get a seven-year-old in school? I have to really go through all this?' My baby was out of school for a long time before she went back to school. That was so upsetting to me, because I'm so strict. I don't play no games when it come down to their school."

Although Shay moved multiple times between different doubled-up households over the next year and a half, she kept Kyla enrolled in the suburban school. Providing the transportation necessary to maintain this stability took substantial time and money, and Kyla spent many school nights at her grandmother's house without Shay. To Shay, keeping her daughter in the same school was worth the sacrifices she made; she did not want her daughter to experience the same level of school instability that she had as a child. "Because I know how it is going from school to school to school. . . . When you transfer to another school, they need your transcript. And they looking at it like, 'Oh no, this child done been to three schools this year. She won't be here long.' No, I don't want that look for her. I want them to see that she was in a stable school district and she was doing good. So that's why I kept her where she was at." The final time I spoke with her, Shay had finally received a housing voucher and was living in her own apartment. The apartment was not in the suburban school district where Kyla attended school, so Shay was planning to transfer her again for the coming school year, this time to a Dallas elementary school down the street from their new apartment.

Doubling Up and Subjective Feelings of Instability

Parents described doubled-up households as inherently precarious. This subjective feeling of insecurity made doubling up a particularly stressful source of support for both hosts and guests. As sociologist Bruce Western and his colleagues point out, income insecurity and subjective feelings of insecurity shape how "forward looking" families can be.[12] When guests did not know how long they would have housing and hosts did not know how long to expect to have guests coresiding with them, it impeded the ability of both parties to plan for the future and to reap the benefits of doubling up.

Doubling up often fostered subjective feelings of precarity, particularly for guest families like Simone and Darnell's. Dependent on Darnell's mother for housing, they had little control over the timing of their residential move. Simone felt that, living in someone else's home, "anything could happen. Like right now. We thought we were going to be settled here for at least until the end of the year. . . . So it's stuff like that's unpredictable." The lack of agency that they felt over their mobility decisions helps explain why many parents described living doubled up in someone else's home as unstable, even those who had lived in the same household for months or even years.

Although doubled-up households often dissolved unexpectedly, many parents knew—and often intended—that doubling up would be a short-term arrangement. Many guests sought to use doubling up to weather temporary setbacks or to pursue upward mobility, and hosts often planned to provide housing support to guests temporarily until they could move out on their own. The assumption that doubled-up households were merely short-term arrangements, rather than permanent household forms, could prevent families from planning for the future. For example, Shay's sense that her doubled-up household was temporary made it difficult for her to plan even a month ahead for her daughter's school year. "I really didn't know where we was gonna live at, so I didn't know what school to even go look at to try to even enroll the little one in school." Even for parents like Shay, who looked forward to being able to move on from their doubled-up arrangement, the temporary nature of these arrangements shaped how they experienced living doubled up.

"It's Good to Have My House Back": Hosts' Experiences of Household Instability

Doubling up provided important support for many hosts, but given its instability, this support was often temporary and rarely fostered lasting benefits. Household dissolutions sometimes left hosts—particularly those who benefited from economic or in-kind assistance from their guests—without the support they needed. In my sample, roughly two-fifths of hosts who were living independently by the end of the fieldwork period reported that they needed something that the guest previously provided—such as income, childcare, or food—or that they found residential independence undesirable in some other way.

Although doubled-up household dissolutions often left hosts without needed support, many hosts were eager to return to a nuclear family household. Paula, a thirty-two-year-old Hispanic mother, had separated from her husband in response to domestic violence about three months before her first interview. She lived with her four children, who ranged in age from seven to fifteen, in a tidy, three-bedroom rental home on a tree-lined street in a majority-Hispanic neighborhood of Cleveland. Paula hosted her cousin Mary, Mary's husband, and their one-year-old daughter after a disagreement with their landlord forced them to leave their previous rental. When going through recertification for food stamps, they had asked the landlord for a letter stating the amount that they paid in rent each month. The landlord—who had not been reporting income from the rental property and was worried about being discovered, according to Paula—refused to provide this documentation and told them to move out. Because they could not afford to move to a new rental, Paula offered them space in the attic of her home.

The arrangement also stood to benefit Paula, who was living on less than $20,000 a year ever since a car accident about a year before had left her unable to work. She asked Mary's family to contribute $150 a month; this amount would cover the full cost of her subsidized utility plan, which she struggled to pay on her own, sometimes resulting in utility disconnections. Mary also helped her cook, clean, and take care of the children.[13] Such help was particularly valuable to Paula, who was a newly single parent and had struggled with depression and chronic pain since the accident, which left her unable to be as active as she used to be. Yet, to Paula, the benefits of coresiding with Mary and her family did not outweigh the disadvantages.

When Paula offered housing to Mary and her family, she imagined that it would take them about two months to get back on their feet and move out. When the family had been living in her house for over six months—far longer than expected—Paula began encouraging them to move. She saw a rental home available just a few blocks from her own home, so she spoke to the landlord about the move-in costs. Then she reported back to Mary and her husband: "I told them, 'Well, you need this much money.' So they started counting their money, and they said that they didn't have enough, so they couldn't give me the whole money [they owed me that month]. I was like, 'Okay.' I just left it at that, because the main thing was that they needed to find a place, because they were not going to keep staying here." Eager for them to move out of her home, Paula accepted $75 that month instead of the full $150 they owed her.

Even after paying the deposit and first month's rent at their new home, Mary's family remained in Paula's home for an additional month. "I told her, 'So, when are you guys planning to leave? Because you guys have the house.' Then [the landlord] made them put the water into their name, because obviously it's a rental. That was another big issue for that too. They couldn't get the water under their name. They needed $250 to get it connected." Paula thought her cousin's family was financially ready to move into a home of their own, but they had a higher threshold and wanted to continue saving. Having expected to provide only short-term housing, Paula interpreted their longer stay as taking advantage of her generosity. "I felt more like her husband was just leaning against the help. They had the money saved up and everything, but they wanted to keep saving, and they wanted to stay."

Paula was relieved when Mary's family finally moved. She had found Mary's husband to be an unpleasant houseguest. "His attitude, because one moment he's fine and the other day he would have this phase, like he wouldn't even talk to nobody." Moreover, although their coresidence brought additional income into the home, it was accompanied by additional financial stress. Paula was glad she no longer needed to repeatedly ask for their monthly rent or argue with Mary's husband about his tendency to help himself in her kitchen but hide his own snacks and drinks in the attic.

Most host parents in my sample echoed Paula's sentiments about doubled-up household dissolutions: even if the arrangement provided benefits, they were eager to return to a nuclear family household. Yet not all parents felt that the disadvantages of doubling up outweighed the benefits. Recall Lauren, the thirty-eight-year-old Black mother of two from chapter 2 who appreciated having her mother Debra living with her because "it takes a village to raise a child." She planned to have her mother live with her indefinitely, but the first weekend immediately after the school year ended, Debra moved back to her other daughter's home.

Debra justified the move by telling Lauren that the cost of living was lower in Abilene, where her other daughter lived, but Lauren was skeptical. Her mother was on a fixed income, but Lauren had paid for her housing, groceries, and YMCA membership in Dallas. "To me, it seemed like she would have enough to do whatever she wanted. Because that was really all she would have to buy, was groceries, and I was buying that [too]. She didn't have electric bills or water bills or anything like that to pay." Although Lauren did not agree with her mother's motivations for moving, she did not try to dissuade her. "I just said, 'Okay.' So, okay. I mean, she pretty much had it easy as far as I could tell. You kind of could do whatever you do during the day. You just do you. Go wherever you want to go and whatever. 'Cause there was nobody [home except] her during the day. I mean, some days I would ask her to watch [my son], but that would only be like two hours. . . . So, I don't know . . . maybe that's just where she wants to just be."

Lauren was ambivalent about whether her mother's move was for the best. Although she appreciated Debra's help, after a year of living with two adults and two children crowded into a one-bedroom and loft apartment, she had been ready for a change. After Debra moved out, Lauren reported that "it's good to have my house back"—a sentiment expressed by many hosts. She described the joy of sleeping in her own bed again and having more space in the apartment. In retrospect, she thought, "I don't know if I really wanted to stay with my mom for too long. I don't know. I need my space."[14]

When doubled-up parents like Lauren referenced the need for space for their family, they often meant more than just reducing the crowding.[15] Asked to tell me more about what she meant by "space," Lauren replied, "I mean, you are used to being on your own. I have been on my own since almost right after I graduated college. . . . And then I got married. And even then, it's still your own space. It's your house together, but it's still like, 'It's my house.' You know. It's your house. But staying with your parents is like, 'Oh God.'" This response invoked far more than just physical space; Lauren was emphasizing the difference between living in a nuclear family household and sharing a household with someone outside the nuclear family unit.

Despite Lauren's positive feelings about her mother's departure, it was clear that she had lost a critical source of support. The summertime—when we last spoke—was a more relaxed time of year for her: she had summers off from her job as a schoolteacher, and her son's summer camp schedule was far less taxing than his school-year lineup of early morning drop-offs and after-school sports. Because her youngest child's father also had more time in the summer to spend with his son, she frequently had only one child at home. Yet despite the relative calm of the summer schedule, she already missed having her mother's help with the children and around the house. "Just coming home and having to cook dinner and still clean up and all that stuff. Because she would do that when she was here. Because she was here by herself, so sometimes she would just have stuff already made or clean up the bathroom and the kitchen. I didn't have to worry about that kind of stuff. But now I have to do that again. . . . When she is here for over a year, you kind of get used to not having to worry about that." Lauren anticipated that once the school year began and she again had to balance work and her children's busy schedules, she would miss her mother's support even more.

"We Are Never Going to Move in with Anybody Ever Again": After Doubling Up as a Guest

For guests, household instability often involved moving between different hosts. Guests could be asked to move from a household unexpectedly and before they had planned to move; even when not forced to move, tensions in the household could push guests to try to move before they felt financially ready. Lacking adequate resources and unprepared to move to a unit of their own, guest parents making forced moves often had little choice but to move into another doubled-up household. Although guest parents' households changed frequently, most parents who doubled up as guests during the fieldwork period remained guests by the end of the fieldwork period.[16] Although most hoped to obtain residential independence, few achieved their goal during the years I spoke with them.

Moreover, parents who did obtain residential independence sometimes did so at substantial cost. Of the guest parents who had managed to move into independent housing by the end of the fieldwork period, approximately half were in housing that they found undesirable or appeared unable to afford. The challenges that guests faced when they searched for housing of their own— challenges like criminal backgrounds and eviction histories, limited incomes, and rushed timelines for the housing search—are not unique to doubled-up guests. Many lower-income families who rent their own unit also face these barriers. Likewise, even non-doubled-up lower-income parents are often forced to make reactive moves with tight timelines, which can compel them to accept housing that is poorly matched to their long-term residential goals.[17] Yet the challenges that guest parents faced when moving out on their own were notable because they had often intended to use living doubled up as a temporary housing solution that they could leverage to overcome such challenges and pursue their ultimate residential goals. Instead, they found that the time they spent doubled up rarely substantially improved their residential trajectory.

Simone and Darnell spent years living doubled up in the hope of eventually being able to secure desirable housing for their family. Their goal was to rent a three-bedroom home in a safe neighborhood on the west side of Cleveland, near their extended families and within an easy commute to Simone's workplace. However, when they decided to move out of his sister's home, they were not in a better position to achieve this goal than they had been before they began doubling up. At that time, Simone worked nearly full-time at Subway, where she made just $8 an hour, and Darnell brought in about $100 a week from his odd jobs. Because they could save very little from their meager income, they had to rely on an advance payment from Darnell's employer to pay their deposit and first month's rent.

Doubling up for multiple years had done little to mitigate the barriers that Simone and Darnell faced in their housing search. They calculated that they could afford only $400 to $500 a month in rent. Given this financial reality, they did not search for the housing they wanted. Instead, they described their criteria as "whatever's the cheapest place we can find that's a two-bedroom in the paper." Darnell's criminal record also made them ineligible for many units. "The places on the west side, a lot of them had background checks, and he has a felony, so . . . we couldn't get the place because as soon as they do a

background check on him—boom. They don't want nobody with felonies living in their unit, then fine." To avoid being rejected, Simone applied for some
apartments without including Darnell on the application, even though she worried about how they would hide his coresidence if they moved in. Still, perhaps
because of her limited income and bad credit, Simone's applications garnered
few responses. "I applied for some, I just never got called back for some of them.
Most of them were no callbacks, and some of them I didn't even put his name
on. Some of them I just put my name on, and I didn't get accepted."

Simone and Darnell also did not have time to undertake a lengthy housing
search for a desirable, affordable rental that would overlook their histories.
When they began their housing search, they were mere days away from owing
his sister her $300 monthly rent, and paying her that sum would make it even
more financially difficult to move. "Because we had called about ten places, we
had been to about three or four places, so by the time we got here, we were
exhausted. We didn't do too much looking, but we were desperate at this point
because it was like, 'Hey, her money is going to be due in like three days.'" They
accepted a unit that had no other prospective tenants and would allow them
to move in immediately. With more time, the couple might have had more
options, as they discovered when some of the apartment complexes where
Simone put in applications called her back after they had already moved to
their new home.

In previous interviews, Simone had repeatedly emphasized that she would
never choose housing on the east side of Cleveland. Most of their extended
family lived on the west side, and Darnell characterized the east side as "the
hood," saying, "It's just out of control over there." Yet they moved to the east
side to double up with his brother and also with his sister. Even more surprisingly, they accepted an apartment of their own that was located squarely in the
very area on the east side that they had said they would avoid. Simone herself
was surprised: "I just didn't expect to move in this neighborhood ever. If you'd
ask me would I have moved to the east side last year, I'd have told you, 'Hell no.
No way.' But when I got put in a bind and I had nothing else to do, I had to move
to the east side." Their fears about the neighborhood would soon be confirmed.
Just a couple of weeks before we spoke, someone had "shot up all the houses
on the street, including ours," while the family was out grocery shopping.

Despite the housing challenges, Simone described how having a nuclear
family household fostered an idyllic family life. "Our relationship, the moods,
I get up and cook dinner every day in my own kitchen. I like coming home and
cooking and cleaning and being responsible for my own house. We try to do

our little family thing and have family dinner every night. I kind of like doing the mom thing." For the first time since they moved in together, the couple had their own room, and Darnell's son also had a room of his own. Life felt easier without the stress of "other people's bullshit, their rules," and with less stress, Simone said, "we're just happier. We don't argue as much anymore, we don't have nothing to argue about."

Simone and Darnell's $425 rent was higher than the $300 they were paying while doubled up, and they struggled to afford it. Although they had not yet missed paying a bill by the time of the first interview in their new home, she said, "I'm sure it will happen eventually because once the electric bill gets high enough, the gas bill gets high enough, we'll be able to pay it, but the problem will be, we'll be broke. And we won't have money to pay for the necessities at the end of the month." In order to save for essentials, like bus tickets for Simone's commute to her job on the west side of Cleveland, the family no longer had spending money, and they no longer went out. "The first thing we pay at the beginning of the month is the rent," Simone reported, but despite their careful budgeting, they fell behind on rent about three or four times over the next year. Luckily, the landlord had never filed an eviction, and each time they fell behind, they managed to pay off their debt over the next month.

Simone's low-wage job at Subway and Darnell's odd job employment were simply insufficient to meet their basic needs and pay for housing. The federal minimum wage has remained $7.25 an hour since 2009, and as of 2024, its inflation-adjusted value was over 40 percent lower than it was in 1970.[18] The declining value of the minimum wage is increasingly out of step with rising costs in the housing market. Of course, states and localities can increase their minimum wage beyond the federal level; Simone may have benefited from a recent increase in the Ohio minimum wage to over $10.00 an hour and the state's policy of adjusting the minimum wage annually for inflation (unlike the federal minimum wage).[19] Still, even after accounting for higher state and local minimum wages, the average minimum-wage worker in the United States would need to work nearly three full-time jobs to afford a modest two-bedroom rental.[20] Moreover, because Black workers are disproportionately paid the minimum wage,[21] its low value contributes to Black families' unequal vulnerability to housing unaffordability.

The last time I spoke with Simone, the couple was again behind on rent. In the hope of increasing her income, she had quit her low-paying job at Subway to take a two-week course to become a state tested nurse assistant. While unemployed, she was carefully deciding which bills to pay. "All my bills are allowed to lapse over a month. So if I skip out on this month paying any one of my bills, it's all right, it'll still be on because I'm not in debt like that. I only owe them maybe a hundred bucks. They're not going to cut my stuff off for a hundred bucks." Although money was tight, Simone and Darnell received help from family and friends, "so it's not like it's that bad. It's not like we're starving and we don't have what we need at the house." She hoped that once she was making $12 an hour as a nurse assistant, she could use her first paycheck to get out of debt. Whatever happened, she swore she would never again double up as a guest.[22] "Money gets tight, I swear to God, I will borrow, rob, steal, anything I can do to get my rent paid first. I told you, rent is the first thing. We are never going to move in with anybody ever again."

Conclusion

This chapter has highlighted the ramifications of doubled-up household instability across many dimensions of families' lives, including their social environment, economic well-being, residential stability, and subjective sense of precarity. The many forms of instability that often accompanied household transitions may help explain why such transitions are linked to less favorable child outcomes. Changes in household composition caused by extended family and nonrelatives entering and leaving the household are negatively associated with children's educational attainment and positively associated with teenage childbearing.[23] In fact, the effects of household composition changes involving extended family and nonrelatives appear to be about as large as the negative effects of changes involving biological, adoptive, and step parents.[24] The mechanisms uncovered in this chapter may contribute to these associations.

Although instability—especially unexpected instability—introduced challenges, parents were often ambivalent about household dissolutions. Both hosts and guests often expected and wanted doubled-up arrangements to be temporary. However, dissolutions could leave both hosts and guests with unmet needs. Moreover, although guest parents typically hoped that doubling up would help them achieve their longer-term residential goals, these arrangements often left them little better off than they had been before doubling up. This chapter has emphasized the challenges that doubled-up household instability poses for parents. Yet, as the next chapter will show, household stability could likewise be problematic.

8

Getting By and Getting Ahead
by Doubling Up

KEVIN, A FIFTY-TWO-YEAR-OLD BLACK FATHER, and his nine-year-old daughter lived in a three-bedroom home toward the end of a dead-end street in Dallas with Kevin's mother, May.[1] May said she bought the home for less than $6,000 in 1960 and had lived there ever since, despite a couple of floods that required dramatic renovations. Kevin had moved into the home with his daughter about seven years before I met them. His eleven-year-old son spent some weekends with them, and at one point, his twenty-year-old son stayed on the couch in the den for a couple of months before moving in with his girlfriend. Yet the core household composition—May, Kevin, and his daughter—had remained stable for the last seven years.

It was easy to see why the arrangement would be so long-lasting: sharing a household provided a range of benefits for both May and Kevin. Before doubling up, Kevin had been paying $650 a month for a two-bedroom rental, but he was dissatisfied with the landlord and his upkeep of the property. After bees in the yard became so bad that he could no longer allow his daughter to play outside, he decided to move. When his housing search led him to an apartment complex that offered units for $600 a month, all bills paid, he gathered his proof of income and applied. "And I got approved and everything else. I went over there one day at nighttime, and I'm seeing all kinds of cars, where you get drug dealers and everything else. I said no, I can't do this right here. I don't want to sit here and have my kids around [this] . . . you're doing the best thing for your kids, everybody has got their certain standards." Yet the housing options in more desirable neighborhoods were beyond his budget.

Unable to afford any of the neighborhoods where he would want to raise his daughter, Kevin asked May if they could move into her home, and she eagerly agreed. He knew that her neighborhood—a mix of vacant lots, older homes, and brand-new homes with Habitat for Humanity signs out front— was a safe area. "I moved here because I could leave my kids in the front yard, you know? I know they're getting older now, but I know they'll be watched out for because my neighbors are real, I'm not going to say nosy—I think I might just say nosy, okay. [They] sit there on [the] couch [the] whole day . . . they're watching." At May's house, his daughter could safely play on a new-looking trampoline that sat in the grassy front yard, while her grandmother kept an eye on her through the window.

Before moving into May's home, Kevin's employment in a warehouse with six-day workweeks and mandatory overtime kept him from spending much time with his daughter, but he could not afford to quit. Working such long hours, he relied heavily on childcare, but since his divorce a series of bad experiences had left him believing that "you can't trust a lot of people with your kids." He could trust May. "That's why I decided to move here, because . . . I can go work and everything else. I'd need to work overtime, I can do this right here." Living with his mother, he said, gave him a "comfort level with my daughter."

Kevin now worked as a security guard, with evening and overnight shifts. When he was at work, May helped her granddaughter with her homework and was home with her overnight. When he got home each morning, he got his daughter ready for school and helped with any homework questions May could not answer. May also washed the girl's clothes, did most of the cooking, and acted as a female role model. "Because I can't raise a little girl . . . I can't tell a girl how to be a woman," Kevin explained. It was apparent after just a few minutes of talking with him that he doted on his daughter. He described the active childhood he curated for her: "I do a lot of things with my daughter. I don't have a lot of money, so I do things in my budget. Piano lessons. And we're taking karate at the same time." The nurturing environment that May's home provided was invaluable to him. May explained, "I helps him with the girl. I keep her at night while he goes to work. So that really meant a lots to him."

When Kevin moved in with May, he "agreed to help her out if she helps me out," and both had kept this pledge. She had paid off the mortgage to her home decades before he moved in, so her housing costs were limited to utilities and insurance. However, he contributed $500 a month, explaining, "Ain't [anyone] going to let you stay free. Everybody needs help. So I pay her rent and she said thank you." He was satisfied because the amount was far less than he would need to pay for his own home, especially if he were to rent in a desirable neighborhood. May described herself as poor, but Kevin's help, along with her Social Security payments and the income she brought in from work for Habitat for Humanity, ensured that she could pay her bills and avoid material hardship.

Living with May also helped Kevin weather fluctuations in his income. Soon after he moved in with his mother, he was fired from the warehouse where he worked, which required long overtime hours. "I was so happy to get fired. I thought I'd never be happy to get fired," he recalled. He found a job as a nighttime security guard two days later, a position without mandatory overtime but one that paid only $9 an hour. After buying his work uniforms and having insurance and child support deducted from his check, he earned just $250 a week in those first weeks. "I wasn't paying [May] very much money. She never complained about it, so when I got a better job, I started giving her more money. . . . Then when my job went down, she never said anything. I couldn't pay very much because I still had to get to work."

Keeping her home in good repair was important to May, who planned to "spend the rest of my days here." Although she did most of the housework, Kevin helped with the work that she could not do. "He helps clean up the house and do things, cutting the yard yesterday," she explained. Indeed, the home appeared well maintained, down to the fresh-looking coat of paint on the light-yellow siding and green shutters. Historic and present-day racist practices have left older Black women like May particularly likely to own homes that need repairs, putting them at risk of what sociologist Robin Bartram calls "routine dilapidation," which can lead to health problems or even displacement.[2] Kevin's help allowed May to keep her home in good repair, despite her limited income, and to comfortably age in place.

Kevin and his daughter also helped seventy-seven-year-old May with her day-to-day care needs. "I'm at the age where I need the help," she admitted. For instance, after a recent hospitalization, Kevin monitored his mother's medication because "my remembering wasn't all there," she explained. Another time, May fell, and her granddaughter was there to help her. Kevin and his daughter also provided company. "It's so good to have company in your house and you not living alone," May said. "If they wasn't here, I'll be here all alone. Nobody sitting . . . nobody coming in and out, nobody—you know what I'm saying? It just be empty space in here and just me walking in and out trying to do things that they can do for me."

———

Chapter 7 focused on the ways in which doubled-up households can perpetuate instability. It described how most doubled-up households are short-term arrangements and household dissolutions often leave parents without needed support. Yet not all households dissolve quickly and not all household dissolutions leave parents with unmet needs. This chapter focuses on parents who were able to use doubling up as either a long-term source of support or as a stepping-stone toward their ultimate housing or economic goals. These were parents who might have considered doubling up to have "worked" for them, at least in part.

Scholars of social support draw a helpful distinction between support that facilitates coping and support that promotes economic mobility.[3] Social support can help families "get by" and meet their daily needs without changing their overall economic status. It can also help families "get ahead" in ways that improve their economic well-being, such as by helping parents further their education or find higher-paying employment. Similarly, doubling up successfully provided two types of support: long-term coping support and temporary support that helped families achieve their residential or economic goals. Both types of support were important for families, but they had very different implications for families' residential trajectories. This chapter examines how doubled-up households provided each of these two forms of support. It also explores the circumstances that enabled long-term coping support and those that enabled families to "get ahead," as well as how these circumstances differed from those of the households described in chapter 7.

Kevin and May's household was particularly effective at providing coping support that helped both parties get by on a day-to-day basis. May provided Kevin with housing that he would have been unable to afford on the private market, and in a neighborhood where he felt comfortable raising his daughter. She also provided trustworthy and reliable childcare at no cost. He provided his mother with live-in assistance with daily activities, like cooking, and he and his daughter provided companionship that was critical to her well-being. His assistance with the home maintenance that she was no longer able to do helped her remain in the home she loved, and his financial assistance provided an additional source of income.

Households like Kevin and May's stood in stark contrast to the unstable households in chapter 7 that dissolved quickly and left families little better off. However, not all doubled-up household dissolutions left household members without needed support; some families were able to leverage temporary support from doubling up to advance their ultimate housing or economic goals. Because parents often intended doubling up to be a temporary arrangement, this kind of instability reflected a *positive* outcome: some households dissolved because the household members no longer needed the support that the household was formed to provide, or because they had achieved the goal that doubling up was intended to support. Other parents were able to leverage doubled-up arrangements to make progress toward their goals despite facing undesirable household instability.

The families in this chapter show that doubling up sometimes provided critical support. In many ways, however, this private safety net simply built on existing inequalities, rather than equalizing them. Parents with stable, well-paying employment, well-off social networks, and other advantages were most likely to be able to use doubling up to achieve their goals. Less advantaged parents, like Kevin, could receive long-term coping support through doubling up, but these households rarely made dramatic changes to parents' incomes or housing prospects.

Stable Coping Support from Doubling Up

Multigenerational households, like Kevin and May's, tend to be more stable than other doubled-up household types. National survey data show that 47 percent of children who live doubled up as a guest with a grandparent and 39 percent of those who live doubled up as a host with a grandparent remained in the same household type over a three-year period—far more than remained doubled up as a guest (29 percent) or a host (17 percent) with other extended family or as a guest (18 percent) or a host (9 percent) with a nonrelative.[4] To understand household stability in my sample, I focused on households that had remained intact—with the host and guest coresiding—for at least two years, a relatively rare milestone. In this subsample, doubled-up households had remained intact for a median length of about five years.[5] Consistent with national trends, a large majority of these stable households were multigenerational, typically with the older generation hosting the younger generation.[6]

Kevin and May had coresided for over seven years, and there were no signs that the household would dissolve anytime soon. Two factors seemed to contribute to household stability. First, Kevin and May shared a strong sense of household solidarity. As was clear from their day-to-day interactions around money and childcare, they both looked out for the other's interests and felt that they could count on the other to do the same.

Second, they had a shared understanding of their relationship and expectations for their relationship. They both acknowledged the help that the other provided, and they frequently expressed gratitude. For example, May thanked Kevin for his rent payments, and she knew how much he valued the childcare she provided. She did not feel the need to set many household rules. For instance, they had a shared sense of propriety and never had to discuss having romantic partners overnight. "They respect home. It's very respect[ful]—they don't bring nobody to spend the night, and I don't either," May reported. Moreover, she respected that Kevin had authority over his own decisions. "You got to let them be grown, let them do what they want to do. That's the way I do it," she explained. "He going to go in there and take his shoes and lay down, then go do it. He going to get in his car and go for a ride, go do it. You're grown now. You don't have to ask me no question. You grown."

Of course, May and Kevin had moments when they were not fully in agreement, but disagreements diffused quickly. For example, she was quick to recognize when she had overstepped her authority. "I asked him the other day, 'How come you didn't tell me you going to work?' [He responded,] 'You didn't ask me.' He kept walking. I didn't. So that closed my mouth up, didn't it? That's what we do. 'You didn't ask me.'" As the next section makes clear, Kevin continued to link residential independence to adulthood and autonomy; however, he rarely needed to assert his autonomy in daily life, in part because of the care that May took not to "boss him." As she explained, "He can do anything he want to do. He take and put his money where he wants it to go. And I can't say nothing because he's a grown man . . . I don't try to. That's him and his life. And he living it like he please."

May took an active role in Kevin's daughter's life, but her role was clearly differentiated from that of a parent—parenting was his domain. Asked whether she talked to her granddaughter's teachers, she responded, "I haven't, but my son goes all the time. . . . That's his job, that's his child. I don't take nobody's responsibility." Kevin and May did not always agree on how his daughter should be raised, but she deferred to his authority as a parent. For example, she disapproved of the unnecessary purchases that he made, but when she raised these concerns, he responded, "You won't tell me what to buy for my child," and she accepted his decision. "I shut up. And get out the way. What you want me to do? He's right. It's his money. It's his money, his child."

Kevin and May's doubled-up arrangement was an archetype of household peace. Few households in my sample, even relatively stable and peaceful ones, matched the level of agreement they had about their household roles; other stable households often experienced at least some of the challenges described in chapters 3 through 6. Examining Kevin and May's household dynamics yields insights into how a doubled-up household could remain intact, with minimal conflict, for years.

"You're Supposed to Have Your Own Place": The Problem of Household Stability

Kevin and May's doubled-up arrangement provided them both with countless benefits, and they had little conflict in their day-to-day lives together. In nearly all ways, the household appeared to be a clear success story. Unlike the families in chapter 7, May, Kevin, and his daughter were not subject to any of the social, economic, or residential instability that could accompany doubled-up household dissolutions. The stability of their household was thus protective in a way. On the other hand, the stability of their household was the product of barriers that prevented Kevin from achieving his goal of residential independence. Although the doubled-up arrangement enabled him to get by on a day-to-day basis, it was insufficient to allow him to surmount the structural barriers that prevented him from getting ahead and achieving his residential goals. In his experience, doubling up was *both* a life-changing, critical lifeline and an imperfect and incomplete safety net.

Kevin made just $9 an hour and paid $200 in child support for his son each month, which left him with a limited income even though he worked forty hours or more each week. He was unable to afford a home of his own in the type of neighborhood he wanted to provide for his daughter—a place that was safe, familiar, and close to May so she could continue providing childcare. He had looked for alternative housing. He had applied for a housing choice voucher about a year before his interview, but he had not yet heard back. He had applied for an income-restricted apartment before that but decided that he could not raise his daughter in that neighborhood. "It's got drug dealers on every corner. You got crackheads and prostitutes over there. But at the time, it's what I can afford." At this point, his hopes of residential independence were tied to landing a job that would allow him to afford desirable housing on the private market. "Once I find a better job, I plan on moving down and I can have my own apartment. But I'm not able to do it [now] because the job I got is not paying enough money. . . . I've been there for a year, I haven't got a raise, so I'm looking for a better job."

Living doubled up was a rational response to the barriers that Kevin faced: high housing costs, low-wage employment, and difficulties finding affordable quality childcare. However, his internalized expectations about nuclear family independence prevented him from being satisfied with the arrangement. "If I had money, I'd move out because you're supposed to have your own place, you know?" These emotional costs weighed heavily on him, despite the many benefits of living doubled up. In fact, he suggested that if it were not for his daughter, he would have already moved out of May's home. "My biggest thing is not about me myself, because I can live in an RV and just be comfortable. But for my daughter, it's the best thing to be here with her."

Each of the guest parents in my sample who were stable—that is, they had lived in a doubled-up household for two or more years—planned to move to a home of their own in the future, and Kevin was no different. Although he had lived with May for seven years, he still saw her home as a temporary stop on his way to residential independence. When he first moved in, he put his furniture in storage, imagining that he would stay just a couple of years before again moving out on his own once he found a better-paying job. This economic security had eluded him, yet he continued to pay for the storage unit. "I don't want to start over. Because I could get a house—well, if I get a better job—but I'm going to have no furniture. . . . And realistically, I can't afford to get new stuff. . . . And if I can get an apartment or a house, I don't want to sit there and say I got a house, but now I don't have no bed, I don't have anything, I'm going to sleep on the floor. I'd rather keep the stuff I have till I can afford something, before I get a place, and then I can get my stuff in storage."

May did not seem to judge her household against a nuclear family ideal, and she described the doubled-up arrangement as an unqualified success. She never wanted Kevin and his daughter to move out; for her, the emotional costs of doubling up came from having little control over this decision. When asked how long she thought they would remain in her home, she was resigned. "Who knows? They may move out tomorrow. They may move out next week. Who knows? When Daddy ready to go, he going to tell her go get your clothes, and you going to pack them. 'Let's go. We going to stay in an apartment for a while.' And that's what's going to happen. And you know what I say? Nothing. Nothing. That's his family." May felt it was natural that her son wanted a home of his own. "He's a grown man. He's fifty years old. Don't grown men that age like to have their own homes?" she asked rhetorically. Yet she remembered the loneliness of living alone. "It's giving me company. I don't want to stay here by myself. Ain't nobody come here. I don't see nobody. I don't want that."

When Stability Is Temporary

Kevin and May lived together throughout the fieldwork period, but stability was not always such a constant characteristic. Other households appeared stable at one point but later experienced unexpected instability. This was the case for Sonya, a forty-three-year-old Black mother who lived in a beige, two-story house in Cleveland with her three minor children, ages twelve, nine, and three, her twenty-one-year-old daughter Keneisha, and Keneisha's three-year-old daughter. After Sonya married, her husband moved in as well. Sonya was not stably employed, but she was able to afford the home—a six-bedroom single-family house with a fenced-in backyard that rented for over $1,000 a month—with the help of a housing voucher.

Keneisha had lived with her mother since birth, and in the first two years of fieldwork, their household remained a model of stability. She had her first child not long after graduating from high school. While planning the baby shower for her grandchild, Sonya learned that she too was unexpectedly pregnant. They navigated pregnant life together—"She was evil, I was evil, but we still made it," she recalled—and gave birth to daughters just seventeen days apart. They described themselves as "best friends," and Sonya was also close to her granddaughter. Asked about her favorite part of living with Keneisha, she responded, "What's my favorite part? That we all stay together. And then I can see my grandbaby every day."

Sonya and Keneisha had a strong sense of solidarity. As Keneisha described it, "Me and my mom help each other out. If my mom needs something, I'm going to help her get it, and then if I need something, she's going to help me get it." She received about $700 a month in supplemental security income (SSI), which she used primarily to take care of her young daughter. During the school year, she began working in a school cafeteria and contributed $200 to $300 a month to Sonya for household bills. Sonya said that Keneisha had offered to contribute even more. "She like, 'Mom, I told you, if I ever get a job, I'm going to help you out, I always told you that when I was younger.'" Her daughter offered half of her paychecks, but Sonya told her that was too much: "'You got to work for you and your daughter. You gotta worry about y'all. We going to be all right.'" Since then, Keneisha had contributed to the household regularly, but Sonya did not press for the money when her daughter was not working and unable to pay. "That's why it really don't bother me when she say, 'Mom, I can't pay rent. Can't pay rent nothing until I go back to work.' I told her that's fine, but she's trying to find a job. She trying."

Sonya and Keneisha also shared childcare duties. They both had unstable employment, but when they both worked, they had complementary schedules. Keneisha worked at the school cafeteria in the mornings, so Sonya woke the children up and got them ready for their 7:20 AM drop-off at school. She then went to work at a day care, and Keneisha watched the children in the evening. The children were often asleep by the time Sonya returned home.

Although Sonya enjoyed living with her daughter and granddaughter, the household was far from peaceful. She described Keneisha as "stubborn," and tempers flared frequently. For instance, Sonya recently told her granddaughter to say "sorry" for stepping on her young daughter when getting into the backseat of her truck. "My daughter [Keneisha] got mad, like, 'Shit, she don't gotta say nothing, she [your daughter] should move. Just drop me off.'" Sonya was so angry that she let Keneisha out of the truck and sped home. Although these incidents were common, "we always make up the same time it happens," Sonya said, and the arguments had not threatened the stability of their household.

During the first two years of fieldwork, Sonya did not expect Keneisha to move out anytime soon. "She have ADHD, so she'll be living with me a long time, probably the rest of her life." She had discouraged her from signing up for the housing choice voucher wait-list in the past, Keneisha said, "'cause she just felt like I wasn't just ready to be on my own with a child." Keneisha followed the advice and continued to live in her mother's home. However, by the time I met her, she was hoping to move into a home of her own, saying that, given her age, "it was time to move on, move along. . . . I just wanted my own space. I have my own family now." Sonya wanted her daughter to achieve this goal: "I want her to move. I want everybody to see how it takes. I want everybody to get they own house key." At the same time, she worried that Keneisha could not afford a private market rental; she helped her apply for public housing, but they were told to expect a two- to three-year wait.

Initially, Sonya wanted Keneisha to remain in her home. She described how her daughter threatened to move out before getting housing assistance, especially when she was angry—"When it's time to clean up, 'Oh, I really gotta move.'" But Sonya knew that her daughter simply could not afford private market rent. "She got to pay her car note and her insurance . . . keep gas in it, and it don't go that way. That $600 dollar check ain't gonna [be enough]—it's going to crash." If her daughter moved out despite her advice, Sonya expected that she would soon want to return to her home. "It's not going to work. I told her she can't come back. My grandbaby can come back."

While hosting, Sonya did not have to worry about whether her daughter and granddaughter had an appropriate home. "I don't want my daughter to be in the house by herself because a lot of her friends that got they own house now, or with they boyfriend, they have fights, it's a flophouse—you don't want everybody be piled up at your house. Your friends' boyfriends—and you got a grandbaby." Keneisha and her partner fought frequently, but they typically avoided physical altercations in front of Sonya and her husband. Sonya worried about what would happen if Keneisha lived on her own. "At least I ain't gotta wake up, or be woke out of my sleep, [with someone] saying, 'Girl, hurry up. You gotta get over here, something done happened.'"

Sonya and Keneisha's household revealed how unpredictable doubled-up household stability could be. Although Keneisha had lived with Sonya consistently since her childhood and Sonya expected her to remain there for years to come, this seemingly stable household dissolved suddenly. Keneisha's boyfriend had been living with his own mother, but when his mother lost her home, he began—without permission—to spend every day at Sonya's. "It wasn't no sit-down and having a conversation saying he was staying here," she explained. She quickly grew tired of having another person in the house, particularly someone who did not contribute financially. "No job, no nothing. No. You can't keep taking care of a grown person."

Moreover, she and her daughter still argued frequently. Keneisha was pregnant with her second child, and that made her moody, Sonya said. When Sonya's brother was put out by his wife, she allowed him to start sleeping on her couch, and Keneisha complained that the house was too full. Sonya eventually tired of her daughter's moods and complaints and told her and her boyfriend that they had to move out. She recalled, "People run they mouth, [saying I'm] grown. Right. You grown. So, you go do grown stuff. Mmm hmm. That's what my mama taught me. You run your mouth, you grown, go get your own shit." With a slight shift in circumstances, Sonya and Keneisha's seemingly stable household quickly became unstable.

The sense of solidarity that Sonya and Keneisha shared was insufficient to keep the household intact with the added pressures introduced by Keneisha's partner. At her next interview, Sonya continued to emphasize that she cared for and wanted to support her daughter, who was now a mother of two. She reasoned that Keneisha was now more prepared to live independently than she had been when she was younger. "You know, she had ADHD, but now she is better. She doing good. She know how to count her money. Her reading level, at [age] twenty, was still . . . fourth grade." Moreover, Sonya knew that Keneisha, her daughter, and her newborn son—although not her boyfriend—would be welcome at her father's house, and also that she could stretch her savings and employment income to move into a rental unit of her own if absolutely necessary. "So I wasn't worried about her being outside," she explained. As Sonya predicted, her daughter responded to being kicked out of her mother's home by moving with her children to her father's home.

Using Doubling Up to "Get Ahead"

The two households described in this chapter so far were both stable doubled-up arrangements that provided long-term support for household members so that they could more easily get by on a day-to-day basis. That is, each of these households was a stable source of coping support over a multiyear period. In both cases, however, the guest was unable to leverage this support to make progress toward their long-term residential goals. For parents like Kevin and Keneisha, doubling up alone was insufficient to allow them to surmount barriers that kept them out of the private housing market, like low-wage or unstable employment and the limited availability of desirable affordable housing. Although a stable doubled-up household could protect families from the negative experiences of instability described in chapter 7, its support was limited to helping parents cope with daily needs.

Some parents were able to leverage doubling up to make progress toward their long-term residential or economic goals. Guests often intended for doubling up to provide a springboard toward their ultimate goals—that is, they hoped that doubling up would be a short-term arrangement rather than a stable, long-term one. Thus, parents who were able to make progress toward their goals—those who were able to "get ahead" and not merely "get by"—were often not stable because they moved into a home of their own. These parents understood the short-term nature of doubling up as a *positive* outcome.

Jennifer, a twenty-four-year-old Hispanic mother, her partner of ten years—whom she called her husband—and their three sons, ages seven, five, and two, lived in an apartment in a complex immediately off a highway in North Dallas. During her interview, she sat on one of the black leather sofas in the living room and talked as the younger boys sat in front of the large entertainment center and played Xbox. The two-bedroom apartment was neat but in transition; the family was preparing to move to Jennifer's mother's home in Garland, a suburb near Dallas. Unconstructed moving boxes sat in one corner of the living room, and there were few pictures on the walls. During the interview, her mother, Magda, arrived and began transferring boxes from the porch to a truck to help with the move.

Jennifer's lease was ending that month. Before deciding to move in with Magda, she and her husband Daniel had been considering whether to renew the lease for their current apartment or find new housing in Fort Worth, where he worked for her father, Gilbert, who owned a janitorial company. They hoped to buy a house, but with Jennifer in school and her husband covering all the bills, they were struggling financially—in fact, they often needed loans from her mother and father. "We struggle with everything, not just like the kids, but raising them, I mean it's pretty expensive. Paying for rent, paying for a car, and sometimes we're like struggling with money and stuff."

Magda suggested they move in with her while they saved to move to Fort Worth. She had three minor children of her own, ages twelve, ten, and nine, and was in the process of separating from her partner. Jennifer reported that her mother had been stressed about how she would be able to cover the bills by herself with the income she brought in as a hairstylist. Jennifer saw an opportunity for them to help each other: "I moved in with Mom to kind of help her out, but then at the same time I thought we can be helped out too ... because we were living in apartments so we could buy a house and just—I guess what every family wants, eventually [to own] their own house."

Jennifer's family moved into Magda's three-bedroom townhouse. With three adults and six children, "we were really tight. I mean, there was no room for anything." She explained that they managed through a combination of bunk beds and sharing beds with the children. Their arrangement was financially beneficial for everyone. Magda had initially asked them to pay for two-thirds of both the $900 rent and the utility bills, reasoning that Jennifer and Daniel would be two-thirds of the adults in the household, but Jennifer talked her into splitting the bills evenly between them with a promise that she and Daniel would help more when possible. She kept this promise by occasionally paying the entire electricity bill.

Because her mother could watch her children, Jennifer was able to begin working in the evenings in an office of her father's janitorial service. "It's a lot easier for her to help me if I was [living] with her, than ... if I wasn't living with her," Jennifer explained. She had hesitated to ask her mother to watch her children before they lived together because she worried that Magda might sometimes forget when she needed childcare. Likewise, she appreciated the structure her mother helped her enforce for her sons, such as stricter bedtimes. "And those are little rules that I picked up and which were good."

Despite these benefits, Jennifer said that, overall, "It wasn't nice living together." She and Magda argued frequently about the children. "Even though my mom loves my kids . . . my kids are little. Her kids are more grown. So having the little kids at home all the time and the noise and all that, it bothered her, and then it bothered me that it bothered her, and it was just crazy." She recalled her mother telling her sons to quiet down when they got too excited over cartoons. "And then I would be like, 'Oh my God, well, you know they're in the living room. They're not [in] your room.'" Likewise, Magda's sons would pick on her sons, but when she complained, her mother would remind her that they were her children. As she recalled these moments when "any little thing can be turned into a big thing," she said, "I think there was just too many people in the house, and it just gives you a tension, you just feel tense."

Daniel had never wanted to move to Magda's home. "He just didn't want to share his space, or he didn't feel comfortable. . . . It was different to him just coming home and turning on the TV and not worrying about 'Oh, they're asleep already,' or something like that." Although they paid more than half of the bills, "we always felt like it was her home . . . she was here first." While living doubled up, Daniel worked long days out of the house and had little sympathy for the challenges his wife faced during the day. "When he was there, I would be like, 'Oh, this happened today with the kids.' And he would be like, 'Yeah, I told you. I told you.'"

Jennifer expected to stay with Magda for a year, but the household dissolved after just four months. Before moving in with her mother, she had been uncertain about leaving Dallas, but when Gilbert offered to allow them to move into his home in Fort Worth, she immediately accepted her father's offer. "Like two months [after] moving in with my mom, I was ready to just move out. I didn't care where. Anywhere, just out." Despite her financial need, Magda felt similarly. Jennifer explained, "I think that even for her, she was ready—she was like, 'No, I think both of us was just used to our own space.' . . . I think she was [at] a point where [she felt like,] 'I don't care if I have to struggle.'"

Gilbert lived alone in a two-story, four-bedroom house, so Jennifer and Daniel had a bedroom to themselves, and their sons shared another bedroom. Her father was close to both her husband and sons, and Jennifer imagined that he would have preferred them to stay for a long time. "I guess he wanted the company. He lived by himself for so many years. Even now, he probably still feels lonely."

However, Jennifer continued to feel like her family needed to have "their own space." Given how spacious her father's house was, I inquired further about this sentiment, and she explained, "Because I still—even though I was there and it was my dad's house, we still—it was his house. We weren't going to invade someone else's house. . . . I was just used to just us alone. So I told him. He's like, 'Well, you guys can stay here.' He did offer. We were like, 'No . . . we have to move out.'" To Jennifer, doubling up was a temporary arrangement intended to help her make progress toward homeownership. A nuclear family household continued to be her ideal. "I think that you can only live for so long. I think that once there's two families, you know, each family needs their space. It doesn't matter if it's through your mom or dad, whoever it is, everybody needs their space."

Jennifer and Daniel achieved their dream of homeownership when they paid cash for a house about one year after first doubling up. By doubling up with Magda, they had been able to save money from their reduced housing costs and the work Jennifer was able to do with Magda providing childcare. Once they moved in with Gilbert in Fort Worth, Daniel no longer spent as much gas money on his commute and Gilbert paid nearly all the bills, so they were able to save even more. Her father, who was eager to support their effort to save toward homeownership, "never really asked for anything," Jennifer said, but they insisted on contributing to some bill payments because "we just felt like we weren't going to live there for free." Still, living with Gilbert enabled them to save rapidly compared to when they were living on their own or even when they lived with Magda.[7] Jennifer thought it would be "scary having a big mortgage," so if they had not doubled up, she said, "I think I would still be living in apartments."

Doubling up allowed them to have a flexible timeline for their housing search and move, and it also freed them from the lease renewal cycle. "It was nice to live with him and spend time with him, but it was nice also just not having to rush into [something because] when you lease you have to sign a contract, and then it was just really nice to [take time to] look for something that you knew was going to be yours." They decided to buy a three-bedroom, one-bath home located on a street of neat one-story brick homes with square front yards in a predominantly Hispanic suburb of Fort Worth. The home's exterior matched the modesty of the other homes in the neighborhood, with its beige brick and light brown awning. The inside of the home, after months of renovations, was far more lavish, from the brightly painted walls to the beautiful glass tile backsplash in the kitchen. These renovations were also made possible by doubling up. Jennifer and Daniel were able to buy a home that was "completely destroyed," knowing they had time to make the renovations they wanted before moving in.

Which Parents "Get Ahead" by Doubling Up?

Although Jennifer was able to achieve her residential goals while living doubled up, her doubled-up household trajectory was not particularly stable; she made three residential moves in one year and was doubled up with her mother and then with her father for less than six months each. What distinguished Jennifer from parents, like those in chapter 7, for whom doubling up perpetuated instability?

It was not that the instability was particularly easy for Jennifer to navigate. She described how rapidly her family's circumstances changed that year: "It was really crazy. It was an adventure. We were like on a roller coaster.... We still had difficult times because we had so many bills and expenses. Then to move in with my mom and not paying as much but having all that pressure with just so many people in the house, then to move in with my dad." Her children's frequent school changes also weighed heavily on her. In her very first interview—even before their move to Magda's home—she had recounted her experience of changing schools frequently as a child and said, "I don't want my kids to move around different schools. I want them to actually have a home school where they've been from first grade to fifth grade." That had not been their experience in the previous year, however, and Jennifer was not surprised that the moves had taken a toll on her children. "Once we moved and we had them moving, I had problems with them like not following directions.... I kind of saw their reflection with the moving, with their grades and the behavior." She worked hard in the year after the moves to try to catch her sons back up to academic level.

It was Jennifer's comparatively privileged economic position—and the economic position of her father—that allowed her to use doubling up to achieve her residential goals. Doubling up provided her and Daniel with temporary housing while they saved for and renovated their own home. However, it was Jennifer's father's financial help and the stable employment he provided for Daniel that truly made it possible for them to leverage doubling up to achieve their homeownership goal. In this way, doubling up gave more advantaged families, who were in a position to be able to accumulate resources, time to do so. In contrast, parents like Kevin, whose low-wage employment left him unable to afford rent in neighborhoods he thought were safe for his daughter, were unable to use doubling up as a springboard toward their ultimate housing goals. Doubling up might provide time to accumulate resources, but it rarely dramatically changed families' access to resources.

For some guest families, time was all they needed in order to move on from their doubled-up household to a desirable housing situation. For example, Sonya's brother moved in with her after he and his wife separated; after a month, he reconciled with his wife and returned to her home. Sonya's daughter Keneisha doubled up with her father after leaving her mother's home. After only about a month in this household, she received the subsidized apartment she had applied for a year earlier and was able to move out on her own. Lisa, the mother from chapter 6, hosted her cousin's family after they moved to Cleveland; her cousin quickly landed a job and after four months found a rental home of her own. In each of these cases, the doubled-up household was short-lived because the guest's support needs were temporary.

Chapter 7 described several parents whose needs outlasted their doubled-up arrangement. Some host parents in my sample dissolved their doubled-up household with few negative ramifications for themselves but while their guest was still in need of support. These hosts were not harmed by household instability. Yet neither they nor their guests would likely have categorized the household dissolution as a positive resolution to the doubled-up arrangement.

Conclusion

This chapter has focused on doubled-up arrangements that helped parents either "get by" on a day-to-day basis or "get ahead" and advance their goals. Some doubled-up households served as a long-term safety net for their residents by providing benefits such as economic assistance, help with household work and childcare, and emotional support. These households were predominantly multigenerational and often characterized by household solidarity and more shared understandings of household relationships. However, stability was not always permanent; stable households could quickly become unstable as circumstances changed.

Some families leveraged doubled-up households to make progress toward their residential or other goals. These households typically supported time-limited needs, most commonly the guest's needs, and dissolved once the need was met. Doubling up sometimes provided an economic safety net that enabled guests to temporarily reduce their housing costs, and many hosts expressed a willingness to provide this kind of temporary support. For guests who were already well positioned to achieve their goals—due to their own economic position, their social network, and other advantages—this temporary support was all they needed to achieve goals like buying a home or completing a degree. For other parents, doubling up provided a temporary stopgap while they waited for months or even years to access the public housing assistance they were eligible for.

As chapter 7 demonstrated, doubling up was often insufficient in itself to allow families to make progress toward their goals. Only parents who had social ties who were willing and able to host with little payment in return were able to save, and, as described in chapter 4, some hosts exploited guests' housing needs by charging excessive rent. There are racial disparities in whose hosts can afford to not charge rent; national data show that doubled-up White mothers are more likely than doubled-up Black or Hispanic mothers to not pay rent.[8] However, having a generous host was insufficient to allow families to achieve their goals unless they were already well positioned to do so. For instance, doubling up sometimes allowed parents with low-wage and unstable employment to save enough to afford move-in costs or even several months' worth of rent, but it could not ease concerns that, on the private housing market, they would always be just a few paychecks away from not being able to pay their rent. In this way, even stable doubled-up households provided insufficient support for guests to overcome longer-term imbalances, such as the limited supply of desirable and affordable housing and a fundamental mismatch between wage and housing price growth.

The benefits of household stability should not be understated. Kevin's family experienced none of the challenges of unstable households highlighted in chapter 7. Moreover, they had access to a critical stable safety net. Neighborhood contexts influence children's development and later life outcomes,[9] and doubling up allowed Kevin to raise his daughter in a neighborhood where they felt safe and socially connected. If he had not doubled up, he would have likely lived in unaffordable housing, leaving less room in his budget to invest in other material needs and child-centered activities. And the kind of safe and stable childcare that May provided for his daughter has benefits for both parents and children.[10] Thus, doubling up can provide an incredibly valuable safety net, even when it does not propel parents toward other long-term goals.

However, it is not clear that doubled-up household stability should be a policy goal. Cultural norms valorizing independent nuclear family households pose a formidable barrier to making long-term doubling up as a guest a desirable option for families, even if policymakers were somehow able to transform unstable and conflictual households into longer-term arrangements. For parents like Kevin, who had internalized the cultural ideal of the nuclear family household, long-term coresidence as a doubled-up guest came with emotional costs and a sense that his family was in a temporary residence. As described in chapter 2, some hosts, likewise expecting working-age adults to pursue independence, were hesitant to provide long-term housing. Parents were more likely to approve of long-term coresidence when the younger generation hosted an older adult. Because assistance to the older generation is broadly viewed more positively than assistance to the younger generation, these households may be best equipped to achieve a stability that leaves all household members satisfied with the arrangement. However, such arrangements are possible only when the younger generation can obtain housing of their own.

The Imperfect Private Safety Net

AFTER LIVING IN HER mother-in-law's home for about three years, Eva, the White and multiracial mother featured in chapter 5, moved with her partner Dylan and their two children into their first independent home, a small single-family rental in a neighborhood close to downtown Cleveland. They searched for a full year before finding something they could afford and were willing to accept, and the new home was still far from ideal. In fact, Dylan wanted to reject it because of damage from previous tenants and their pets, but Eva persuaded him that they could fix it up. "And then he seen we weren't finding anything else that was in our price range that was on our list, so he had no other choice," she explained.

Eva was thrilled to be out of her mother-in-law's home and eager to make the rental their own. They installed carpet and painted the children's bedroom in a bright blue and orange, colors their children selected themselves. After years of doubling up, moving between the homes of her mother-in-law and her mother and stepfather, Eva was proud to have a home of her own. "I never had anything that was mine. That's why this place is very important to me, because it's mine. It has my name on it, so I don't have to listen to nothing."

For the first time, Eva could build the family life she wanted. At her mother-in-law's home, she had been reticent to have guests over. "I felt bad because, again, it's not my house and that's an extra kid running around. . . . She wouldn't want to hear a bunch of kids screaming and running around her house tearing it up." Now she hosted friends for regular family dinner parties, and she held a large gathering for her son's birthday. "That was another big thing that I felt so good about because I got to do it all by myself. I cooked all the food. I decorated everything."

Living independently had also reduced Eva's parenting stress level. "We don't have anyone telling us, 'Can't do that. You shouldn't do that. It's not the right parenting.'" With a home of her own, she was able to provide her children with both more freedom and more structure. "My kids can run free and I don't have to be like, 'Shh, they're sleeping.'" Instead of responding to other household members' schedules, she built a routine that worked for her family. "I love bedtime. It was hard to put them to sleep when you live with somebody because that person might not be going to bed at that time or they may be having company over. . . . Now it's lights off, in the bed . . . they go right to sleep. I love that so much because that's my time to wind down, relax."

Eva and Dylan also had more privacy as a couple. They no longer needed to share their bedroom with their children, and it was more difficult for extended family members to interfere in their relationship. "We can tell each other more stuff now because we don't have other people switching the story around or giving their opinions and whatever," she explained. "We just communicate so much better."

Despite their joy at having an independent home, Eva and Dylan's first year on their own was difficult. They faced problem after problem with their new rental. First, they had to purchase a fridge and stove for the kitchen. Then pipes burst in the bathroom and the shower stopped working for over a year. At multiple points, mold and pet waste and dander from previous tenants made the home unsafe for their son's asthma, and the children stayed with Eva's mother while they made repairs and cleaned.

Eva and Dylan also sorely missed the economic support that their doubled-up arrangement had provided. Dylan, Eva recalled, had bemoaned, "Man, it seems like as soon as we get where we want to be, something happens and we fall back. . . . It wasn't never like that before." He lost his job as a tire tech just a couple of months after they moved. Although he quickly found a job at U-Haul, it was part-time and paid just $8 an hour. Eva began working at a department store, working her way up from a cleaning position to cashier. Yet she still made just $8 an hour and had been turned down for another promotion after she called off work a couple of times for emergencies with her children. "I'm the only one there that has small kids at home still. . . . Maybe that's not the position for me, because you never know what's going to happen. Like, [my daughter] broke her arm and I had to take off work. I didn't mean for that to happen," she explained exasperatedly, motioning toward her small daughter's cast.

Eva's and Dylan's part-time, low-wage work did not cover their family's needs. Their rent was $450 a month, which they typically paid in increments and sometimes not at all. They even received an eviction notice before one of my visits. At the time, Eva had taken a week off work to attend a string of medical appointments for her own recent unexplained fatigue and her daughter's broken arm. After the eviction notice, she had to return to work to help pay the bills, even if that meant relying on energy drinks to get through her shifts. With their landlord pressuring them to pay $450 by that Friday, they planned to use every dollar of her next paycheck on rent and ask family for help with the rest. They were also behind on their utilities and paying only a little each month to prevent a shutoff. Despite the challenges of living independently, Eva was determined to make it work. "I don't care if we don't have a dollar in our pocket, our bills and our rent will be paid. I don't care if we don't have a dollar to take the kids somewhere. As long as we have our own house, that's all I care about."

———

For Eva and Dylan, doubling up had a complicated relationship with family well-being. In some ways, they represented a best-case scenario for doubling up: living with his mother had provided clear economic benefits, stable housing, and an environment that was safe for them and their children. Not all doubled-up guests had this security. Yet, even for them, these benefits were only one small part of how they experienced life in a doubled-up household. Doubling up prevented Eva from enacting her ideals of family life, took a toll on her sense of self-worth and her stress level, and added challenges to her romantic relationship and parenting. The amount of mental energy that parents like Eva needed to devote to navigating the complicated relationships and shared space of doubled-up households cannot be understated. Parents had different levels of tolerance for these challenges—and different housing alternatives available to them—but for Eva they were so burdensome that she vowed to never live doubled up again.

Moreover, although Eva remained doubled up for years, trying to save and search for a way to meet her residential goals, she had made little progress. Although she and Dylan eventually moved into a home of their own, the time they spent doubling up had not addressed the layers of precarity they faced from the housing and labor markets. The last time I spoke with her, Eva hoped to find a home that was in better repair, but she was scared to move because she worried that another landlord might be quicker to evict them when they inevitably fell behind on rent again. Even when doubled-up households provided vital support, they failed to fully address the broader barriers faced by families like Eva's.

Critical Support in Precarious Times

Doubled-up households are home to more than eleven million children, an increase of roughly 40 percent from just two decades prior.[1] What does it mean that so many families with children now live doubled up? The stories of the families in this book show that doubled-up households have become an integral part of families' tool kits for survival and mobility. Doubling up is an individual, private response to overwhelming structural problems: a lack of adequate, affordable housing for low- to moderate-income families, a labor market that leaves too many parents in precarious and low-paid work, historic and ongoing racism that amplifies these challenges for families of color, and the inadequacies of existing public supports.

In recent years, the housing landscape has become increasingly daunting for low- to moderate-income families as the number of available low-cost rentals has declined, rent prices have outpaced wages, and barriers to homeownership have persisted. The challenges that families face in the current housing market are reflected in the high rate of families who are living in unaffordable housing; nearly one-third of all households, and about half of all renter households, are cost-burdened—that is, they pay more than 30 percent of their income for housing.[2] Families living in unaffordable housing make difficult trade-offs between paying their rent and spending on other necessities, like health care and food.[3] Housing challenges are also reflected in the millions of evictions that are filed.[4] The number of informal evictions—families being pushed out of their homes, often because they are unable to afford their ever-rising rent—is even greater. And housing challenges are reflected in the large majority of renters who want to be homeowners but are limited by financial and credit constraints,[5] as well as the dramatic disparities by race and ethnicity in homeownership rates.[6]

This book highlights yet another way in which high housing costs are shaping families' lives: by changing their household arrangements. Because of their larger household size, doubled-up hosts and guests are less likely to be counted among the housing cost–burdened, and because guests are often not evicted through formal channels, their departures from households are not reflected in eviction rates. Measures like cost burden and eviction pick up families who are in the private housing market, but not guests who were pushed out of this market and sought an alternative through doubling up. Yet like cost burdens and evictions, the prevalence of doubling up reflects the pressures of the current housing market. As chapter 1 showed, doubling up helped a range of families address the burden of high housing costs, from very low-income families struggling to keep a roof over their heads to moderate-income families seeking to prevent housing expenses from stifling their dreams for upward mobility.

High housing costs are compounded by other challenges. Many of the doubled-up parents in my sample were among the fifty-three million working-age adults in the United States who earn low wages. Earning a median rate of about $10 an hour, low-wage workers find it challenging to make ends meet even with full-time, year-round work. Moreover, many low-wage workers are not consistently offered full-time hours and are stuck working part-time, often with unpredictable schedules.[7] For parents working low-wage jobs, chronically small and unpredictable paychecks and a lack of job security contribute to the need to double up. Some parents and young adults double up to lower their housing costs and receive other support while pursuing educational goals, in response to a labor market in which higher education credentials are increasingly necessary for economic stability but are time-consuming and expensive to obtain. Employment challenges are heightened for Black and Hispanic adults and for women, who disproportionately work low-wage jobs.[8] Black and Hispanic workers also face higher rates of unemployment than White and Asian workers.[9] In these ways, the challenges of the labor market compound the challenges of the housing market; in response, the families in this book turned to doubling up. Moreover, the intractability of such labor market difficulties kept many families doubled up for far longer than they intended.

On top of the challenges posed by the labor and housing markets, parents—especially mothers of young children—must balance work and caregiving needs. The United States has one of the least supportive policy environments for working mothers in the developed world; companies are largely left to set their own policies around paid family leave, vacation, and sick days, so where these benefits do exist, they accrue primarily to the most privileged workers.[10] Thus, even when lower-income parents manage to save toward their housing goals, they are too often forced to start over when they face a medical emergency or family care needs. Childcare costs have also skyrocketed in recent decades, such that this expense now rivals housing costs for many families; the average childcare expenditure is equal to roughly half the median mortgage payment and nearly 80 percent of the median rent.[11] Moreover, with the limited availability of childcare providers, even parents who can afford private care or who receive a childcare subsidy still struggle to find an acceptable provider.[12] Childcare assistance is an important benefit for hosts and guests in many doubled-up households, filling in for gaps left by the market and public supports.

In response to the compounded challenges they face, many families with young children—especially single-parent families, families of color, and families with lower levels of educational attainment—turn to doubling up. The doubled-up households in my sample were a response to challenges, yet they also reflected resilience and the role of social networks in helping families weather these challenges. Doubling up provided guest families with housing support that helped them avoid having to live in housing that they found unacceptable, being burdened by the high cost of rent, or turning to emergency shelter or falling into unsheltered homelessness. As chapter 2 showed, some hosts provided housing support to others even at a substantial personal cost to themselves. Moreover, both hosts and guests often received economic support from other household members—support that, however imperfect, did at times provide flexibility in families' budgets or prevent material hardship, as chapter 4 demonstrated.

Additionally, it is impossible to overstate the value of the care work that doubled-up household members provided. As chapter 6 demonstrated, doubling up with a trusted adult, particularly a grandmother, often allowed both host and guest parents to receive help with the care and oversight of children. Household members frequently provided regular childcare, and coresiding made it easier to schedule care and eliminated the need for transportation. More casual childcare assistance was also valuable for doubled-up parents, many of whom were raising their children without a coresident romantic partner. For instance, having another adult in the home who could take responsibility when they stepped out for groceries or who could join in child-centered activities alleviated pressure on parents. Living together also facilitated other types of care work, such as assistance for older adults who needed help with daily personal care.

Beyond these practical and tangible benefits of doubling up, many of the parents in my sample experienced undeniable moments of joy from sharing a home with their loved ones. They laughed around the kitchen table, drew comfort from having a listening ear for their problems, and took pleasure in watching their children's daily interactions with an older grandparent or great-grandparent. In her book on skipped-generation households (in which a grandparent is raising a grandchild, without the parent present), scholar

LaShawnDa Pittman writes that for grandmothers with custody of their minor grandchildren, raising their grandchildren is an act of both love *and* coercion. The custodial grandmothers' deep love for their grandchildren does not undermine the fact that they feel forced to provide care that they did not choose and without the support that they need.[13] Likewise, doubled-up households can be filled with joy and love, and often are (though certainly not always). This reality exists alongside the fact that doubling up too often is a response to the compounded challenges families face and the insufficiencies of public supports, rather than a choice freely made.

When their extended family and friends were in need, the parents in my sample felt obligated to help by sharing their housing, sometimes alongside the hope that doubling up could help them meet some of their own economic or care needs. When higher-income families want to support needy family members, they can choose to help fund independent housing; for instance, a recent survey found that parents help 17 percent of young adults with their rent or mortgage payments.[14] In contrast, most of the hosts I interviewed were not financially able to help support a separate household. When their family and friends needed help with housing, these parents bore the burden of hosting them in their home.

Furthermore, support from doubling up was often insufficient to allow guests to overcome the other barriers they faced. Doubling up could reduce parents' housing and childcare costs. But it did not ensure that they could find stable employment that paid a living wage, nor did it give them access to affordable, adequate housing of their own. At its best, doubling up helped parents meet their day-to-day needs, but it could not reshape the resources and opportunities available to them. With some exceptions—for example, parents who were already relatively advantaged—doubling up often left guest parents no closer to achieving their goals than they had been before doubling up.

How Doubling Up Reshapes Family Life

When I began this study, I was interested in families' *housing* experiences. Informed by the expansive literature on the importance of housing and neighborhoods for family well-being,[15] I sought to understand how families chose units and neighborhoods and what effect these physical environments had on them. I found that, for so many families, understanding their housing situation required thinking of housing not just as a *physical* phenomenon but as a *social* one as well. Social networks determined the housing options available to families when they doubled up as guests. Perhaps even more importantly, sharing the physical home environment structured social interactions and relationships for both hosts and guests. In short, I found that leaving families reliant on the private safety net not only affected where they lived, it *reshaped family life*.

Doubled-up household arrangements are certainly not new, but they remain incompletely institutionalized. Taken-for-granted assumptions about how a household should function are based on the nuclear family household, and these norms provide limited guidance for how to share household space and navigate relationships with coresident adults beyond the nuclear family. Because doubled-up households remain "culturally uncharted"—there is no standard set of norms around household authority, romantic relationships, child-rearing, or economic exchange—the household members in my sample were left to negotiate among themselves about the most intimate aspects of family life.[16] When household members drew upon competing scripts about appropriate roles and relationships, it caused conflict and confusion, with negative impacts on household functioning as well as the well-being of both adults and children.

Moreover, although doubling up is common in the United States, ideals of family life remain based on the independent nuclear family household consisting of a parent, their children, and sometimes a romantic partner. This cultural context made navigating relationships with extended family and non-kin household members difficult, as parents in my sample often believed that these roles were not "supposed" to exist at all. Many of the realities of doubled-up life were incompatible with expectations based on single-family households, such as the expectation of relationship privacy or of parental control over children's home environments. In part because of the inconsistencies and ambiguity in doubled-up household expectations, this private safety net "solution" created many unique challenges for doubled-up families.

In non-shared households, the home forms a physical and symbolic boundary around the private affairs of the nuclear family, setting these affairs apart from the outside world. Doubling up blurred these boundaries, reducing the level of privacy available to families in my sample. With shared household members surveilling their day-to-day activities and cleanliness levels, parents felt that they were treated like children. Household members monitored and criticized parents' decisions about their own children, undermining their authority as primary caregivers. They easily overheard private conversations and interfered in parents' romantic relationships. Overcrowded household conditions could limit physical privacy, leaving parents and children sharing a single bedroom or even sleeping in common areas of the home. And families who lived doubled up often treated their shared home like a public space rather than a private one—for instance, in how they dressed.

Sharing intimate household space also increased families' exposure to adults beyond the nuclear family. Other adults interfered in parenting by undercutting parents' rules, disrupting children's routines, and teaching or interacting with children in ways that parents found inappropriate. Parents struggled to protect their children from being negatively influenced by other household members and household guests. For example, living with unruly children made it difficult for parents to enforce rules for their own children. At other times, parents sought to shield their children from having their feelings hurt by coresident adults who, for example, refused to engage with the children or treated the children in the household unequally. Most concerningly, some doubled-up household environments forced parents to consider how to guard their children from dangers like verbal or sexual abuse, exposure to drug use, and the presence of unknown visitors in the home. These risks posed immediate dangers for children, and they also put an additional burden on parents, particularly mothers, who took responsibility for insulating their children against these risks.

In shared homes, even the most basic everyday activities required careful timing and negotiation. In households with multiple adults and few bathrooms, finding time to shower was a constant puzzle, as was keeping showers to an acceptable length. When sharing a kitchen, making dinner for children might require finding a time when no other adult wanted to use the stove, ensuring that other household members had not eaten the ingredients the parent planned to use for the meal, and doing the dishes immediately after to satisfy the other household members' expectations for cleanliness. Bedtimes could be disrupted by an unexpected household visitor or, especially for children and adults who slept in common areas, the return home of another household member. In sum, the rhythms of daily life simultaneously required more planning and more flexibility in shared spaces.

For guests, who typically held little household authority, householders' rules compounded the challenges of sharing space. For instance, some householders decreed that laundry could be done only on a specific day each week, leaving parents unable to clean up after a child's mess or to wash their uniforms after working for hours in a fast-food restaurant. Householders also set rules for children, such as when they could run the water hose, how loud they could be in the home, and whether they could host other children for playtime or a birthday party. Any one of these rules might not seem that troublesome on its own, but together they added substantial inconvenience to parents' lives. Moreover, householders' rules sent a consistent message to guests that they were not in charge and would not be until they had a home of their own.

One particularly important form of authority involved making rules about who could be inside the home. Some hosts had rules that limited whether biological or social fathers could live with their partner and children and sometimes even whether and when they could visit. Guest parents, but perhaps especially fathers, faced stigma when they were unable to afford a home for their nuclear family. Rules against coresidence and visiting further labeled as disposable those fathers who failed to meet an economic bar. Research on disadvantaged fathers shows that given limited opportunities to fulfill the breadwinner ideal, these men often redefine good fatherhood to emphasize quality time.[17] Relying on others for housing can limit fathers' ability to meet this redefined ideal of fatherhood as well.

Household regulations took a toll on hosts too, even though they had a home of their own and typically set the rules. Parents often made rules for their guests in an effort to limit the costs of providing housing assistance. They set rules against visitors to keep their children safe and stave off negative influences inside the home. Rules about cleaning and how guests could use the home were intended to avoid mess and damage to their belongings; recall, for example, how the new couches on which Leeann in chapter 3 spent her limited income were promptly ruined when her guests spilled drinks without cleaning up. Hosts' rules about water use were intended to prevent their bills from skyrocketing while doubled up, adding to the financial cost of hosting. Hosts saw rule-setting as necessary, and enforcing these rules became an added burden of doubling up.

For both hosts and guests, navigating the complex relationships and routines in their doubled-up household imposed an immense emotional and cognitive burden. As research in behavioral economics has emphasized, individuals have a limited amount of mental "bandwidth."[18] When doubled-up parents—whose bandwidth is often already taxed by poverty—must devote more of their bandwidth to navigating the complexities of day-to-day life in a shared household, they are left with less bandwidth for other efforts, including investing in their familial relationships and pursuing their economic and housing goals.

Of course, even parents who do not live doubled up can have ambivalent relationships with family and friends. For instance, parents who have a home of their own may still feel that a grandparent gets too involved in their child-rearing. Yet after their children spend a weekend with the grandparents, such parents can bring them home, where the parent is fully in control and can take a break from negotiating the grandparent-grandchild relationship. Parents who live with a child's grandparent do not have this ability; they have to constantly devote mental energy to navigating this relationship day in and day out. Moreover, guest parents' reliance on householders for housing infuses challenging power dynamics into these already complex negotiations.

Beyond the interpersonal challenges, doubled-up families often experience dissonance between the way things *should* be—often informed by their nuclear family household ideal—and the way they *are*. The idealized image of the independent nuclear family places immense pressure on parents to maintain a home of their own. Thus, even when parents in my sample recognized that doubling up was the best option available to them, they also invoked norms labeling such a household as insufficient. Poverty often places people in positions like this, where internalized societal expectations are inconsistent with the opportunities available to them. Mothers hold marriage as an ideal even when they are unable to clear the economic and relationship bars that would enable them to obtain this ideal.[19] Low-income workers find dignity in earning a paycheck, even when their wages and benefits are insufficient to make ends meet and jobs are hard to find.[20] Parents who drop out of community college continue to be influenced by larger cultural discourses around the value of education and often plan to return to finish their degree, even when life circumstances make it impractical to do so.[21] So long as lower-income families do not have the supports needed to attain societally sanctioned goals, such conundrums are inevitable.

There is no reason that the independent nuclear family must be the archetypal family form in the United States. If societal ideals could be shifted away from the independent nuclear family and begin to valorize supportive social networks instead, parents might experience less dissonance between doubling up and their ideals of family life. In my sample, hosting, especially hosting older relatives, sometimes enhanced parents' sense of self-worth, even as they experienced the challenges of sharing space. However, reducing the undesirability of doubling up as a guest and ensuring that hosts have more flexibility to choose *not* to double up would require public supports and housing and labor markets that do not leave parents feeling forced into these households.

If the only parents who live doubled up were those who freely chose this arrangement, despite having alternative paths to pursue their goals, it is likely that far fewer families would face the challenges described in this book.[22] Moreover, doubling up by choice could be a more stable arrangement, and household stability has positive impacts on child well-being.[23] In my sample, the understanding that doubling up as a guest was a temporary stop for working-age adults in the pursuit of their residential and economic goals made these households inherently unstable. And as demonstrated in chapters 7 and 8, the sense of instability that accompanied doubling up affected how parents planned for the future—even when they remained in the same household for years.

Accounting for Doubled-Up Household Dynamics in Policy

The doubled-up households in my sample defied simple systems of classification. Distinguishing between doubled-up households formed by choice and those formed by economic necessity requires value judgments about when economic necessity is dire enough to no longer constitute a choice. As chapter 1 showed, guests' needs largely compel them to double up; that is, their choice to double up or not is constrained. Such constraint makes it challenging to draw a clear line between doubling up by choice and doubling up out of economic need. Is a parent who refuses to live in a neighborhood where they are scared for their children's safety doubled up by *choice*? When a low-wage parent puts off renting a home of their own because they know they will always be one missed paycheck away from potential eviction, are they *choosing* to remain doubled up? Facing a housing market that is increasingly out of sync with the low- to moderate-wage labor market, guest parents are often left with only bad options. Likewise, as chapter 2 argued, hosts' household formation decisions are constrained by the needs of their social ties and their loyalty to these ties, as well as their own financial and care needs.

Today's high rates of doubling up are the consequence of policy decisions, and this book has highlighted the need for policymakers to endeavor to reduce the constraints that lead families to rely on doubling up for support. Parents should be able to choose to raise their children in a home of their own, not as a guest in someone else's home. Parents should not be torn between providing housing for their family and friends and letting them flounder in a broken housing market. And rather than rely on extended family members and friends to stand in as private safety nets, we should strive for a housing market, a labor market, work-family supports, and public safety nets that leave fewer people behind. Until these lofty goals are reached, however, policymakers and practitioners should recognize the prevalence of doubled-up households and make explicit decisions about how to treat them.

Over eleven million children live in doubled-up households, and far more move in and out of them at some point during childhood, so keeping these families in mind is key to making effective and equitable policy. White, higher-income, and married-parent families are more likely to maintain the non-shared households that often serve as the presumptive family form in the United States. Thus, the failures of policy and research to consider and accommodate doubled-up families' needs fall disproportionately on the backs of families of color, lower-income families, and unpartnered-parent families.

The complex roles and relationships in doubled-up households have implications for how programs can best serve them. For instance, lines of authority in doubled-up households challenge guests' sense of autonomy and leave hosts struggling to maintain control over their home environment. Such intrahousehold dynamics may impact how families respond to programs' efforts to gather information on all household members; for instance, some guests may be unable or unwilling to ask for personal details from their hosts. These dynamics may also shape how families respond to and engage with program rules. For instance, recall that Ron from chapter 3 preferred taking the risk of housing unauthorized residents in his subsidized apartment over adding them to his lease and risking the loss of some of his household authority. As these examples show, understanding household relationships and the daily patterns of life in doubled-up households is important for policies that interface with doubled-up parents, children, or other household members.

Parents' stories of the challenges they faced while living doubled up also call into question common assumptions about what families need. Consider relationship education programs that focus on building skills like communication.[24] Or the range of institutions, from the federal Centers for Disease Control and Prevention to state university extension programs, that disseminate information to parents on the importance of consistent rules and routines for child well-being.[25] Chapters 5 and 6 showed that doubling up can undermine families' efforts to nurture their romantic relationships and to establish consistent rules and routines for their children. Of course, doubled-up parents, like all parents, may benefit from building their skills and knowledge around romantic relationships and parenting. But these chapters underscore that meeting parents' housing needs, as well as the needs of the extended family members and friends that parents might feel pressure to host, is key to truly empowering families to thrive in other domains of family life.

Likewise, doubled-up parents endeavored to provide safe homes for their children. However, their efforts were not always recognized by rigid definitions of what makes a home adequate. When Annalise in chapter 6 moved her children to the unfinished basement of her grandmother's home, she sought to insulate them from her verbally abusive uncle and the questionable visitors her stepfather brought to the home. Yet the unfinished basement sparked concerns from child protective services. Likewise, when Lisa allowed her cousin's family to join her crowded household, the social worker overseeing her foster parenting of her niece and nephew was concerned about crowding. Yet, by hosting, she was protecting another child—her cousin's young son—whom she was unwilling to "let sit out on the street." These cases demonstrate the difficult trade-offs that doubled-up parents face—trade-offs that do not always fit neatly into expectations about safe home environments.

Rethinking What It Means to Be a Household

The experiences of doubled-up families should lead us to reconsider at least two aspects of what it means to be a household. First, doubled-up households are rarely cohesive economic units that practice the risk-pooling we expect to see in households. As chapter 4 discussed, the official poverty measure defines a resource unit as members of a household who are related by blood, marriage, or adoption. Within this unit, resources and expenses are assumed to be shared; the entire unit is in poverty if its total income falls below a threshold that is determined by the number of people in the resource unit (or not in poverty if their total income falls above that threshold).

Yet, as chapter 4 showed, patterns of resource exchange in doubled-up households, including those formed with close family, are complicated, and coresidence does not imply full economic integration. Although doubling up does typically increase the total level of resources in the household, not all doubled-up families reap the full economy-of-scale benefits assumed by household equivalence scales, which adjust income levels for household size.[26] For example, to fully take advantage of economy-of-scale benefits for food purchases, household members must agree on types of food to have on hand and coordinate their shopping, and they should eat similarly to how they would if they were solely paying for the food. Yet food in doubled-up households is often a source of contention rather than a collaborative undertaking.

Moreover, patterns of exchange are often unpredictable. Guests who promise to pay their host a set amount are sometimes unable or unwilling to follow through. Hosts sometimes unexpectedly demand higher contributions from their guests. Sharing food with a household member at one point in time does not guarantee that this help will be reciprocated in the future. Resource-sharing practices sometimes change day by day and even hour by hour. Because doubled-up parents lack ownership over other household members' resources—and often do not even fully know what resources other household members have—treating the household as a single economic unit overstates the benefit that other household members' resources convey for doubled-up families.

More than 13 percent of children live doubled up with an extended family member.[27] These extended family members' incomes are treated as if they are available to the child's family when we determine resource units based on blood, marriage, and adoption. When doubled-up households are treated as a single resource unit, we are more likely to overlook the hardships faced by the individual families within these households. It can also become more challenging for them to qualify for the public support they need, as I discuss in the next section.

Second, we often think of household composition as relatively fixed, but the composition of doubled-up households is rarely static. In unstable households, household income reflects, at best, a brief snapshot of the average economic situation of household members. This instability poses a challenge for policies and programs that rely on household composition to determine eligibility, as frequent changes are unlikely to be picked up by programs that require recertification, say, annually. On the other hand, allowing benefits to fluctuate in response to every change in household composition, especially if these adjustments are delayed rather than immediate, would undoubtedly increase the instability and feeling of unpredictability that many doubled-up families already experience.

Furthermore, in my sample, parents' expectations about how long their doubled-up arrangements would last were often incorrect. Some guests were put out of the home by their hosts before they were ready to move. Others were doubled up for longer than they expected because of difficulty finding housing alternatives. Some hosts had guests who lingered, outstaying their welcome. Others had guests who exited unexpectedly, leaving the host scrambling to make up for the resources the guests had contributed. This unpredictability directly impacted families' well-being; some parents described a subjective sense of instability when living doubled up, even in relatively stable households. It also poses a challenge for policy efforts to identify stable and unstable households. For example, subsidized housing occupancy regulations that require householders to document long-term residents but not short-term guests assume that householders know how long their guest will coreside.

Acknowledging and Supporting Doubled-Up Households in Policy Design

The diverse ways in which shared households are encoded into policy reflect the incompletely institutionalized status of roles and relationships in these households, and it also creates a confusing system to navigate for families seeking public benefits. As described earlier, the official poverty measure includes household members related by familial ties (blood, marriage, or adoptive), but not nonrelatives. A wide range of programs rely on the official poverty measure to set eligibility rules, including Head Start, the National School Lunch Program, and the Low Income Home Energy Assistance Program.[28] However, the information that families can access about program eligibility rules is not always clear about whose income is included in eligibility determinations. For instance, a description of income eligibility for the National School Lunch Program thoroughly documents what kinds of income should be counted to determine eligibility, but it provides little guidance around *whose* income counts in shared households, and it seems to use the terms "household" and "family" interchangeably.[29]

Other social policies are based on Internal Revenue Service tax units, including subsidies in health insurance marketplaces and the Earned Income Tax Credit, one of the nation's most impactful antipoverty programs.[30] The IRS defines tax units based on marriage and a strict definition of financial dependency.[31] Under this definition, doubled-up households would typically contain multiple tax units. However, the lines defining the different tax units within doubled-up households can be confusing, and there may be multiple adults (such as a grandparent and a parent) who might claim the same child, though only one is allowed to do so.[32]

The Supplemental Nutrition Assistance Program (SNAP, also known as food stamps) has yet another set of rules for doubled-up households. In general, SNAP eligibility rules consider everyone who lives together and purchases and prepares meals together to be a single household.[33] This rule appears logical for a program providing food assistance, yet, as chapter 4 showed, the question of whether doubled-up household members shared food was often far too complex to be answered with a simple "yes" or "no." Moreover, even household members who shared most groceries with one another typically kept other resources separate, so looking at household-level income would not accurately reflect the resources available to each subfamily to use for food.[34]

In addition to the complexity that doubled-up families face in determining their program eligibility, program rules often penalize them for living doubled up.[35] In some means-tested public programs—like SSI benefits, subsidized housing, and some states' Temporary Assistance to Needy Family (TANF) cash assistance—program recipients can receive reduced benefits if doubling up has reduced their housing costs.[36] Other programs penalize doubling up less explicitly by determining benefits and eligibility using household equivalence scales that disadvantage larger, shared households.[37] For instance, a two-person household might qualify for SNAP with up to approximately $2,140 of income each month. But if two two-person households combine to form a four-person household, their income will have to be below $3,250 a month in order to qualify.[38]

Accounting for all resources that may be available to the family and the potential impacts of economies of scale may seem like a laudable goal when determining eligibility for public programs and benefit amounts. Yet as chapter 4 showed, this goal is far more complicated than it may appear. The current system of inconsistent, often confusing program rules seems unlikely to accurately capture the complexity and fluctuations of resource-sharing in doubled-up households.

Moreover, program rules that penalize larger households may discourage doubling up. For example, lowering housing costs was a main goal of guest families and an important benefit for economically precarious hosts. Reducing public benefits to account for these savings increases the costs of using the private safety net for guests and of providing this safety net for hosts. Given that doubling up is often a *response* to inadequate public support for lower-income adults and families, making doubling up a less viable option risks undermining an important stopgap for the public safety net.

Conclusion

At the end of one of her interviews, Eva asked what the research team would do with her story. As I explained my goal—of informing people and policy-makers about the lives of families like hers—she interjected, "You guys are basically the voice for us who can't necessarily take this to a higher power." Parents like Eva hoped that their stories will convince policymakers of the challenges that they experience on a day-to-day basis and prompt these officials to respond. Like so many families, she and Dylan responded to the economic and housing barriers they faced by doubling up. This safety net solution brought problems of its own; the challenges of navigating adulthood, child-rearing, her romantic relationship, and finances while living under someone else's roof overwhelmed her. Moreover, despite years of living doubled up in the hopes that, with enough time and hard work, everything would eventually work out—that they would become financially stable and find affordable, desirable housing—it simply never happened. Their housing options remained limited: they could either live doubled up or spend every penny they had to live precariously in independent, but substandard, housing. Doubling up cannot solve the challenges that parents like Eva face, even if it can help them weather those challenges for a time. These families need policies that address the compounded challenges they confront daily and that free them from reliance on the private safety net.

ACKNOWLEDGMENTS

FIRST AND FOREMOST, I am grateful to the families who shared their stories with me and made this book possible.

This book also would not have been possible without the efforts of the How Parents House Kids (HPHK) study team. I am grateful to HPHK co-PIs Kathryn Edin and Stefanie DeLuca for leading the study, and also for their indispensable mentorship in qualitative methods, generous feedback on the manuscript, and enthusiastic support for this book project from beginning to end. HPHK was made possible by the generosity of the Annie E. Casey Foundation and the John D. and Catherine T. MacArthur Foundation. Data collection was truly a team effort, and I am grateful to the entire HPHK team. HPHK fieldwork was conducted by Eva Rosen, Melody Boyd, Asad Asad, Monica Bell, Angela Simms, Siri Warkentien, Kelley Fong, Meredith Greif, Philip Garboden, Ann Owens, Beth Schueler, Kristin Perkins, Kathryn Reed, Hilario Dominguez, Holly Howell Koogler, Barbara Kiviat, Kaitlin Edin-Nelson, Sophie Damas, Jennifer Darrah, Anna Rhodes, Elizabeth Talbert, Jessica Tollette, Margot Moinester, Brielle Bryan, Jennifer Ferentz, and myself. Crucial logistics support was provided by Terri Thomas, Megan Prior, and Jessie Albee.

I am grateful to Jennifer Bouek, Christina Cross, Kelley Fong, Anna Rhodes, and Casey Stockstill, who provided feedback on many chapter drafts. Their insights improved this book in so many ways, and their camaraderie made the book-writing process far more fun. Brian McCabe, Jennifer Randles, Jennifer Silva, and Laura Tach generously read the book in full and participated in a book conference. Having four scholars whose research I so admire read my book and spend a day discussing it was a highlight of my career so far, and their feedback was invaluable for revising and improving this manuscript. Edward Morris, Brielle Bryan, and Margot Moinester read early writing for the book and also gave thoughtful feedback. I cite research by Natasha Pilkauskas, Kristin Perkins, and Mariana Amorim throughout the book, and my conversations with each of them have also deeply shaped my thinking on doubling up. I received research support from University of Kentucky students Andrew Sullivan, Jessica Thomas, Tanya Gardner, Samanta Laskar, and Vinh Dao. Lisa Adams expertly helped me navigate the book publishing process.

I was in graduate school when I began studying doubled-up households and collected my qualitative data, and this book would not have been possible without the support I received at that time. I am grateful for my dissertation committee members who guided me in data collection and analysis and helped me develop as a scholar: Sasha Killewald, Devah Pager, Mario Small, and Kathryn Edin. I also greatly appreciate the support and mentorship that Rachel Dunifon, Laura Tach, and Kelley Musick provided during my postdoc. Their advice and collaborations helped me continue to grow as a scholar, and they expanded my understanding of doubled-up households and the private safety net more broadly.

My research was generously supported by several funders. Besides the support from the Annie E. Casey Foundation and the John D. and Catherine T. MacArthur Foundation that made the HPHK study possible, the MacArthur Foundation also funded my supplemental fieldwork on doubling up. The Harvard University Center for American Political Studies funded pilot interviews for this research. I received additional support and funding from the Radcliffe Institute for Advanced Study at Harvard University, the Harvard Joint Center for Housing Studies, the Penn Social Science and Policy Forum Summer Institute on Inequality, and the Harvard Multidisciplinary Program in Inequality and Social Policy.

Finally, I thank my family. Your love and support have made this book, along with everything else in my life, possible.

Methods Appendix

Definitions of Doubling Up, Hosts, and Guests

In this book, I define doubled-up households using the demographic definition, which is relatively broad. According to this definition, a doubled-up household is any household that includes an adult besides the householder and the householder's romantic partner. The demographic research that employs this definition has shown that this type of household is very common among families with children in the United States and has increased rapidly in recent decades. These findings motivated my interest in this household type, but I was open to adjusting my definition of doubled-up households based on what I found in my fieldwork. However, despite the broadness of this definition, it seemed to resonate with the perspectives of the families in my sample. They did not typically use the term "doubled up," and in fact no clear term emerged from my fieldwork for doubled-up households. But parents did draw a sharp distinction between nuclear family households and other arrangements. In this way, doubled-up households are defined more by what they are *not* than by what they are. As I discuss in the introduction, this definition reflects assumptions around the independent nuclear family.

Consistent with the idea that doubling up involves adults beyond the nuclear family, doubling up was seen as distinct from cohabiting. Multiple parents brought up differences between sharing a household with a romantic partner and sharing a household with someone else. For instance, whereas parents said that they could be a co-householder with their romantic partner—with one "lady of the house," as Lauren in chapter 3 put it—they were more likely to suggest that other adults could not share householder status in the same way. This assumption reflected and reinforced the importance of householder status in doubled-up arrangements.

During fieldwork, I also met families whose living arrangements seemed similar to doubling up, including parents who paid less than market rate rent for housing owned by an extended family member and parents who lived in duplexes with extended family members in a separate unit. I considered including such families in my sample, but my conversations with them suggested that their experiences were distinct from those of doubled-up families. Primarily because these families did not have to share household space with others, they were able to maintain physical boundaries around their nuclear family life and avoid many of the day-to-day challenges that the doubled-up families in my sample faced.

The definition I use is broader than the definition for doubled-up homelessness. Scholars of homelessness typically limit the term "doubled up" to guest families whose financial need has compelled them to live temporarily in someone else's home. As chapter 1 discussed, the line between doubling up as a guest for economic reasons and doubling up by choice is often gray, and differentiating between these categories is not clear-cut. And as chapters 7 and 8 showed, parents were not always able to predict how temporary or permanent their doubled-up arrangement would be. Thus, the line between doubled-up homelessness and choosing to double up appeared ambiguous in my sample, and I did not limit my sample based on where families fell along this continuum.

Finally, I use the terms "host" and "guest" in this study to refer, respectively, to doubled-up householders and the people they house. The importance of householder status emerged inductively from my interviews, but parents did not use the terms "host" and "guest." I chose to use the terms "host" and "guest" because they are concise and hold intuitive meanings for readers. Although these terms convey the importance of householder status and the authority this status conveys, they are imperfect. It seems unlikely, for example, that a mother who has lived her entire life in her natal home considers herself a "guest" there; however, in my sample, it was meaningful to such mothers that they were living in a home that was not their own. Likewise, the term "guest" may invoke more hospitality than guest parents typically experienced. For instance, we might not associate paying rent with being someone's "guest." In doubled-up households, parents living in someone else's home often contributed financially but still held a subordinate ("guest") position in the household. Despite these shortcomings, I use the terms "host" and "guest" because of the importance of distinguishing between these two roles and because I have not found alternative terms that are more precise. Other research has used the terms "host" and "guest,"[1] "householder" and "additional adults,"[2] and "informal housing providers" and "guests."[3]

Sampling and Recruitment

The data presented in this book come from a subsample of the How Parents House Kids study. The HPHK data are the product of collaborative efforts from a team of interviewers led by Stefanie DeLuca and Kathryn Edin. The Annie E. Casey Foundation and the John D. and Catherine T. MacArthur Foundation funded data collection. The HPHK interviewing team included Eva Rosen, Melody Boyd, Asad Asad, Monica Bell, Angela Simms, Siri Warkentien, Kelley Fong, Meredith Greif, Philip Garboden, Ann Owens, Beth Schueler, Kristin Perkins, Kathryn Reed, Hilario Dominguez, Holly Howell Koogler, Barbara Kiviat, Kaitlin Edin-Nelson, Sophie Damas, Jennifer Darrah, Anna Rhodes, Elizabeth Talbert, Jessica Tollette, Margot Moinester, Brielle Bryan, and Jennifer Ferentz. As a member of the HPHK team, I served as an interviewer at the Cleveland site in the summer of 2013, co-managed the Cleveland site in the summer of 2014, and also completed interviews in Dallas in the summer of 2014. As described later, I completed independent data collection with doubled-up families in both Dallas and Cleveland as well. Because the HPHK data collection process was collaborative, I use the first-person plural ("we") to describe the sampling, recruitment, and interviewing process.

As described in the introduction, HPHK sampled households with young children from Dallas County, Texas, and Cuyahoga County, Ohio, which are relatively low- to moderate-cost housing markets. The HPHK team took a sample of census block groups from Dallas and Cuyahoga Counties stratified by racial composition (majority-White and majority-Black in Cuyahoga County and majority-White, majority-Black, and majority-Hispanic in Dallas County) and median income (under $25,000, $25,000 to $50,000, and over $50,000). We oversampled lower-income block groups (three under-$25,000 block groups: two $25,000-to-$50,000 block groups: one over-$50,000 block group). To identify households with children, we visited randomly selected addresses in the sampled block groups. In households with at least one child between the ages of three and eight, we invited the children's primary caregiver to participate in the study. The majority of these primary caregivers were mothers, but my sample also included seven fathers, one grandfather, and five grandmothers. Most parents chose a pseudonym for themselves.

The two-year response rate for HPHK was 80 percent, achieved through repeated visits to households on different days and at different times to ensure that we spoke to as many parents as possible. This response rate reflects the number of households that were interviewed relative to the total number of households that were interviewed, declined to be interviewed, or were not contacted (some of which were likely to have been ineligible). Vacant addresses and households without children ages three to eight are not included in this calculation.

HPHK interviewers conducted in-depth narrative interviews. We were trained to view parents as *experts* about their lives from whom we hoped to *learn*.[4] We began our interviews by asking parents to tell us "the story of your life," from the beginning to the present time. This question garnered valuable life history, but it was also intended to get parents used to talking and to convey our interest in hearing long responses. The HPHK interviews focused primarily on residential decision-making, but interviewers also sought to understand the context around these decisions and asked questions about children, romantic partners, and making ends meet. We interviewed parents in the summer of 2013 and completed follow-up interviews in the summer of 2014. By typically conducting the interviews in parents' homes, we were able to observe the neighborhood, the home environment, and sometimes interactions between household members. After the interviews, we asked parents to give us a tour of their home, and most of them obliged, often pointing out aspects of their housing that they particularly liked or disliked.

From the HPHK sample, I identified all parents who reported doubling up at any point during the fieldwork years (2013 and 2014). For seven respondents, I also included in my sample a coresident adult with whom they were doubled up. I conducted additional interviews focused specifically on doubling up from the winter of 2013 to the spring of 2014, in the summer of 2014, and in the summer of 2015. These interviews were sometimes conducted in the home, but as needed, I invited parents to join me at a restaurant or another area away from other household members, where they might feel freer to discuss their living situation. During the course of fieldwork, over two-thirds of parents completed three or more interviews about their housing arrangements. Thirteen were interviewed once, six twice, sixteen three times, and twenty-five four or more times.[5]

In keeping with the narrative interview approach, I sought to learn how doubled-up families experienced their living arrangement. Many interview questions were very open-ended, such as asking parents "what works well" and "what doesn't work so well" about their housing situation. Their answers allowed me to learn what topics were most important to them. The respondents and I together determined the flow of the interview, and I sought to cover the topics in my interview guide as they came up organically. This approach also offered parents opportunities to share information that I had not planned to ask about. Of course, even if the topic did not arise naturally, I asked specific questions about household members' interactions around child-rearing, household rules, and resource exchanges to ensure that I had as much detail as possible about the household. I framed doubled-up households as a common household form I was interested in learning more about, and I sought to avoid imposing any preconceived notions about what it was like to live doubled up. In introducing the topic of doubling up, I attempted to convey interest in the arrangement without judgment, positive or negative, and to convey my eagerness to hear about both the challenges and joys of parents' households.

All interviews were recorded and professionally transcribed. I read the interview transcripts in full, going in chronological order for each parent in the sample. As I read, I wrote summaries of each episode of doubling up, a task that was surprisingly challenging because of the sometimes circuitous household history of some parents. Informed by my inductive analysis of the data and consultation of the literature, I wrote memos on emerging themes, then coded the interviews with these emerging themes. My analysis was an iterative process of cycling between these various steps—coding emerging themes in the data, reading transcripts, updating the case summary for each episode of doubling up, and writing memos. Along with the summaries of each episode of doubling up, I cataloged characteristics of each doubled-up household (for example, whether the parent was a host or guest, or whether a guest made a financial contribution to the host), as well as characteristics of each parent's full household trajectory (why they initially doubled up, whether they lived independently by their final interview, and so on). In my analysis, the relatively small sample limited the extent to which I could identify differences by demographic subgroups, although I do note throughout the book when differences were apparent.

My identity as a college-educated White woman without children and a Harvard PhD student undoubtedly impacted how I was seen by the parents I interviewed, who were predominantly lower-income Black and Latina mothers with young children. That they understood me to be an outsider was made clear in small moments, such as when a parent walked me to my car after an interview, worried that I was not used to neighborhoods like hers. Although

I was an outsider, my background was not what they might have guessed; I grew up in a low-income family who lived in subsidized housing and was the first in my family to attend college, I am the granddaughter of a first-generation Mexican immigrant, and although I have never personally lived doubled up, several of my family members have. As I entered fieldwork, I considered whether I could use anything from my own background to build some commonality with the parents I interviewed, but I found that, in many ways, being seen as a complete outsider was helpful. It allowed parents to easily take on the role of expert, teaching me about their lives. For the most part, I spoke as little as possible during the interviews, allowing parents to take the lead in our conversation.

In interviews, one of my primary concerns was that parents might express an opinion or preference because they thought it was what I thought they should say. I tried to mitigate the risk of social desirability bias as much as possible through narrative interviewing techniques and, in some cases, by probing further into interviewees' motivations. Conducting repeated interviews helped me develop rapport as the parents in this study and I got to know each other over the three years and our interactions allowed them to share their perspective multiple times. Not all interviews were as easy as others; a couple of parents very bluntly kept me at a distance, and when they did not want to talk more about a subject, they were more than willing to let me know. I am sure that others were wary of me but less forthcoming about it. But, for the most part, parents seemed pleased to have someone who was genuinely interested in quietly listening and trying to understand their life from their perspective. This book is possible because parents welcomed me into their homes and entrusted me with the stories of their lives and the details of their hopes and dreams for the future, and I am grateful for all that they shared.

Sample Characteristics

Like doubled-up parents nationally, the parents in my sample were disproportionately unmarried, more likely to be Black and less likely to be White, and had relatively low levels of education and income. As mentioned earlier, my sample is the product of a stratified random sample of households in Cuyahoga and Dallas Counties, with an oversample of lower-income block groups. This sampling strategy captured a broad picture of the doubled-up population. However, there were also several important differences between my sample and doubled-up parents nationally. Some of these differences probably

APPENDIX TABLE 1: Sample Characteristics, by Host/Guest Status

	Guest (n = 22)	Both (n = 11)	Host (n = 27)
Guest[a]			
Multigenerational	0.95	0.82	
Extended family	0.14	0.36	
Non-kin	0.14	0.45	
Host[a]			
Multigenerational		0.18	0.78
Extended family		0.64	0.44
Non-kin		0.27	0.22
City			
Cleveland	0.50	0.73	0.56
Dallas	0.50	0.27	0.44
Race			
White	0.09	0.09	0.15
Black/African American	0.73	0.73	0.67
Hispanic/Latino	0.18	0.18	0.15
Asian	0.00	0.00	0.04
Gender			
Male	0.09	0.18	0.15
Female	0.91	0.82	0.85
Education level			
Less than high school	0.23	0.09	0.19
High school	0.41	0.36	0.30
Some college	0.32	0.55	0.41
Bachelor's or higher	0.05	0.00	0.11
Relationship status			
Married	0.14	0.27	0.41
Cohabiting	0.32	0.09	0.19
No coresident partner	0.55	0.64	0.41
Income (median)[b]	$17,760	$12,000	$19,800
Age (median)	29	29	39

Source: How Parents House Kids (HPHK) study, 2013–2015.

Note: Individual characteristics measured at the summer 2014 interview (if available). Values reported in other interviews were used if 2014 values were unavailable.

a. Proportions do not sum to one because individuals could live in multiple types of doubled-up households over the fieldwork years.

b. Income includes formal and informal employment, benefits from SSI (supplemental security income) and SSDI (Social Security disability insurance), and child support. If the parent shared income with a coresidential romantic partner, the partner's income is included in this amount as well.

resulted from the specific characteristics of the two metropolitan areas represented in my sample. Cuyahoga and Dallas Counties were relatively low- to moderate-cost urban housing markets, so future work should explore how well my findings match the experiences of parents in other housing markets, such as extremely high-cost areas and rural areas.

Compared to parents with children (of any age) nationally, the doubled-up parents in my sample were less likely to have a bachelor's degree.[6] Parents with some college were disproportionately represented in my sample, so it is possible that some of these parents will complete their education at a later point. The parents in my sample also had income levels below the national average for doubled-up families, especially for hosts. Some of the differences in education level and income between my sample and national samples may reflect the relatively low housing costs in Cuyahoga and Dallas Counties. In higher-cost areas, where housing unaffordability is common even further up the income ladder, doubling up may be necessary for an even wider array of families.

My sample was almost entirely comprised of White, Black, and Hispanic/ Latino parents. Compared to doubled-up parents nationally, Black parents were disproportionately represented in my sample, most likely reflecting the demographics of the two metropolitan areas sampled. Although Asian families have high rates of doubling up as hosts of multigenerational households,[7] this population is underrepresented in my sample, probably because of the cities and block groups that HPHK sampled.

Because my sample includes only HPHK parents who preferred to complete their interviews in English, more recent immigrants are also underrepresented in my sample. As I note in the introduction, other scholars have documented the important role of doubling up in immigrant communities.[8] This book captures only a piece of that experience. Likewise, my sample does not provide insight into how cultural differences may influence experiences of doubling up. For instance, familistic values are commonly posited to drive Latino immigrants' high rates of doubling up, though research on Latino immigrants finds that structural forces play an important role in household formation differences that are often assumed to be driven by cultural factors.[9] My sample, however, does not allow for an analysis of potential cultural differences in experiences of doubling up.

My sample was disproportionately unmarried and particularly likely to live without a romantic partner, especially those who were guests. The marital status of parents in my sample was quite similar to statistics from national data, though hosts in my sample were somewhat less likely to be married than hosts nationally, again potentially reflecting the negative selection into doubling up in my two research sites.

My findings were shaped by the child age ranges that HPHK sampled. Because children ages three to eight require substantial supervision, their presence may provide more opportunities for both child-rearing support and interference than households with older children. Likewise, young children's grandparents tend to be relatively young, given that the median age at transition to grandparenthood in the United States is forty-nine for women and fifty-two for men.[10] Samples of doubled-up households with older children might include more households that involve parents providing care support for aging grandparents. Some parents in my sample did provide care for aging parents or grandparents—for example, Gabby in chapter 1, LaTonya in chapter 4, and Kevin in chapter 8—but this support may be even more important in older samples. Likewise, given the ages of the sampled parents' children, combined with the relatively low price of housing in Dallas and Cleveland, many households of recent college graduates who "boomeranged" back to their parents' homes are likely to have been omitted. There are many reasons to expect that this population has different—and likely more positive—experiences of doubling up than the largely lower- and moderate-income parents of young children in my sample.[11]

Doubling up as a guest is particularly common among mothers of infants and mothers giving birth to their first child. In my sample, some mothers described a greater acceptance of the need to double up as a guest as they made the transition to motherhood. Recall Isa from chapter 6, who described initially wanting her mother's help when she first became a young mother, even though she now wanted to live independently and with less interference from her mother. Some mothers who lived doubled up when they had their first child suggested that the child-rearing advice they received from their own mothers had taught them how to be a mother, and they did not suggest that this advice was unwelcome. It is impossible to know from my data whether this sentiment was driven by rosy retrospective reporting or a true difference in how mothers experience doubled-up households at different points.

For this book, I focused on the experiences of doubled-up families. Because I selected on doubled-up status, my findings do not speak to differences in propensity to double up. For instance, I did not find distinct experiences by race and ethnicity among parents who were doubled up (though my sample size and sample characteristics limited this analysis), but rates of doubling up do vary dramatically by race and ethnicity. These differences are in part explained by the disproportionate burden that the precarity of the modern labor and housing markets places on families of color. Yet racial and ethnic variation in rates of doubling up remain even after adjusting for economic need.[12] What forces shape families' decisions about whether or not to double up, and how this may vary by race and ethnicity, is an important question for future research.

Finally, my data collection took place between 2013 and 2015. Rates of doubling up began increasing before this period and have continued to grow in the years since.[13] Growth in doubling up has been greatest among more advantaged groups, such as older, more educated, and married mothers.[14] Disadvantage remains highly correlated with doubling up, but it will be interesting to explore how the changing composition of the doubled-up population may (or may not) shift how parents experience and interpret living doubled up. My data collection also took place prior to the Covid-19 pandemic, when rates of doubling up increased dramatically before returning to their expected levels.[15] This book has provided insights into the childcare and economic support that parents may have sought by doubling up during the pandemic, as well as the challenges they may have faced in these households. However, it remains an open question how doubling up during a national emergency may differ from or be similar to doubling up at other times.

APPENDIX TABLE 2: Characteristics of Quoted Parents

Name	City	Age	Race/ Ethnicity	Number of Minor Children	Coresident Partner	Income	Education Level	Doubling Up Episode(s) Described
Annalise	Cleveland	26	White	2	None	$8,000	Some college	Guest of grandmother, ex-boyfriend's mother
Anrisa	Dallas	27	Black	2	Partner	$12,000	High school	Guest of mother, friends, brother, sister, uncle-in-law, cousin-in-law; host of siblings and cousins
Dana	Dallas	28	Black	2	Partner	$6,000	Less than high school	Host of mother-in-law
Eva	Cleveland	22	Multiracial	2	Partner	$20,000	Less than high school	Guest of mother-in-law
Gabby	Dallas	38	Black	2	None	$35,000	Some college	Guest of stepfather
Gail	Dallas	54	Black	2	None	$27,000	Some college	Host of adult daughter, sister; guest of father
Hope	Cleveland	47	Asian	3	Spouse	$150,000	BA	Host of mother-in-law and father-in-law
Isa	Dallas	29	Hispanic	3	None	$6,000	Some college	Guest of mother
JC	Dallas	47	Black	4	None	$37,000	High school	Host of nephew, niece, niece's husband
Jennifer	Dallas	24	Hispanic	3	Partner	$22,000	High school	Guest of mother, father
Joe	Cleveland	52	White	3	Spouse	$84,000	Some college	Host of sister-in-law
June	Cleveland	23	Black	2	None	$11,000	High school	Guest of aunt; host and guest of sister-in-law, brother-in-law
Katy	Dallas	38	Black	2	None	$17,000	Less than high school	Guest of mother
Keneisha	Cleveland	21	Black	1	None	$13,000	High school	Guest of mother, father
Kenya	Cleveland	39	Black	5	Partner	$16,000	Some college	Guest of friend
Kevin	Dallas	52	Black	2	None	$19,000	High school	Guest of mother
LaTonya	Cleveland	29	Black	2	None	$30,000	Some college	Guest of mother
Lauren	Dallas	38	Black	2	None	$55,000	BA	Host of mother
Leeann	Cleveland	26	Black	4	None	$13,000	Less than high school	Host of father and father's girlfriend, ex-boyfriend's adult daughter, brother and sister-in-law, cousin and cousin's boyfriend; guest of brother
Lisa	Cleveland	40	White	4	Partner	$18,000	Some college	Host of cousin and cousin's husband
Lola	Cleveland	29	Hispanic	3	None	$2,000	Some college	Guest of mother

(continued)

Name	City	Age	Race/Ethnicity	Number of Minor Children	Coresident Partner	Income	Education Level	Doubling Up Episode(s) Described
Lorraine	Dallas	30	Black	4	None	$20,000	High school	Guest of mother
Moke	Cleveland	34	Black	3	None	$16,000	Less than high school	Host of friend
Noelle	Dallas	25	Black	2	None	$22,000	High school	Guest of mother
Papi	Cleveland	59	White	5	None	$35,000	BA	Host of brother, adult daughters, adult granddaughter, granddaughter's friend
Paula	Cleveland	32	Hispanic	4	None	$16,000	Some college	Host of cousin and cousin's husband
Ron	Dallas	31	Black	1	Spouse	$10,000	Some college	Host of friends, brother-in-law; guest of friend, mother
Samantha	Dallas	30	Black	2	None	$9,000	High school	Host of mother-in-law, brother-in-law, sister-in-law; guest of grandmother, mother-in-law
Shay	Dallas	27	Black	2	Partner	$7,000	High school	Guest of godmother's niece, cousin-in-law, cousin, mother
Simone	Cleveland	24	Multiracial	1	Partner	$10,000	Some college	Guest of father, friends, mother-in-law, brother-in-law, sister-in-law
Sonya	Cleveland	43	Black	3	Spouse	$0	High school	Host of adult daughter and daughter's boyfriend, brother
Starr	Cleveland	36	Black	3	None	$15,000	High school	Host of adult daughter, friend, sister and sister's boyfriend, nephew and nephew's girlfriend
TaKayla	Cleveland	23	Black	2	None	$13,000	High school	Guest of grandmother, mother
Teresa	Dallas	29	Hispanic	2	Spouse	$20,000	Some college	Guest of parents
Tina	Dallas	36	Hispanic	4	Spouse	$15,000	Less than high school	Host of friend and friend's girlfriend, sister-in-law, brother, nephew, adult daughter
Toni	Dallas	28	Black	3	Spouse	$19,000	High school	Guest of nephew

Source: How Parents House Kids (HPHK) study, 2013–2014.

Note: Demographic characteristics measured as of the summer 2014 interview (when available). Income, coresidence with a romantic partner, and number of children often changed over the fieldwork period. Income is rounded to the nearest $1,000 and includes formal and informal employment, SSI/SSDI benefits, and child support. If the parent shared income with a coresidential romantic partner, the partner's income is included in this amount as well. The last column (Doubling Up Episode[s] Described) summarizes the incidents of doubling up described in the book. I use the term "in-law" to refer to extended family of the parent's spouse or romantic partner.

NOTES

Introduction: The Rise of Doubled-Up Households

1. All names in this book are pseudonyms. Parents typically chose a pseudonym for themselves during the interview. I present quotations verbatim with the exception of filler words and repetition, which have sometimes been removed for clarity.

2. Harvey, Dunifon, and Pilkauskas, "Under Whose Roof?" Despite growing attention to doubling up, researchers and advocates define these households in a variety of ways. The broadest definition considers a household "doubled up" if it includes at least one adult besides the householder and the householder's romantic partner. Other definitions do not include coresidence with adult children as "doubling up," with some exceptions depending on whether the adult child is married, has children of their own, or is out of school. Finally, scholars of homelessness limit the term "doubled up" to guest families who are living in someone else's home because of financial need, though they conceptualize financial need in a variety of ways (Richard et al., "Quantifying Doubled-Up Homelessness"). I use a broader definition, in keeping with the demographic and sociological literature (see the methods appendix), but notably, determining which families in my sample would be considered doubled-up guests under the narrow definition of economic need is not straightforward. As I discuss in the next chapter, doubling up as a guest is often motivated by economic need, but parents have a range of alternatives.

3. Joint Center for Housing Studies, "The State of the Nation's Housing 2022."

4. Joint Center for Housing Studies, "America's Rental Housing 2024."

5. Joint Center for Housing Studies, "America's Rental Housing 2020."

6. National Low Income Housing Coalition, "Out of Reach: Texas."

7. Joint Center for Housing Studies, "The State of the Nation's Housing 2022."

8. Hacker, *The Great Risk Shift*; Seefeldt, *Abandoned Families*.

9. Kalleberg, "The Social Contract in an Era of Precarious Work"; Kalleberg, *Precarious Lives*.

10. Glass, Andersson, and Simon, "Parenthood and Happiness"; Schneider and Harknett, "Paid Family and Medical Leave in the US Service Sector."

11. Joughin, "Latest Economic Data Underscores the Need for Significant, Sustained Investment in Child Care and Early Learning"; Swenson and Simms, "Increases in Out-of-Pocket Child Care Costs: 1995 to 2016"; US Department of the Treasury, "The Economics of Child Care Supply in the United States."

12. A 2020 Economic Policy Institute report found that the average cost of childcare for a four-year-old in Texas was $7,062 a year. Costs for infant care were even higher, at $9,324. Economic Policy Institute, "Child Care Costs in the United States."

13. Chien, "Factsheet: Estimates of Child Care Eligibility and Receipt for Fiscal Year 2019"; Bouek, *Everything Is Broken*; US Government Accountability Office, "Child Care."

14. Bouek, *Everything Is Broken*.

15. Western et al., "Economic Insecurity and Social Stratification."

16. US Census Bureau, "Historical Living Arrangements of Children."

17. Gornick, Maldonado, and Sheely, "Single-Parent Families and Public Policy in High-Income Countries."

18. Ross and Bateman, "Meet the Low-Wage Workforce."

19. Bartram, "Routine Dilapidation"; Faber, "The Future of Segregation Studies"; Hyde and Fischer, "Latino Homeownership"; Rucks-Ahidiana, "Housing as Capital"; Rothstein, *The Color of Law*; Pager and Shepherd, "The Sociology of Discrimination"; Rosen, Garboden, and Cossyleon, "Racial Discrimination in Housing"; Krysan and Crowder, *Cycle of Segregation*.

20. Joint Center for Housing Studies, "The State of the Nation's Housing 2023"; Hepburn, Louis, and Desmond, "Racial and Gender Disparities among Evicted Americans."

21. Hepburn, Louis, and Desmond, "Racial and Gender Disparities among Evicted Americans"; National Equity Atlas, "Housing Burden"; Choi, "Unmasking the Real Gender Homeownership Gap."

22. Rosen, *The Voucher Promise*.

23. Joint Center for Housing Studies, "America's Rental Housing 2024."

24. Joint Center for Housing Studies, "America's Rental Housing 2024."

25. Administration for Children and Families, "LIHEAP FAQs for Consumers."

26. Tach and Edin, "The Social Safety Net after Welfare Reform."

27. Halpern-Meekin et al., *It's Not Like I'm Poor*. Nonetheless, the EITC does impact housing outcomes. Increases in the EITC improve housing outcomes for single mothers and reduce their rates of doubling up. Pilkauskas and Michelmore, "The Effect of the Earned Income Tax Credit on Housing and Living Arrangements."

28. Edin and Shaefer, *$2.00 a Day*; Edin and Lein, *Making Ends Meet*; Ryan, Kalil, and Leininger, "Low-Income Mothers' Private Safety Nets and Children's Socioemotional Well-being." Given the many potential benefits of doubling up for families like Isa's, doubled-up families could be considered relatively advantaged. The precarity of the modern labor market and the insufficiency of public supports make it nearly impossible for many families, particularly lower-income families, to get by without help from family and friends (Hansen, *Not-So-Nuclear Families*; Mazelis, *Surviving Poverty*). However, lower-income families also face constraints that limit the amount of social support available to them, such as disadvantaged social ties and distrust in their social networks (Menjívar, *Fragmented Ties*; Roschelle, *No More Kin*; Smith, *Lone Pursuit*). Such barriers to forming and maintaining supportive networks leave many parents feeling that no support is available to them. In a sample of mothers with young children living in urban areas, poor mothers perceived particularly low rates of support availability: roughly one in four had no one they could count on to provide financial assistance, and a similar share had no one who would provide housing. About one in five poor mothers had no one who would help with emergency childcare (Harknett and Hartnett, "Who Lacks Support and Why?"). By definition,

doubled-up guests who are living in someone else's home have housing support available. More broadly, for both hosts and guests, living in a doubled-up household suggests that parents have an active social support network, which many lower-income parents lack. In this book, I acknowledge doubling up's potential benefits—benefits that parents who do not have the option to double up may not have access to—while also attending to the unique challenges it introduces to families' lives.

29. Harvey, "Cumulative Effects of Doubling up in Childhood on Young Adult Outcomes"; Pilkauskas, Garfinkel, and McLanahan, "The Prevalence and Economic Value of Doubling Up."

30. In my sample, most households had a clear host and guest. I classified parents as hosts if they were the person named on the mortgage or lease. For households without a resident named on a mortgage or lease, I classified as the host the subfamily that would remain in the home if the doubled-up arrangement were to dissolve. The use by a small share of parents of the language of "roommates" suggested more equality than the host/guest distinction conveys. Even in these cases, however, householder status (and ultimate control over the home) tended to be concentrated in one subfamily.

31. Important exceptions include Vacha and Marin, "Doubling Up"; Keene et al., "Filling the Gaps in an Inadequate Housing Safety Net"; Ratliff and Seefeldt, "There's No Room, Not Even for a Dog."

32. Harvey, Dunifon, and Pilkauskas, "Under Whose Roof?"

33. For a discussion of cohabitation, see Sassler and Miller, *Cohabitation Nation*.

34. I use the demographic definition of "doubling up" (living in a household that includes any adult besides the householder and the householder's romantic partner) because it aligns with parents' understandings of these arrangements. Although parents in my sample did not use the term "doubling up," many subscribed to the nuclear family household ideal and treated shared household arrangements as something distinct, even if they did not have a term to describe it. See the methods appendix.

35. Harvey, Dunifon, and Pilkauskas, "Under Whose Roof?"

36. Amorim, Dunifon, and Pilkauskas, "The Magnitude and Timing of Grandparental Coresidence during Childhood in the United States"; Harvey, "Cumulative Effects of Doubling up in Childhood on Young Adult Outcomes."

37. Harvey, "Cumulative Effects of Doubling up in Childhood on Young Adult Outcomes."

38. Harvey, Dunifon, and Pilkauskas, "Under Whose Roof?"

39. Cross, "Extended Family Households among Children in the United States"; Harvey, Dunifon, and Pilkauskas, "Under Whose Roof?"; Pilkauskas and Cross, "Beyond the Nuclear Family"; Pilkauskas, Garfinkel, and McLanahan, "The Prevalence and Economic Value of Doubling Up."

40. Harvey, Dunifon, and Pilkauskas, "Under Whose Roof?"

41. DeParle, "The Coronavirus Class Divide"; Desmond, "Disposable Ties and the Urban Poor"; Edin and Shaefer, $2.00 a Day; Olsen, "Doubled-up for Dollars." Indeed, doubling up as a guest is considered akin to homelessness under certain conditions. For example, doubled-up students are considered homeless under the McKinney-Vento Act if they "lack a fixed, regular, and adequate nighttime residence" and "are sharing housing of other persons due to loss of housing, economic hardship, or a similar reason" (National Center for Homeless Education,

"Determining Eligibility for McKinney-Vento Rights and Services," 1). The definitions used by researchers to define doubled-up homelessness vary widely but focus on characteristics like the income level of the guest family and/or the entire household, whether the doubled-up arrangement is temporary, the relationships between the coresident adults, and household crowding. See, for example, Richard et al., "Quantifying Doubled-Up Homelessness."

42. Ruggles, "The Transformation of American Family Structure," 104.

43. Bashi, *Survival of the Knitted*; Domínguez and Watkins, "Creating Networks for Survival and Mobility"; Garrett-Peters and Burton, "Tenuous Ties"; Hansen, *Not-So-Nuclear Families*; Menjívar, *Fragmented Ties*; Pattillo, *Black Picket Fences*; Sarkisian and Gerstel, "Kin Support among Blacks and Whites"; Stack, *All Our Kin*; Ruggles, "The Transformation of American Family Structure."

44. Cross, Fomby, and Letiecq, "Interlinking Structural Racism and Heteropatriarchy"; Jarrett, "Living Poor"; Ruggles, "The Origins of African-American Family Structure."

45. Hansen, *Not-So-Nuclear Families*, 4.

46. Folbre and Nelson, "For Love or Money—Or Both?"; Parsons, "The Social Structure of the Family."

47. Hansen, *Not-So-Nuclear Families*; Mazelis, *Surviving Poverty*.

48. Brooks, "The Nuclear Family Was a Mistake."

49. Hansen, *Not-So-Nuclear Families*; Sherman, "Surviving the Great Recession."

50. Sarkisian and Gerstel, *Nuclear Family Values, Extended Family Lives*.

51. These differences may be shrinking, as countries with higher rates of shared households have shifted toward nuclear family households in the last fifty years. Esteve and Reher, "Trends in Living Arrangements around the World."

52. Esteve and Reher, "Trends in Living Arrangements around the World."

53. Hogendoorn and Härkönen, "Single Motherhood and Multigenerational Coresidence in Europe"; Esteve and Reher, "Trends in Living Arrangements Around the World." Among single mothers, multigenerational households also tend to be more stable in eastern Europe compared to northern and western Europe (Hogendoorn and Härkönen, "Single Motherhood and Multigenerational Coresidence in Europe"). Comparative research across Australia, the United Kingdom, and the United States shows that American children are more likely to live in multigenerational households at some point during early childhood, but multigenerational households in the United Kingdom are somewhat more likely to be stable over early childhood. Pilkauskas and Martinson, "Three-Generation Family Households in Early Childhood."

54. Reher, "The Aftermath of the Demographic Transition in the Developed World"; van den Berg, Kalmijn, and Leopold, "Explaining Cross-National Differences in Leaving Home."

55. Harvey, Dunifon, and Pilkauskas, "Under Whose Roof?"

56. Amorim and Pilkauskas, "'Excess' Doubling Up during COVID."

57. Differences in rates of multigenerational coresidence by maternal education level and race and ethnicity have strengthened over time. Rates of multigenerational coresidence began to diverge by maternal education level around 1980, and trends by race and ethnicity diverged after 1940. Black children experienced a sharp increase in multigenerational coresidence from about 1920 to 1950, compared to a more gradual increase for White children. Compared to Hispanic and Asian children, White children experienced a particularly steep decline in multigenerational coresidence after 1950. These trends have produced the sharp differences by race

and ethnicity we see today, with far lower levels of multigenerational coresidence for White children than for Black, Hispanic, or Asian children. Pilkauskas, Amorim, and Dunifon, "Historical Trends in Children Living in Multigenerational Households in the United States."

58. Carlson and Meyer, "Family Complexity," 7.

59. Carlson and Meyer, "Family Complexity."

60. Cross, Fomby, and Letiecq, "Interlinking Structural Racism and Heteropatriarchy"; Jarrett, "Living Poor." Of course, nonresident kin also often play important roles in families' lives, and the support of nonresident extended families is another important extension of family research. Cross, Fomby, and Letiecq, "Interlinking Structural Racism and Heteropatriarchy"; Jarrett and Burton, "Dynamic Dimensions of Family Structure in Low-Income African American Families."

61. Westrick-Payne and Wiborg, "Children's Family Structure, 2021."

62. Prager, "When the Forms Don't Fit Your Family."

63. Although FEMA later introduced more discretion to decisions about who within shared households should be considered separate, the rental assistance process remained ambiguous for families who had lived in shared households, and their doubled-up housing status subjected them to further delays in assistance receipt as they waited for approval to be considered a separate household (Reid, "Social Policy, 'Deservingness,' and Sociotemporal Marginalization"). Likewise, federal disaster relief is often provided to the "head of household," leaving adults who later double up in someone else's home no longer eligible for assistance. Bosick, "'Pushed Out on My Own.'"

64. Michelmore and Pilkauskas, "The Earned Income Tax Credit, Family Complexity, and Children's Living Arrangements."

65. Fong, *Investigating Families.*

66. Head Start ECLKC, "The Importance of Schedules and Routines."

67. Although there are exceptions, including Dunifon, Ziol-Guest, and Kopko, "Grandparent Coresidence and Family Well-being"; Fomby and Johnson, "Continuity and Change in US Children's Family Composition, 1968–2017"; Kalil, Ryan, and Chor, "Time Investments in Children across Family Structures."

68. Carlson and Meyer, "Family Complexity"; Cherlin, "Remarriage as an Incomplete Institution"; Cherlin, "The Deinstitutionalization of American Marriage"; Cherlin, "Degrees of Change."

69. Cherlin, "Remarriage as an Incomplete Institution"; Manning and Smock, "Measuring and Modeling Cohabitation"; Cherlin, "The Deinstitutionalization of American Marriage"; Cherlin, "Degrees of Change"; Nock, "A Comparison of Marriages and Cohabiting Relationships."

70. Cavanagh and Fomby, "Family Instability in the Lives of American Children"; Wu and Martinson, "Family Structure and the Risk of a Premarital Birth."

71. Cavanagh and Fomby, "Family Instability in the Lives of American Children"; McLanahan and Sandefur, *Growing Up with a Single Parent*; Desmond and Perkins, "Housing and Household Instability."

72. Mollborn, Fomby, and Dennis, "Extended Household Transitions, Race/Ethnicity, and Early Childhood Cognitive Outcomes"; Perkins, "Household Complexity and Change among Children in the United States, 1984–2010"; Raley et al., "Estimating Children's Household Instability between Birth and Age 18."

73. US Census Bureau, "Cuyahoga County Quick Facts."

74. US Census Bureau, "Dallas County Quick Facts."

75. Flanagan and Schwartz, "Rental Housing Market Condition Measures."

76. Flanagan and Schwartz, "Rental Housing Market Condition Measures."

77. This number reflects, for guests, the number of different hosts they had, and for hosts, the number of different family units they hosted. For hosts, I count adults who are closely connected (like romantic partners) as a single guest unit even when they move in and out at different times.

78. Although not a common occurrence in my sample, some households were formed with relatively new acquaintants, similar to the "disposable ties" described by Desmond, "Disposable Ties and the Urban Poor."

79. Parents who doubled up as both hosts and guests at different points during the fieldwork had a lower median income level than either parents who doubled up only as hosts or parents who doubled up only as guests, perhaps because this group is defined by their instability (that is, they must have lived doubled up as both a host and a guest during the fieldwork period).

80. Harvey, Dunifon, and Pilkauskas, "Under Whose Roof?" More research is needed to understand how doubled-up households' functions may vary within the diverse Asian population in the United States. See, for example, Kang and Cohen, "Household Extension and Employment among Asian Immigrant Women in the United States."

81. Menjívar, *Fragmented Ties*; Bashi, *Survival of the Knitted*.

82. Menjívar, *Fragmented Ties*; Bashi, *Survival of the Knitted*.

83. Amuedo-Dorantes and Arenas-Arroyo, "Immigration Enforcement and Children's Living Arrangements"; Van Hook and Glick, "Immigration and Living Arrangements"; Landale, Thomas, and Hook, "The Living Arrangements of Children of Immigrants"; Hall, Musick, and Yi, "Living Arrangements and Household Complexity among Undocumented Immigrants"; Sarkisian, Gerena, and Gerstel, "Extended Family Integration among Euro and Mexican Americans."

Chapter 1: Doubling Up as a Guest

1. Lee, Tyler, and Wright, "The New Homelessness Revisited," 503.

2. For instance, Matthew Desmond's ethnography in the city of Milwaukee describes many families who weathered eviction by moving in with family, friends, or even new acquaintances (*Evicted: Poverty and Profit in the American City*). Likewise, interviews with low-income mothers in Philadelphia showed that many families lived doubled up in someone else's home as a "temporary refuge" to meet their basic housing needs until they could afford residential independence again (Edin and Kefalas, *Promises I Can Keep*, 63; Clampet-Lundquist, "Finding and Keeping Affordable Housing"). In their study of the housing histories of very low-income families in Minnesota, Kimberly Skobba and Edward Goetz found that 89 percent of families had used doubling up, often in combination with homeless shelters, to meet their emergency housing needs ("Mobility Decisions of Very Low-Income Households"; "Doubling up and the Erosion of Social Capital among Very Low Income Households"). Doubling up is also common among low-income families with children who have experienced homelessness. Bush and Shinn, "Families' Experiences of Doubling Up after Homelessness."

3. Popular attention has also focused on young adults who live in, or "boomerang" back to, their parents' home (Settersten and Ray, *Not Quite Adults*; Newman, *The Accordion Family*; Blassingame, "The Joys and Pains of Multigenerational Households"; Sassler, Ciambrone, and Benway, "Are They Really Mama's Boys/Daddy's Girls?"). Much of this discourse has centered well-educated young adults from middle-class families who doubled up in their parents' homes to pursue financial or career goals that would facilitate economic security in adulthood. This pathway is similar in motivation to the parents in this chapter who made deliberate decisions to double up. However, the experiences and interpretations of doubling up as a guest in my sample of predominantly lower-income parents differed substantially from those of the primarily middle-class young adults in previous research. Elsewhere I have discussed how interpretations of doubling up may differ by parenthood status and class (Harvey, "When Mothers Can't 'Pay the Cost to Be the Boss,'" 278). Katherine Newman likewise contrasts the "decidedly middle-class perspective" of her mostly college-educated sample of young adults in a wealthy Boston suburb with the experiences of young adults from lower-income families. Newman, *The Accordion Family* (14, 115, 134).

4. National Alliance to End Homelessness, "State of Homelessness."

5. National Center for Homeless Education, "Determining Eligibility for McKinney-Vento Rights and Services," 1.

6. One mother did not fit into these categories. She had doubled up in her senior mother's home after moving from out of state to help her, but economic limitations had kept her doubled up by the time she entered the sample.

7. Higher rates of doubling up among Black, Hispanic, and Asian families compared to White families may reflect, in part, a greater affinity for household sharing among these groups. Income is negatively associated with living doubled up, especially as a guest, regardless of race and ethnicity (Cohen and Casper, "In Whose Home?"; see also Pilkauskas and Michelmore, "The Effect of the Earned Income Tax Credit on Housing and Living Arrangements"). However, race and socioeconomic class seem to interact in producing rates of doubling up (Angel and Tienda, "Determinants of Extended Household Structure"), and differences by race/ethnicity often remain even after controlling for economic resources and other family characteristics (Cross, "Extended Family Households among Children in the United States"; Harvey and Dunifon, "Why Mothers Double Up"). These findings suggest that there may be differences by race and ethnicity in whether families choose to live doubled up, even in similar economic circumstances. Because this book focuses on the experience of families who double up, examining racial and ethnic differences in the propensity to double up is beyond the scope of the data. The guest parents in my sample, regardless of race and ethnicity, broadly expressed a preference for being a householder if they could obtain desirable, affordable housing.

8. Taylor, *Race for Profit*; Bartram, "Routine Dilapidation."

9. McCabe, *No Place Like Home.*

10. Barnes and Jaret, "The 'American Dream' in Poor Urban Neighborhoods"; McCabe, *No Place Like Home*; Rothstein, *The Color of Law*; Korver-Glenn, *Race Brokers*; Haurin, Herbert, and Rosenthal, "Homeownership Gaps among Low-Income and Minority Households"; Oliver and Shapiro, *Black Wealth/White Wealth.*

11. Hall and Crowder, "Extended-Family Resources and Racial Inequality in the Transition to Homeownership"; Heflin and Pattillo, "Kin Effects on Black-White Account and Home

Ownership"; Heflin and Pattillo, "Poverty in the Family"; Sharp, Whitehead, and Hall, "Tapped Out?"

12. Joint Center for Housing Studies, "America's Rental Housing 2024"; Joint Center for Housing Studies, "America's Rental Housing 2020."

13. Pelletiere, "Getting to the Heart of Housing's Fundamental Question."

14. Joint Center for Housing Studies, "America's Rental Housing 2024."

15. Harvey and Dunifon, "Why Mothers Double Up."

16. Silva, *Coming Up Short*; see also Furstenberg et al., "Growing Up Is Harder to Do"; Kalleberg, "The Social Contract in an Era of Precarious Work."

17. Joint Center for Housing Studies, "State of the Nation's Housing 2024."

18. Flanagan and Schwartz, "Rental Housing Market Condition Measures."

19. In national data, the end of a coresident romantic partnership is associated with an increased likelihood of forming a shared household (Harvey and Dunifon, "Why Mothers Double Up"). In my sample, some parents sought support by doubling up after a romantic relationship ended. But as chapter 5 shows, some of the association between being unpartnered and living doubled up may also be driven by the difficulties of coresiding while living doubled up.

20. Harvey et al., "Forever Homes and Temporary Stops."

21. Eviction Lab, "National Estimates."

22. Lloro et al., "Economic Well-being of US Households in 2022."

23. Cleveland Housing Authority, "Frequently Asked Questions."

24. Abt Associates et al., *Study of Rents and Rent Flexibility*.

25. Dallas Housing Authority, "DHA Fact Sheet."

26. Acosta and Guerrero, "Long Waitlists for Housing Vouchers Show Pressing Unmet Need for Assistance."

27. Docter and Galvez, "Public Housing Fact Sheet."

28. Joint Center for Housing Studies, "Housing America's Older Adults 2023."

29. Scommegna, "Family Caregiving."

30. Joint Center for Housing Studies, "Housing America's Older Adults 2023."

Chapter 2: Doubling Up as a Host

1. Economic Policy Institute, "Child Care Costs in the United States." The financial benefits for Lauren of having Debra coresiding with her varied over time. When Debra first moved in, she provided full day care for Ezra. After back pain left her unable to care for the baby all day, Lauren put him in daycare at a cost of $400 to $500 a month, and Debra provided care only in the evenings, when Lauren went to the gym with her older son. Chapter 6 describes child-rearing assistance and interference.

2. Vacha and Marin, "Doubling Up"; Keene et al., "Filling the Gaps in an Inadequate Housing Safety Net"; Ratliff and Seefeldt, "There's No Room, Not Even for a Dog."

3. Harvey and Dunifon, "Why Mothers Double Up."

4. Bouek, *Everything Is Broken*; US Government Accountability Office, "Child Care."

5. Economic Policy Institute, "Child Care Costs in the United States."

6. Watkins-Hayes and Kovalsky, "The Discourse of Deservingness."

7. Leopold, "The Housing Needs of Rental Assistance Applicants."

8. Keene et al., "Filling the Gaps in an Inadequate Housing Safety Net"; Ratliff and Seefeldt, "There's No Room, Not Even for a Dog"; Harvey, Dunifon, and Pilkauskas, "Under Whose Roof?"

9. Mpondo-Dika, "Adversity, Ambivalence, and Mental Health."

10. In representative samples of US adults, hosts are more likely to have poverty-level personal incomes than are adults in non-shared households (Mykyta and Macartney, "Sharing a Household"). Likewise, for mothers, poverty- and near-poverty-level incomes are positively associated with becoming a host (Harvey and Dunifon, "Why Mothers Double Up"). Average maternal earnings for children whose families host non-multigenerational extended family are substantially lower than for families in non-shared households. Average maternal earnings for children whose families host multigenerational and non-kin households are similar to average maternal earnings for children in non-shared households, but compared to mothers in non-shared households, hosts of non-kin are much less likely to be married—and therefore do not have a second potential earner in the family (Harvey, Dunifon, and Pilkauskas, "Under Whose Roof?"). See the methods appendix for more discussion of how my sample compares to doubled-up parents nationally.

11. Wherry, Seefeldt, and Alvarez, "To Lend or Not to Lend to Friends and Kin," 6.

12. Gail entered my sample because she identified as the primary caregiver of her five-year-old grandson. Her interviews later revealed that Gail and her adult daughter shared caregiving.

13. These findings also echo previous work showing that cultural stereotypes shape the provision of social support. In her seminal study of the role of social networks in the job searches of poor Black adults, Susan Sandra Smith found that employees deciding whether to make a job referral to a friend or family member drew upon logics that were similar to those that employers deployed when making hiring decisions—logics painting poor Black adults as unmotivated job-seekers and risky hires (Smith, "'Don't Put My Name on It'"; see also Anderson, *Code of the Street*; Newman, *No Shame in My Game*). Job-holders worried that adults in their social networks were too unmotivated to follow through on a referral, that they would need too much help securing and later maintaining employment, and that they would be irresponsible workers who reflected poorly on the job-holder. These logics led the employed to carefully evaluate a job-seeker's history and reputation when deciding whether and how much to assist with their job search (Smith, *Lone Pursuit*, 58–59; Smith, "'Don't Put My Name on It'").

14. Soss, "Making Clients and Citizens"; Steensland, "Cultural Categories and the American Welfare State"; Watkins-Hayes and Kovalsky, "The Discourse of Deservingness."

15. Rosen and Garboden, "Landlord Paternalism."

16. Hughes, "From the Long Arm of the State to Eyes on the Street."

17. Guetzkow, "Beyond Deservingness."

18. Unger and Cooley, "Partner and Grandmother Contact in Black and White Teen Parent Families"; Hao and Brinton, "Productive Activities and Support Systems of Single Mothers"; Gordon, Chase-Lansdale, and Brooks-Gunn, "Extended Households and the Life Course of Young Mothers"; see also Kang and Cohen, "Household Extension and Employment among Asian Immigrant Women in the United States."

19. Seltzer, Lau, and Bianchi, "Doubling Up When Times Are Tough."

20. Watkins-Hayes and Kovalsky, "The Discourse of Deservingness."

21. Fictive kin terms were common among doubled-up household members, and parents often revealed that the familial relationship was fictive only after direct questioning. Given the frequency with which parents used fictive kin terms when describing their relationships, it seems

plausible that fictive kin may sometimes be misclassified as extended family members in survey household rosters. If so, researchers may underestimate the number of shared households formed by nonrelatives. For further discussion of the challenges of studying doubled-up households with existing survey data, see Harvey and Perkins, "Shared Housing and Housing Instability."

22. Abt Associates et al., *Study of Rents and Rent Flexibility*.

23. Kurwa, "The New *Man in the House* Rules."

24. Harvey and Dunifon, "Why Mothers Double Up."

25. Bashi, *Survival of the Knitted*; Menjívar, *Fragmented Ties*; Nelson, *The Social Economy of Single Motherhood*; Edin and Lein, *Making Ends Meet*; Newman, *No Shame in My Game*; Hogan, Hao, and Parish, "Race, Kin Networks, and Assistance to Mother-Headed Families"; Garrett-Peters and Burton, "Tenuous Ties."

26. Stack, *All Our Kin*, 123.

27. Garrett-Peters and Burton, "Tenuous Ties"; Portes and Sensenbrenner, "Embeddedness and Immigration"; Stack and Burton, "Kinscripts."

28. Wherry, Seefeldt, and Alvarez, "To Lend or Not to Lend to Friends and Kin."

Chapter 3: Authority and Autonomy

1. When initially asked, TaKayla was unsure about whether the household had a mortgage. "I don't want to tell you the wrong thing," she said as she ran to the other room to confirm with her mother. In later interviews, Rose provided details of the household bills. Like many householders, Rose claimed that she did not *need* TaKayla's contributions to make ends meet.

2. Although parents drew a strong link between adulthood and residential independence, it is important not to overstate the stigma of doubling up as a guest. Guests worried about not having their own home, and hosts sometimes disparaged the idea of relying on others for housing. Yet guest parents rarely mentioned feeling stigmatized for doubling up. As LaTonya, a mother described in chapter 4, put it, "We live in a world now where everything is really tight. And it's a lot of families that's moving back with each other because the money is not adding up anymore." As an adult with two children, she found living doubled up as a guest stressful. "I feel like I should be out on my own," she explained. Yet she recognized that her circumstances were common and that doubling up was, for the moment, economically rational, even if she planned to move out on her own when she could.

3. Macmillan and Copher, "Families in the Life Course."

4. Mouw, "Sequences of Early Adult Transitions"; Shanahan, "Pathways to Adulthood in Changing Societies"; Furstenberg, "On a New Schedule"; Furstenberg et al., "Growing Up Is Harder to Do."

5. Booth et al., *Early Adulthood in a Family Context*; Silva, *Coming Up Short*.

6. Schneider and Harknett, "Paid Family and Medical Leave in the US Service Sector."

7. Arnett, "Emerging Adulthood"; Hansen, *Not-So-Nuclear Families*; Mazelis, *Surviving Poverty*.

8. Furstenberg et al., "Growing Up Is Harder to Do."

9. Silva, *Coming Up Short*, 17; see also Mazelis, *Surviving Poverty*.

10. Arnett, "Emerging Adulthood"; Edin and Kefalas, *Promises I Can Keep*.

11. Of course, being the householder may not enable parents to prevent others, particularly their own parents, from trying to regulate their behavior. However, the link between householder

status and authority justified rule-setting. For instance, TaKayla imagined that conflict between her partner and her mother would be greater if she and her partner were the householders: "I know he has his habits and she complains about them. 'He shouldn't be smoking in the house. He shouldn't be drinking in the house.' And I know he's gonna be, 'How she gonna tell me what I can't do in my own house?'" As long as Rose was the householder, she was empowered to set rules, but, if TaKayla and Brandon had a home of their own, pushing back against this interference would be warranted. The potential for this conflict was one of the main reasons that TaKayla had doubts about whether she would want her mother to move in with her if she had a home of her own.

12. Clark, Burton, and Flippen, "Housing Dependence and Intimate Relationships in the Lives of Low-Income Puerto Rican Mothers"; Welsh and Burton, "Home, Heart, and Being Latina."

13. In Katy and Tiji's case, the distinction between host and guest was less explicit than in most households; they chose their house together after Katy found it online, and they sometimes referred to one another as "roommates." However, as the quotes in this chapter demonstrate, Katy was keenly aware that she was not the head of her own household. Tiji expressed no similar concerns. And whereas Tiji planned to live in the home long-term, reliably paid rent, and set and enforced rules in the household, Katy did not. Thus, even though she did not claim the home as solely her own, Tiji occupied a role similar to householders in other doubled-up households.

14. Hansen, *Not-So-Nuclear Families*; Parsons, "The Social Structure of the Family."

15. If Bennie had not moved in, Katy said that she and her siblings would have needed to help her mother pay rent if Katy moved out.

16. For a discussion of symbolic boundaries, see Lamont, *The Dignity of Working Men*; Small, Harding, and Lamont, "Reconsidering Culture and Poverty."

17. Likewise, PHAs may choose to allow voucher recipients to share housing with other voucher holders or unassisted families, pro-rating the total rent for the housing unit by the number of bedrooms for the voucher-recipient family. Corinth, "How Safety Net Programs Tax the Sharing of Housing"; US Department of Housing and Urban Development, "Use of Shared Housing in the Housing Choice Voucher (HCV) Program."

18. DHA Housing Solutions for North Texas, "Administrative Plan for the DHA Housing Choice Voucher Programs," 99.

19. Mazelis and Mykyta, "I Might Stay to Myself."

20. Edin and Lein, *Making Ends Meet*; Newman, *No Shame in My Game*; Sherman, "Surviving the Great Recession."

Chapter 4: Economic Exchange

1. Heflin and Pattillo, "Kin Effects on Black-White Account and Home Ownership"; Heflin and Pattillo, "Poverty in the Family"; Pattillo, *Black Picket Fences*. Likewise, Jody Agius Vallejo documents the family obligations that upwardly mobile Mexican American adults retain to poorer kin (Agius Vallejo, *Barrios to Burbs*).

2. Kochhar and Cohn, "Fighting Poverty in a Tough Economy, Americans Move in with Their Relatives"; Mutchler and Baker, "The Implications of Grandparent Coresidence for Economic Hardship among Children in Mother-Only Families"; Mykyta and Macartney,

"Sharing a Household"; Rendall, Weden, and Brown, "Family and Household Sources of Poverty for Black, Hispanic, and White Newborns"; Reyes, "Mitigating Poverty through the Formation of Extended Family Households."

3. Mykyta and Macartney, "Sharing a Household."

4. Reyes, "Mitigating Poverty through the Formation of Extended Family Households"; Mykyta and Macartney, "Sharing a Household."

5. Kochhar and Cohn, "Fighting Poverty in a Tough Economy, Americans Move in with Their Relatives," 11.

6. Short and Smeeding, "Consumer Units, Households, and Sharing." The supplemental poverty measure (SPM), an updated measure intended to better reflect the social and economic experiences of modern families, goes even further. Researchers developed the SPM in response to the limitations of the official poverty measure (OPM), and poverty rates from this alternative measure are often presented alongside those of the OPM. Whereas the OPM includes only married partners and their family members in the resource unit, the SPM expands the definition to also include cohabiting partners and their family members (Institute for Research on Poverty, "How Is Poverty Measured?"). Reflecting the dominant focus on the nuclear family unit, SPM updates to the poverty measure address the increasing number of romantic couples who cohabit but are unmarried, but they do not address the complicated resource dynamics in shared households. The SPM, like the OPM, treats coresident extended family members as part of the resource unit and coresident unrelated adults as outside of the resource unit.

7. Romantic couples, particularly married spouses, have normative support for pooling their income in what scholar Judith Treas calls a "common pot" approach to family finances (Treas, "Money in the Bank"). A 2013 study of US adults coresiding with a romantic partner (both marital and cohabiting) found that 64 percent pooled all of their money and kept none separate, while 36 percent kept some or all of their money separate (Eickmeyer, Manning, and Brown, "What's Mine Is Ours?"). Likewise, in a sample of mothers who recently had nonmarital births in large US cities, 73 percent of married couples combined all of their money, keeping none separate, and 52 percent of cohabiting couples did. The greater level of income pooling among married couples compared to cohabiting couples has been attributed to their greater level of institutionalization (Kenney, "Cohabiting Couple, Filing Jointly?"). With few clear norms about how economically integrated they should be, doubled-up households seem to have even greater flexibility in how they arrange their household economies.

8. Joint Center for Housing Studies, "The State of the Nation's Housing 2024."

9. Joint Center for Housing Studies, "The State of the Nation's Housing 2024." These numbers reflect today's rental market, but even at the time of my fieldwork (2013–2015), the shortage of low-cost rentals and the rental market shift toward high-end units were already well underway (Joint Center for Housing Studies, "The State of the Nation's Housing 2017").

10. Joint Center for Housing Studies, "The State of the Nation's Housing 2024."

11. Public cash transfers in this study include Temporary Assistance for Needy Families (TANF), Supplemental Security Income (SSI), unemployment benefits, and workers' compensation. Pilkauskas, Garfinkel, and McLanahan, "The Prevalence and Economic Value of Doubling Up."

12. Hardy, "Childhood Income Volatility and Adult Outcomes"; Western et al., "Trends in Income Insecurity among US Children, 1984–2010."

13. As this chapter suggests, payments were sometimes made inconsistently. The numbers presented here represent the expected monetary payment from guest to host, even if this payment was not made consistently.

14. Pilkauskas, Garfinkel, and McLanahan, "The Prevalence and Economic Value of Doubling Up."

15. AARP, "Long-Term Care Cost Calculator."

16. Furstenberg et al., "Growing Up Is Harder to Do"; Silva, *Coming Up Short*.

17. Although LaTonya had lived with her mother for years, doubling up had been intended to be a temporary arrangement, and she linked the efforts she was making to pay rent while living doubled up to the outlook she would need when living independently. "When I do get back out here, I'm not looking for any kind of handouts or anything, because I know I have to pay [rent]. I know I have to be about my business and maintain and be able to provide for [my children]."

18. LaTonya did use her contributions to push back against the idea that she had to give up all her rights by living in her mother's home. For example, she recalled an instance when her mother told her son that he could play his video game after she had told him he could not: "Like I told her, I could see if I was around here having you do it all and not providing any food and not paying any rent and just living off of you. Because when you're that, you keep your mouth closed, because you're not contributing. But I am contributing, so it's like, no, that's not about to happen, you're not going over my head." Although it was not clear that contributions purchased any rights in the home, guests like LaTonya did sometimes use them to claim some household authority and other rights (see also Harvey, "When Mothers Can't 'Pay the Cost to Be the Boss'").

19. After the police sided with her mother, LaTonya turned her attention away from enforcing her tenancy rights and focused on her immediate need for a place to sleep that night. Straightforward and well-publicized regulations around doubled-up guests' rights might improve the housing stability of the doubled-up guest population. At the same time, strengthening the right of guests to remain in doubled-up households would necessarily weaken hosts' control over their home, potentially prolonging negative arrangements. Moreover, as chapters 2 and 3 have shown, hosts greatly value their authority as householders, and more information and enforcement of guests' rights could deter potential hosts, weakening the private safety net.

20. Castner et al., "Benefit Redemption Patterns in the USDA Supplemental Nutrition Assistance Program (SNAP)."

21. Aussenberg and Falk, "Supplemental Nutrition Assistance Program (SNAP)." Although I cannot say for certain why only LaTonya and her children received food stamps, it appears likely that including the retirement incomes of her mother and grandmother in her application would have pushed the household out of eligibility. She said that her grandmother tried to apply for county assistance for insurance but found that her income was far above the eligibility threshold. Her mother and grandmother seemed to occupy a precarious economic position, with incomes too high to receive most public assistance, but too low to meet their needs without LaTonya's help.

22. Western et al., "Economic Insecurity and Social Stratification."

23. Kimbro and Denney, "Transitions into Food Insecurity Associated with Behavioral Problems and Worse Overall Health among Children"; Gundersen and Ziliak, "Food Insecurity and Health Outcomes"; Gee and Asim, "Parenting While Food Insecure."

24. Hochschild, *The Commercialization of Intimate Life*, 105.

25. Some parents hosted multiple guests and had different arrangements with each. This percentage reflects whether the contributions of *any* of the guests during the fieldwork period was an important source of support.

26. Childless young adult children seemed to occupy a unique place in the household. There often were few or even no financial expectations of them, even in households that were financially vulnerable. In contrast to her expectations for her friend, sister, and nephew, Starr tried to minimize the burden she put on her young adult daughter. She spoke in awe of the help her daughter provided in the first few months, and she was now reluctant to burden her with too many bills. Even with the threat of losing her home and having her utilities shut off, she hesitated to ask for money that might limit her young adult daughter's own activities. "She gives a little bit. I don't really try to take none of her money, but she gave me like a little bit here and there. I don't want nothing from her. She likes to shop and get her hair and nails done and all that stuff." Likewise, Tina, who hosted multiple adults with her husband, charged guests like her childless young adult nephews rent because "they needed to put [in] their part and they're grown." However, she did not require rent from her childless young adult daughter, who had been raised by her extended family and only recently had joined Tina's household. "[My children] are part of us," she explained. "She's part of my luggage, yes."

27. Garrett-Peters and Burton, "Tenuous Ties"; Domínguez and Watkins, "Creating Networks for Survival and Mobility"; Menjívar, *Fragmented Ties*; Roschelle, *No More Kin*. Moreover, even for middle-class families, the obligation to assist less well-off extended kin can drain resources that might otherwise strengthen their middle-class status (Heflin and Pattillo, "Kin Effects on Black-White Account and Home Ownership"; O'Brien, "Depleting Capital?").

28. Similar tensions appear in other studies of resource-constrained social support networks. For example, in her analysis of Salvadoran immigrant networks, Cecilia Menjívar shows that limited resources hindered supportive relationships between recent immigrants and their extended kin who immigrated before them; the former were often disappointed with the uneven support and reciprocity expectations of the latter. Yet these extended kin were often resource-poor themselves and felt taken advantage of by newly arrived kin who were unable to fulfill their reciprocity obligations. Menjívar, *Fragmented Ties*.

29. Stack and Burton, "Kinscripts"; Domínguez and Watkins, "Creating Networks for Survival and Mobility"; Garrett-Peters and Burton, "Tenuous Ties"; Portes and Sensenbrenner, "Embeddedness and Immigration"; Stack, *All Our Kin*.

30. Hansen, *Not-So-Nuclear Families*, 158. Similarly, social work scholar Edwina Uehara theorizes a spectrum of exchange types, with different expectations for reciprocity ("Dual Exchange Theory, Social Networks, and Informal Social Support"). On one end is "giving," in which reciprocity expectations are long-term; individuals giving support do not expect an immediate return but have a general sense that when they are in need, the recipient will "do the same for me." On the other end are "deals," like those made in doubled-up households like LaTonya's, in

which individuals engage in direct trades of one resource or service for another. Doubled-up household members sometimes used this contract-like language themselves, such as when Starr recounted her sister's remark that Starr should have made "an agreement" if she wanted her to contribute more to the household.

31. As Linda Burton and her colleagues have identified in their studies of low-income Black and Latina mothers, control over housing is a valuable resource that conveys power for low-income parents (Burton and Clark, "Homeplace and Housing in the Lives of Low-Income Urban African American Families"; Clark, Burton, and Flippen, "Housing Dependence and Intimate Relationships in the Lives of Low-Income Puerto Rican Mothers"; Welsh and Burton, "Home, Heart, and Being Latina"). Even when hosts did not pay rent—for example, because they received housing assistance or squatted in a home rent-free (like Leeann in chapter 3)—householders exercised substantial authority in the home and could charge guests rent.

32. Kochhar and Cohn, "Fighting Poverty in a Tough Economy, Americans Move in with Their Relatives"; Mykyta and Macartney, "Sharing a Household"; Reyes, "Mitigating Poverty through the Formation of Extended Family Households."

33. Clampet-Lundquist, "Finding and Keeping Affordable Housing"; Seefeldt and Sandstrom, "When There Is No Welfare"; National Alliance to End Homelessness, "State of Homelessness"; National Center for Homeless Education, "Understanding Doubled-Up"; Richard et al., "Quantifying Doubled-Up Homelessness."

Chapter 5: Romantic Relationships

1. Of married mothers, 3.9 percent live doubled up as guests and 7.3 percent as hosts; 12.1 percent of previously married mothers live doubled up as guests and 10.1 percent as hosts; and 22.4 percent of never-married mothers live doubled up as guests and 10.3 percent as hosts (Harvey, Dunifon, and Pilkauskas, "Under Whose Roof?"). Cohabiting mothers seem to double up at rates in between those of married mothers and unpartnered mothers. One survey of mothers with young children living in urban areas found that 38 percent of single mothers were doubled up, compared to 25 percent of cohabiting mothers and 13 percent of married mothers. Pilkauskas, Garfinkel, and McLanahan, "The Prevalence and Economic Value of Doubling Up."

2. Harvey, Dunifon, and Pilkauskas, "Under Whose Roof?"

3. Harvey and Dunifon, "Why Mothers Double Up"; Pilkauskas, "Three-Generation Family Households." Likewise, Pilkauskas and Cross find that reduced marriage and increased single parenthood were important contributors to the growth in rates of doubling up in recent decades. This study found that about one-fifth of the increase in three-generation doubled-up households between 1996 and 2009 was attributable to changes in mothers' relationship status. Pilkauskas and Cross, "Beyond the Nuclear Family."

4. Because of relationship and household instability, some parents lived doubled up both with and without a romantic partner during the fieldwork.

5. Other qualitative research likewise describes couples who view doubling up as incompatible with the financial stability expected of married couples and who want to be able to purchase a home before marriage. Gibson-Davis, Edin, and McLanahan, "High Hopes but Even Higher Expectations."

6. Some hosts did threaten to make mothers move out of their household and allow only the children to stay, but I never saw these threats realized. Some guest mothers took their children with them after being forced to move out of the home where they were doubled up, and some mothers left their children in the home where they were doubled up when they exited voluntarily.

7. Conger, Conger, and Martin, "Socioeconomic Status, Family Processes, and Individual Development."

8. Hosts had their own housing and therefore had more control over decisions about romantic coresidence. However, doubling up could affect hosts' romantic relationship progression in more subtle ways. Starr, the host mother from chapter 4, said that her sister, who was living in her home, "ran off my last male friend I was dating." One day when her friend was visiting, her sister cussed at him for making too much noise in the kitchen while cooking and washing dishes. After this altercation, her friend stopped visiting, and Starr blamed her sister. "I never seen him again because of my crazy sister. Nobody wants to bother with her." Although she held authority within the home—for example, she could (and did) kick her sister out of her home— doubling up still negatively affected the progression of her new romantic relationship. Unlike guests, however, hosts rarely described doubling up as a primary reason for living apart from a romantic partner.

9. Harvey, Dunifon, and Pilkauskas, "Under Whose Roof?"

10. Glenna Spitze and Russell Ward's study of intergenerational households suggests that women may also do more household labor than men when living with their parents ("Household Labor in Intergenerational Households"). In their analysis of survey data from 1987–1988, they find that adult daughters in intergenerational households spend more time on housework than do adult sons, and their housework time appears more responsive to household needs.

11. Giddens, *The Transformation of Intimacy*; Cherlin, "The Deinstitutionalization of American Marriage."

12. Coser and Coser, "The Housewife and Her Greedy Family"; Gerstel and Sarkisian, "Marriage."

13. McLanahan, "Fragile Families and the Reproduction of Poverty."

14. Randles, "Partnering and Parenting in Poverty," 399.

15. Sassler and Miller, *Cohabitation Nation*.

16. Edin and Kefalas, *Promises I Can Keep*; Addo, "Debt, Cohabitation, and Marriage in Young Adulthood"; Gibson-Davis, Edin, and McLanahan, "High Hopes but Even Higher Expectations"; Ishizuka, "The Economic Foundations of Cohabiting Couples' Union Transitions"; Schneider, "Wealth and the Marital Divide."

Chapter 6: Raising Children

1. Cross, "Extended Family Households among Children in the United States"; Harvey and Dunifon, "Why Mothers Double Up."

2. Harvey, Dunifon, and Pilkauskas, "Under Whose Roof?"

3. Harvey and Dunifon, "Why Mothers Double Up."

4. Harvey, Dunifon, and Pilkauskas, "Under Whose Roof?"; Cross, "Extended Family Households among Children in the United States."

5. A rich literature documents the important role of grandmothers in the lives of poor mothers and their children. See, for example, Jarrett, "Living Poor"; Stack and Burton, "Kinscripts"; Dunifon, *You've Always Been There for Me*.

6. Kalil, Ryan, and Chor, "Time Investments in Children across Family Structures."

7. Amorim, "Are Grandparents a Blessing or a Burden?"

8. US Government Accountability Office, "Child Care."

9. Dunifon, Ziol-Guest, and Kopko, "Grandparent Coresidence and Family Well-being."

10. Hao and Brinton, "Productive Activities and Support Systems of Single Mothers." These authors do not find evidence that living as a guest in an extended family household prevents unpartnered mothers from exiting school or work activities.

11. Chase-Lansdale, Brooks-Gunn, and Zamsky, "Young African-American Multigenerational Families in Poverty," 389.

12. Head Start ECLKC, "The Importance of Schedules and Routines"; Carroll, "Routines."

13. Hansen, *Not-So-Nuclear Families*; Nelson, *The Social Economy of Single Motherhood*.

14. Chase-Lansdale, Brooks-Gunn, and Zamsky, "Young African-American Multigenerational Families in Poverty"; Unger and Cooley, "Partner and Grandmother Contact in Black and White Teen Parent Families"; Wakschlag, Chase-Lansdale, and Brooks-Gunn, "Not Just 'Ghosts in the Nursery'"; Black and Nitz, "Grandmother Co-Residence, Parenting, and Child Development among Low Income, Urban Teen Mothers."

15. Gordon, Chase-Lansdale, and Brooks-Gunn, "Extended Households and the Life Course of Young Mothers."

16. Chase-Lansdale, Brooks-Gunn, and Zamsky, "Young African-American Multigenerational Families in Poverty."

17. Chase-Lansdale, Brooks-Gunn, and Zamsky, "Young African-American Multigenerational Families in Poverty," 389.

18. Lisa said that because she was a foster parent, she had to report any changes in household composition so that a background check could be done on new household members. Lisa's cousin and her husband did not have any difficulties with this process, but "if there was anything wrong with their background, then they couldn't live here with the kids," she said. Processes like these can create additional barriers to doubling up.

19. Edin and Shaefer, *$2.00 a Day*.

20. As described in the introduction, Isa blamed her relationship dissolution on her mother's interference.

21. Edin and Kefalas, *Promises I Can Keep*; McMahon, *Engendering Motherhood*.

22. Sherman, *Those Who Work, Those Who Don't*.

23. Hansen, *Not-So-Nuclear Families*; Mazelis, *Surviving Poverty*.

Chapter 7: The Challenges of Doubled-Up Household Dissolutions

1. In addition to benefiting from the rent Simone paid, Darnell's sister and her children depended on the food that she brought back from her job at Subway, especially when food ran short at the end of each month. "I'm sure she struggles a little bit too, because we helped a lot. Even though we did live with her, the money that we were giving her and the extra food did help," Simone explained.

2. Here I count individuals who moved in and out together or who were otherwise connected (like romantic partners) as a single unit. Because individuals from these groups sometimes moved in and out at different times, this is a conservative estimate of the instability that these host families experienced.

3. Harvey, Dunifon, and Pilkauskas, "Under Whose Roof?" For other analyses of the length of time that families spend consistently doubled up, see Pilkauskas, "Three-Generation Family Households"; Pilkauskas, Garfinkel, and McLanahan, "The Prevalence and Economic Value of Doubling Up." Because household composition can change even while the household remains the same "type," considering only instability between different types of doubled-up households (such as multigenerational, extended family, and non-kin) provides an incomplete portrait of the overall instability that doubled-up families experience. A parent who remains doubled up in a single type of household may still experience household composition instability; for example, such studies do not account for the kind of instability that Simone and Darnell experienced when they moved from the home of one sibling to the home of another.

4. Cavanagh and Huston, "Family Instability and Children's Early Problem Behavior"; Fomby and Cherlin, "Family Instability and Child Well-being"; Wu and Martinson, "Family Structure and the Risk of a Premarital Birth."

5. Heflin and Iceland, "Poverty, Material Hardship, and Depression"; Huang, Heflin, and Validova, "Material Hardship, Perceived Stress, and Health in Early Adulthood"; Chaudry and Wimer, "Poverty Is Not Just an Indicator"; Gershoff et al., "Income Is Not Enough."

6. Gennetian et al., "Intrayear Household Income Dynamics and Adolescent School Behavior"; Hardy, "Childhood Income Volatility and Adult Outcomes"; Hill et al., "An Introduction to Household Economic Instability and Social Policy."

7. Hill et al., "An Introduction to Household Economic Instability and Social Policy"; Western et al., "Economic Insecurity and Social Stratification."

8. Doubling up may play an important role in driving residential instability for renters. A survey of renters in Milwaukee, Wisconsin, found that 2 percent of renters' moves in the previous two years were due to "situations in which respondents wore out their welcome at temporary arrangements," 10 percent were due to a desire to move out of someone else's home and into their own unit, and 1 percent were due to disputes with roommates (Desmond, Gershenson, and Kiviat, "Forced Relocation and Residential Instability among Urban Renters," 245–46). These are all likely responses to living doubled up. Thus, the instability of doubled-up households appears to be an important contributor to overall renter household instability. (By comparison, formal evictions accounted for just 7 percent of moves.) Moreover, because the survey was typically given to the adult leaseholder, guests' moves from one doubled-up household to another may not be fully represented.

9. Haynie and South, "Residential Mobility and Adolescent Violence"; Mollborn, Lawrence, and Root, "Residential Mobility across Early Childhood and Children's Kindergarten Readiness"; Pribesh and Downey, "Why Are Residential and School Moves Associated with Poor School Performance?"

10. The McKinney-Vento Act defines as homeless those children living doubled up due to a loss of housing, economic hardship, or a similar reason. If Shay's daughter had been identified as homeless by her school, she would have been eligible for special protections to promote school attendance and continuity. Children who are experiencing doubled-up homelessness

may be able to enroll in a new school even if they are unable to meet the full documentation requirements, such as proofs of residence and legal guardianship. When remaining in their school of origin is in their best interest, they can request transportation assistance to and from the school (National Center for Homeless Education, "The Educational Rights of Children and Youth Experiencing Homelessness"). Shay did not seem to be aware of these potential supports.

11. In most cases, public housing authorities and owners of subsidized properties have discretion over whether to allow an adult convicted of criminal activity to live in their properties (Weiss, "Housing Access for People with Criminal Records"). However, given the value of subsidized housing, the perceived risk of disclosing one's criminal record could not be taken lightly by guests like Shay who were in need of housing—or by the hosts who housed them. Tiji, the low-income grandmother in chapter 3 who shared her home with her adult daughter Katy, described not applying for subsidized housing because she wanted to be able to host her brother after his eventual release from prison. "I haven't did any of that because you know they have their rules and regulations. And like I said, my little brother, he's incarcerated and he's ready to come home. If I go on and get Section 8, he can't come stay. And I'm not going to turn him away, and I'm not going to let him go stay in no shelter or leave him out on the streets." This quote shows yet another way that rules around subsidized housing occupancy force low-income adults to choose between needed support and their social ties. See Kurwa, "The New *Man in the House* Rules."

12. Western et al., "Economic Insecurity and Social Stratification," 354.

13. Paula also appreciated the opportunity to get more involved with Mary's daughter. While hosting, she set rules for the child and oversaw her cousin's parenting, for instance, by limiting how much she could spoil her daughter. Of course, as chapter 6 showed, the parenting guidance that Paula enjoyed providing may not have been appreciated by her cousin. According to Paula, Mary returned to her normal way of parenting—"letting them do whatever they want whenever they want"—as soon as she had a home of her own.

14. During her last interview, Lauren expressed more dissatisfaction with multigenerational coresidence than she had when discussing it just a few months prior. It was not clear whether this dissatisfaction had grown over the course of her coresidence with her mother or was simply her perspective in hindsight.

15. Overcrowding was certainly a concern in many doubled-up households, and it is easy to understand how limited space could increase tensions within the home. However, household space was not a reliable predictor of doubled-up household stability. For example, a couple of mothers who remained in their natal home into adulthood began sharing their bedroom with their children when they became parents but did not experience household instability. Likewise, Hope, an Asian mother, shared one bedroom—and a single bed—with her husband and two youngest children throughout the eight years she hosted her in-laws.

16. Most guests in my sample were still living doubled up as guests by the end of the fieldwork, but most parents who lived doubled up as hosts were no longer hosting, either because they were living independently or because they were doubled up as guests.

17. Harvey et al., "Forever Homes and Temporary Stops."

18. Bureau of Labor Statistics, "Real and Nominal Value of the Federal Minimum Wage in the United States from 1938 to 2024 (in 2024 US Dollars)."

19. US Department of Labor, "State Minimum Wage Laws."

20. National Low Income Housing Coalition, "Out of Reach: The High Cost of Housing."

21. Derenoncourt, Montialoux, and Bahn, "Why Minimum Wages Are a Critical Tool for Achieving Racial Justice in the US Labor Market."

22. Simone had recently offered to allow one of Darnell's brothers to stay with them "for a month or two." Although he turned down the offer, she remained open to hosting, especially for extended family members who had helped them in the past. "We don't have enough space anyway, but if we have to make it, for certain people we would."

23. Perkins, "Changes in Household Composition and Children's Educational Attainment"; Perkins, "Household Instability and Girls' Teen Childbearing."

24. Perkins, "Changes in Household Composition and Children's Educational Attainment."

Chapter 8: Getting By and Getting Ahead by Doubling Up

1. May entered the study as her granddaughter's primary caretaker. However, her interview suggested that Kevin held primary authority over parenting decisions.

2. Bartram, "Routine Dilapidation"; see also Taylor, *Race for Profit*.

3. Briggs, "Brown Kids in White Suburbs"; Domínguez and Watkins, "Creating Networks for Survival and Mobility"; Henly, Danziger, and Offer, "The Contribution of Social Support to the Material Well-Being of Low-Income Families." Briggs specifically distinguishes between social support (material and emotional assistance with daily needs) and social leverage (clout or influence that provides opportunities for mobility) ("Brown Kids in White Suburbs"). This distinction is less applicable to doubled-up households, which tend to provide instrumental and emotional support rather than information or connections. However, the distinction between support that helps families "get by" and support that helps families "get ahead," as elaborated by Henly, Danziger, and Offer, is a helpful framework for thinking about doubled-up households. "The Contribution of Social Support to the Material Well-Being of Low-Income Families."

4. Harvey, Dunifon, and Pilkauskas, "Under Whose Roof?"

5. For most parents, this duration is calculated as the time since they first moved in together. For parents who had remained in their natal home continuously since childhood, it is calculated as the time since they first became a parent (and thus eligible for my sample). For parents who hosted their own adult child who had remained continuously in their home since childhood, it is calculated as the time since the adult child turned age eighteen.

6. A couple of households with a parent hosting a grandparent were stable for at least two years, and in these cases the parent expressed a willingness or even desire to be a long-term host for the older relative. In my sample overall, more parents expressed an openness to long-term coresidence in which they would *host* a child's grandparent than were willing to being a *guest* of a grandparent (see chapters 2 and 3). Yet multigenerational households in which the younger generation hosted were not always stable. Chapter 7 described the unexpected departure from the household of Dana's mother-in-law; Dana was left unable to afford rent for the apartment she had shared with her. Likewise, chapter 7 recounted Lauren's experience when her mother moved out; she was left with more space, but also without the childcare assistance she was used to.

7. Jennifer's father also probably made a financial contribution to their home purchase, although the details around this contribution were unclear.

8. Whitehead, "Paying for Their Stay."

9. Leventhal and Brooks-Gunn, "The Neighborhoods They Live In"; Sampson, *Great American City*.

10. Landivar, Scarborough, Collins, and Ruppanner, "Maternal Employment Drops When Child Care Is Expensive and Hard to Find.""

Conclusion: The Imperfect Private Safety Net

1. Harvey, Dunifon, and Pilkauskas, "Under Whose Roof?"

2. Joint Center for Housing Studies, "The State of the Nation's Housing 2024"; Whitney, "More than 42 Million US Households Were Cost Burdened in 2022."

3. Harkness and Newman, "Housing Affordability and Children's Well-Being"; Joint Center for Housing Studies, "The State of the Nation's Housing 2024"; Angst et al., "How Do Renters Survive Unaffordability?"

4. Garnham, Gershenson, and Desmond, "New Data Release Shows That 3.6 Million Eviction Cases Were Filed in the United States in 2018."

5. Lloro et al., "Economic Well-being of US Households in 2022."

6. Joint Center for Housing Studies, "The State of the Nation's Housing 2023."

7. Ross and Bateman define low-wage workers using a threshold of two-thirds of median wages for full-time/full-year male workers. "Meet the Low-Wage Workforce."

8. Ross and Bateman, "Meet the Low-Wage Workforce."

9. St. Louis Federal Reserve Bank, "Comparing Unemployment Rates by Race."

10. Collins, *Making Motherhood Work*.

11. Khater, McManus, and Karamon, "Family Budget Burdens Squeezing Housing."

12. Bouek, *Everything Is Broken*.

13. Pittman, *Grandmothering While Black*.

14. Minkin et al., "Financial Help and Independence in Young Adulthood."

15. Evans, "Child Development and the Physical Environment"; Leventhal and Newman, "Housing and Child Development"; Sampson, Morenoff, and Gannon-Rowley, "Assessing 'Neighborhood Effects'"; Sharkey and Faber, "Where, When, Why, and for Whom Do Residential Contexts Matter?"

16. I borrow the phrase "culturally uncharted" from Furstenberg and Nord, "Parenting Apart," 893.

17. Edin and Nelson, *Doing the Best I Can*.

18. Mullainathan and Shafir, *Scarcity*.

19. Edin and Kefalas, *Promises I Can Keep*.

20. Newman, *No Shame in My Game*; Edin and Lein, *Making Ends Meet*.

21. Deterding, "Instrumental and Expressive Education College Planning in the Face of Poverty."

22. Of course, having the financial means to afford desirable housing of one's own did not guarantee that doubling up would be free from negative social ramifications. For example, Joe, a father in chapter 5, agreed to host his sister-in-law in part because he thought the additional

income would benefit his family. But he had a relatively high income and did not have to double up, and his sister-in-law also could have afforded her own home. By the time I met him, he worried that his sister-in-law's coresidence was weakening his relationship with his wife, but the option of ending the arrangement was no longer readily available to him given how satisfied his wife and sister-in-law were with doubling up.

23. Perkins, "Changes in Household Composition and Children's Educational Attainment"; Perkins, "Household Instability and Girls' Teen Childbearing."

24. Randles, *Proposing Prosperity?*

25. Carroll, "Routines"; Head Start ECLKC, "The Importance of Schedules and Routines"; Centers for Disease Control and Prevention, "Building Structure."

26. In general, poverty rates appear lower when the resource unit definition includes more household adults. See Iceland, "Measuring Poverty with Different Units of Analysis."

27. Harvey, Dunifon, and Pilkauskas, "Under Whose Roof?"

28. US Department of Health and Human Services, "Frequently Asked Questions Related to the Poverty Guidelines and Poverty."

29. US Department of Agriculture, "Child Nutrition Programs."

30. HealthCare.gov, "Who to Include in Your Household"; Michelmore and Pilkauskas, "The Earned Income Tax Credit, Family Complexity, and Children's Living Arrangements."

31. IRS, "Publication 501 (2023), Dependents, Standard Deduction, and Filing Information."

32. Michelmore and Pilkauskas, "The Earned Income Tax Credit, Family Complexity, and Children's Living Arrangements."

33. US Department of Agriculture, "SNAP Eligibility."

34. SNAP policy also imposes an assumption of food-sharing on some multigenerational households; adult children who are under age twenty-two are included in their parent's SNAP household, even if they purchase and prepare meals separately. See US Department of Agriculture, "SNAP Eligibility."

35. Ellen and O'Flaherty, "Social Programs and Household Size"; Corinth, "How Safety Net Programs Tax the Sharing of Housing." Additionally, some zoning ordinances explicitly ban certain doubled-up households, which reifies the nuclear family household ideal and may weaken the private safety net. Some ordinances have limited whether householders can share their home with individuals outside their family, as defined by blood, marriage, and adoption. Other local governments have gone further, narrowing their definition of a family in zoning ordinances to "immediate relatives" or explicitly excluding extended relations, such as cousins, from their definition of a family (see Maldonado, "Sharing a House but Not a Household"; Waters, "Where Living with Friends Is Still Technically Illegal"). In contrast, some localities have expanded their definitions of families to include "functional families"—those individuals who have a permanent emotional bond and act like a cohesive household (for example, by sharing a single household budget and preparing and eating meals together), regardless of their biological or legal relationship (Oliveri, "Single-Family Zoning, Intimate Association, and the Right to Choose Household Companions"; Waters, "Where Living with Friends Is Still Technically Illegal").

36. Corinth, "How Safety Net Programs Tax the Sharing of Housing"; Social Security Administration, "SSI Spotlight on Living Arrangements"; Urban Institute, "Category Descriptions"; US Department of Housing and Urban Development, "Use of Shared Housing in the Housing Choice Voucher (HCV) Program."

37. Likewise, public programs with asset limits often use a single limit, regardless of the size of the household, making it more difficult for families that combine their households to meet the eligibility requirements. Ellen and O'Flaherty, "Social Programs and Household Size."

38. US Department of Agriculture, "SNAP Eligibility."

Methods Appendix

1. Cohen and Casper, "In Whose Home?"

2. Mykyta and Macartney, "Sharing a Household."

3. Keene et al., "Filling the Gaps in an Inadequate Housing Safety Net."

4. DeLuca and Jang-Trettien, "'Not Just a Lateral Move.'"

5. While I conducted supplementary fieldwork focused on doubling up, other HPHK interviewers conducted supplementary fieldwork with other subsets of parents. Because these interviews were not focused on housing and thus typically had little data relevant to the present study, I do not include them in these counts. However, these transcripts did sometimes provide helpful background information or clarifications, and where relevant, I incorporated them into my analysis.

6. Harvey, Dunifon, and Pilkauskas, "Under Whose Roof?"

7. Harvey, Dunifon, and Pilkauskas, "Under Whose Roof?"

8. Bashi, *Survival of the Knitted*; Menjívar, *Fragmented Ties*.

9. Hall, Musick, and Yi, "Living Arrangements and Household Complexity among Undocumented Immigrants"; Van Hook and Glick, "Immigration and Living Arrangements"; Sarkisian, Gerena, and Gerstel, "Extended Family Integration among Euro and Mexican Americans."

10. Leopold and Skopek, "The Demography of Grandparenthood."

11. Harvey, "When Mothers Can't 'Pay the Cost to Be the Boss,'" 278; Newman, *The Accordion Family*, 14, 115, 134.

12. Cross, "Extended Family Households among Children in the United States"; Harvey and Dunifon, "Why Mothers Double Up"; Angel and Tienda, "Determinants of Extended Household Structure."

13. Pilkauskas and Cross, "Beyond the Nuclear Family"; Harvey, Dunifon, and Pilkauskas, "Under Whose Roof?"; Amorim and Pilkauskas, "'Excess' Doubling Up during COVID."

14. Pilkauskas and Cross, "Beyond the Nuclear Family."

15. Amorim and Pilkauskas, "'Excess' Doubling Up during COVID."

REFERENCES

AARP. "AARP Financial and Legal: Family Caregiving: Long-Term Care Cost Calculator." February 9, 2022. https://www.aarp.org/caregiving/financial-legal/long-term-care-cost -calculator.html.

Abt Associates, Urban Institute, and Applied Real Estate Analysis. *Study of Rents and Rent Flexibility*. Report prepared for US Department of Housing and Urban Development, Office of Public and Indian Housing, May 26, 2010. https://www.huduser.gov/publications/pdf /Rent%20Study_Final%20Report_05-26-10.pdf.

Acosta, Sonya, and Brianna Guerrero. "Long Waitlists for Housing Vouchers Show Pressing Unmet Need for Assistance." Center for Budget and Policy Priorities, October 6, 2021. https://www.cbpp.org/research/housing/long-waitlists-for-housing-vouchers-show -pressing-unmet-need-for-assistance.

Addo, Fenaba R. "Debt, Cohabitation, and Marriage in Young Adulthood." *Demography* 51, no. 5 (September 30, 2014): 1677–1701. https://doi.org/10.1007/s13524-014-0333-6.

Administration for Children and Families. "LIHEAP FAQs for Consumers." Office of Community Services, updated June 22, 2020. https://www.acf.hhs.gov/ocs/faq/liheap-faqs -consumers.

Agius Vallejo, Jody. *Barrios to Burbs: The Making of the Mexican American Middle Class*. Stanford, CA: Stanford University Press, 2012.

Amorim, Mariana. "Are Grandparents a Blessing or a Burden? Multigenerational Coresidence and Child-Related Spending." *Social Science Research* 80 (May 2019): 132–44. https://doi.org /10.1016/j.ssresearch.2019.02.002.

Amorim, Mariana, Rachel Dunifon, and Natasha Pilkauskas. "The Magnitude and Timing of Grandparental Coresidence during Childhood in the United States." *Demographic Research* 37 (December 5, 2017): 1695–1706. https://doi.org/10.4054/DemRes.2017.37.52.

Amorim, Mariana, and Natasha Pilkauskas. "'Excess' Doubling Up during COVID: Changes in Children's Shared Living Arrangements." *Demography* 60, no. 5 (October 1, 2023): 10949975. https://doi.org/10.1215/00703370-10949975.

Amuedo-Dorantes, Catalina, and Esther Arenas-Arroyo. "Immigration Enforcement and Children's Living Arrangements." *Journal of Policy Analysis and Management* 38, no. 1 (Winter 2019): 11–40. https://doi.org/10.1002/pam.22106.

Anderson, Elijah. *Code of the Street: Decency, Violence, and the Moral Life of the Inner City*. New York: W. W. Norton & Co., 2000.

Angel, Ronald, and Marta Tienda. "Determinants of Extended Household Structure: Cultural Pattern or Economic Need?" *American Journal of Sociology* 87, no. 6 (May 1, 1982): 1360–83.

Angst, Sean, Jovanna Rosen, Soledad De Gregorio, and Gary Painter. "How Do Renters Survive Unaffordability? Household-Level Impacts of Rent Burden in Los Angeles." *Journal of Urban Affairs* (August 23, 2023): 1–24. https://doi.org/10.1080/07352166.2023.2235039.

Arnett, Jeffrey Jensen. "Emerging Adulthood: A Theory of Development from the Late Teens through the Twenties." *American Psychologist* 55, no. 5 (2000): 469–80.

Aussenberg, Randy Alison, and Gene Falk. "Supplemental Nutrition Assistance Program (SNAP): A Primer on Eligibility and Benefits." Congressional Research Service, September 8, 2023. https://crsreports.congress.gov/product/pdf/R/R42505.

Barnes, Sandra L., and Charles Jaret. "The 'American Dream' in Poor Urban Neighborhoods: An Analysis of Home Ownership Attitudes and Behavior and Financial Saving Behavior." *Sociological Focus* 36, no. 3 (August 1, 2003): 219–39. https://doi.org/10.1080/00380237.2003.10570725.

Bartram, Robin. "Routine Dilapidation: How Homeownership Creates Environmental Injustice." *City and Community* 22, no. 4 (2023): 15356841231172524. https://doi.org/10.1177/15356841231172524.

Bashi, Vilna. *Survival of the Knitted: Immigrant Social Networks in a Stratified World.* Stanford, CA: Stanford University Press, 2007.

Berg, Lonneke van den, Matthijs Kalmijn, and Thomas Leopold. "Explaining Cross-National Differences in Leaving Home." *Population, Space, and Place* 27, no. 8 (November 2021): e2476. https://doi.org/10.1002/psp.2476.

Black, Maureen M., and Katherine Nitz. "Grandmother Co-Residence, Parenting, and Child Development among Low Income, Urban Teen Mothers." *Journal of Adolescent Health* 18, no. 3 (1996): 218–26.

Blassingame, Haili. "The Joys and Pains of Multigenerational Households." 1A, WAMU, November 11, 2022. https://the1a.org/segments/the-joys-and-pains-of-multigenerational-households/.

Booth, Alan, Susan L. Brown, Nancy S. Landale, Wendy D. Manning, and Susan M. McHale, eds. *Early Adulthood in a Family Context.* New York: Springer, 2012.

Bosick, Stacey J. "'Pushed Out on My Own': The Impact of Hurricane Katrina in the Lives of Low-Income Emerging Adults." *Sociological Perspectives* 58, no. 2 (2015): 243–63.

Bouek, Jennifer W. *Everything Is Broken: Inequality and the American Childcare System.* University of California Press, forthcoming.

Briggs, Xavier de Souza. "Brown Kids in White Suburbs: Housing Mobility and the Many Faces of Social Capital." *Housing Policy Debate* 9, no. 1 (1998): 177–221.

Brooks, David. "The Nuclear Family Was a Mistake." *Atlantic*, March 2020, 19.

Bureau of Labor Statistics. "Real and Nominal Value of the Federal Minimum Wage in the United States from 1938 to 2024 (in 2024 US Dollars)." Statista, July 26, 2024. https://www.statista.com/statistics/1065466/real-nominal-value-minimum-wage-us/ (accessed September 10, 2024).

Burton, Linda M., and Sherri Lawson Clark. "Homeplace and Housing in the Lives of Low-Income Urban African American Families." In *African American Family Life: Ecological and*

Cultural Diversity, edited by Vonnie C. McLoyd, Nancy E. Hill, and Kenneth A. Dodge, 166–88. New York: Guilford Press, 2005.

Bush, Hannah, and Marybeth Shinn. "Families' Experiences of Doubling Up after Homelessness." *Cityscape* 19, no. 3 (2017): 331.

Carlson, Marcia J., and Daniel R. Meyer. "Family Complexity: Setting the Context." *Annals of the American Academy of Political and Social Science* 654, no. 1 (July 1, 2014): 6–11.

Carroll, Pattie. "Routines." University of Wisconsin–Madison Extension, Parenting the Preschooler, February 2021. https://fyi.extension.wisc.edu/parentingthepreschooler/relationships/routines/.

Castner, Laura, Breanna Wakar, Carole Trippe, and Kathy Wroblewska. "Benefit Redemption Patterns in the USDA Supplemental Nutrition Assistance Program (SNAP): Fiscal Year 2017 (Summary)." Report prepared by Insight Policy Research for the US Department of Agriculture, Food and Nutrition Service, September 2020. https://www.fns.usda.gov/sites/default/files/resource-files/SNAPEBT-BenefitRedemption-Summary.pdf.

Cavanagh, Shannon E., and Paula Fomby. "Family Instability in the Lives of American Children." *Annual Review of Sociology* 45, no. 1 (2019): 493–513. https://doi.org/10.1146/annurev-soc-073018-022633.

Cavanagh, Shannon E., and Aletha C. Huston. "Family Instability and Children's Early Problem Behavior." *Social Forces* 85, no. 1 (September 1, 2006): 551–81.

Centers for Disease Control and Prevention. "Essentials for Parenting Toddlers and Preschoolers: Building Structure." November 5, 2019. https://www.cdc.gov/parents/essentials/toddlersandpreschoolers/structure/building.html.

Chase-Lansdale, P. Lindsay, Jeanne Brooks-Gunn, and Elise Zamsky. "Young African-American Multigenerational Families in Poverty: Quality of Mothering and Grandmothering." *Child Development* 65, no. 2 (1994): 373–93.

Chaudry, Ajay, and Christopher Wimer. "Poverty Is Not Just an Indicator: The Relationship between Income, Poverty, and Child Well-Being." *Academic Pediatrics* 16, no. 3 (supplement, "Child Poverty in the United States") (April 2016): S23–S29. https://doi.org/10.1016/j.acap.2015.12.010.

Cherlin, Andrew. "Degrees of Change: An Assessment of the Deinstitutionalization of Marriage Thesis." *Journal of Marriage and Family* 82, no. 1 (February 2020): 82–80.

———. "The Deinstitutionalization of American Marriage." *Journal of Marriage and Family* 66, no. 4 (November 1, 2004): 848–61.

———. "Remarriage as an Incomplete Institution." *American Journal of Sociology* 84, no. 3 (November 1, 1978): 634–50.

Chien, Nina. "Factsheet: Estimates of Child Care Eligibility and Receipt for Fiscal Year 2019." US Department of Health and Human Services, Office of the Assistant Secretary for Planning and Evaluation, September 2022. https://aspe.hhs.gov/sites/default/files/documents/1d276a590ac166214a5415bee430d5e9/cy2019-child-care-subsidy-eligibility.pdf.

Choi, Jung Hyun. "Unmasking the Real Gender Homeownership Gap." Urban Institute, March 28, 2023. https://www.urban.org/urban-wire/unmasking-real-gender-homeownership-gap.

Clampet-Lundquist, Susan. "Finding and Keeping Affordable Housing: Analyzing the Experiences of Single-Mother Families in North Philadelphia." *Journal of Sociology and Social Welfare* 30, no. 4 (2003): 123.

Clark, Sherri Lawson, Linda M. Burton, and Chenoa A. Flippen. "Housing Dependence and Intimate Relationships in the Lives of Low-Income Puerto Rican Mothers." *Journal of Family Issues* 32, no. 3 (March 1, 2011): 369–93.

Cleveland Housing Authority. "Frequently Asked Questions." http://clevelandhousingauthority .com/FAQs/tabid/1899/Default.aspx (accessed August 20, 2014).

Cohen, Philip N., and Lynne M. Casper. "In Whose Home? Multigenerational Families in the United States, 1998–2000." *Sociological Perspectives* 45, no. 1 (March 1, 2002): 1–20. https:// doi.org/10.1525/sop.2002.45.1.1.

Collins, Caitlyn. *Making Motherhood Work: How Women Manage Careers and Caregiving.* Princeton, NJ: Princeton University Press, 2019.

Conger, Rand D., Katherine J. Conger, and Monica J. Martin. "Socioeconomic Status, Family Processes, and Individual Development." *Journal of Marriage and Family* 72, no. 3 (June 2010): 685–704. https://doi.org/10.1111/j.1741-3737.2010.00725.x.

Corinth, Kevin. "How Safety Net Programs Tax the Sharing of Housing." *Tax Notes Federal* 149 (December 14, 2015). https://www.taxnotes.com/tax-notes-federal/2015-12-14.

Coser, Lewis A., and Rose Laub Coser. "The Housewife and Her Greedy Family." In *Greedy Institutions: Patterns of Undivided Commitment,* edited by Lewis A. Coser, 89–100. New York: Free Press, 1974.

Cross, Christina J. "Extended Family Households among Children in the United States: Differences by Race/Ethnicity and Socio-economic Status." *Population Studies* 72, no. 2 (2018): 235–51. https://doi.org/10.1080/00324728.2018.1468476.

Cross, Christina J., Paula Fomby, and Bethany Letiecq. "Interlinking Structural Racism and Heteropatriarchy: Rethinking Family Structure's Effects on Child Outcomes in a Racialized, Unequal Society." *Journal of Family Theory and Review* 14, no. 3 (2022): 482–501. https://doi .org/10.1111/jftr.12458.

Dallas Housing Authority. "DHA Fact Sheet." 2012. http://www.dhadal.com/aboutDHA/2/ DHA%20Fact%20sheet (Accessed August 20, 2014).

DeLuca, Stefanie, and Christine Jang-Trettien. "'Not Just a Lateral Move': Residential Decisions and the Reproduction of Urban Inequality." *City and Community* 19, no. 3 (September 2020): 451–88. https://doi.org/10.1111/cico.12515 (accessed September 23, 2020).

DeParle, Jason. "The Coronavirus Class Divide: Space and Privacy." *New York Times,* April 12, 2020. https://www.nytimes.com/2020/04/12/us/politics/coronavirus-poverty-privacy.html.

Derenoncourt, Ellora, Claire Montialoux, and Kate Bahn. "Why Minimum Wages are a Critical Tool for Achieving Racial Justice in the US Labor Market." Washington Center for Equitable Growth, October 29, 2002. https://equitablegrowth.org/why-minimum-wages-are-a-critical -tool-for-achieving-racial-justice-in-the-u-s-labor-market/.

Desilver, Drew. "For Most US Workers, Real Wages Have Barely Budged in Decades." Pew Research Center, August 7, 2018. https://www.pewresearch.org/short-reads/2018/08/07 /for-most-us-workers-real-wages-have-barely-budged-for-decades/.

Desmond, Matthew. "Disposable Ties and the Urban Poor." *American Journal of Sociology* 117, no. 5 (March 1, 2012): 1295–1335.

———. *Evicted: Poverty and Profit in the American City.* New York: Crown, 2016.

Desmond, Matthew, Carl Gershenson, and Barbara Kiviat. "Forced Relocation and Residential Instability among Urban Renters." *Social Service Review* 89, no. 2 (2015): 227–62.

Desmond, Matthew, and Kristin L. Perkins. "Housing and Household Instability." *Urban Affairs Review* 52, no. 3 (2016): 421–36.

Deterding, Nicole M. "Instrumental and Expressive Education College Planning in the Face of Poverty." *Sociology of Education* 88, no. 4 (October 2015): 284–301. https://doi.org/10.1177/0038040715603428.

DHA Housing Solutions for North Texas. "Administrative Plan for the DHA Housing Choice Voucher Programs." September 13, 2021. https://dhantx.com/wp-content/uploads/2022/03/500-1-Admin-Plan-09.10.2021.pdf.

Docter, Benny, and Martha Galvez. "The Future of Public Housing: Public Housing Fact Sheet." Urban Institute, October 21, 2019. https://www.urban.org/sites/default/files/publication/101482/the20future20of20public20housing20public20housing20fact20sheet_0.pdf.

Domínguez, Silvia, and Celeste Watkins. "Creating Networks for Survival and Mobility: Social Capital among African-American and Latin-American Low-Income Mothers." *Social Problems* 50, no. 1 (February 1, 2003): 111–35.

Dunifon, Rachel. *You've Always Been There for Me: Understanding the Lives of Grandchildren Raised by Grandparents*. New Brunswick, NJ: Rutgers University Press, 2018.

Dunifon, Rachel, Kathleen Ziol-Guest, and Kimberly Kopko. "Grandparent Coresidence and Family Well-Being: Implications for Research and Policy." *Annals of the American Academy of Political and Social Science* 654, no. 1 (July 1, 2014): 110–26. https://doi.org/10.1177/0002716214526530.

Economic Policy Institute. "Child Care Costs in the United States." Updated October 2020. https://www.epi.org/child-care-costs-in-the-united-states/.

Edin, Kathryn, and Maria Kefalas. *Promises I Can Keep: Why Poor Women Put Motherhood before Marriage*. Berkeley: University of California Press, 2005.

Edin, Kathryn, and Laura Lein. *Making Ends Meet: How Single Mothers Survive Welfare and Low-Wage Work*. New York: Russell Sage Foundation, 1997.

Edin, Kathryn, and Timothy J. Nelson. *Doing the Best I Can: Fatherhood in the Inner City*. Berkeley: University of California Press, 2013.

Edin, Kathryn, and H. Luke Shaefer. *$2.00 a Day: Living on Almost Nothing in America*. Boston: Houghton Mifflin Harcourt, 2015.

Eickmeyer, Kasey J., Wendy D. Manning, and Susan L. Brown. "What's Mine Is Ours? Income Pooling in American Families." *Journal of Marriage and Family* 81, no. 4 (August 2019): 968–78. https://doi.org/10.1111/jomf.12565.

Ellen, Ingrid Gould, and Brendan O'Flaherty. "Social Programs and Household Size: Evidence from New York City." *Population Research and Policy Review* 26, no. 4 (July 4, 2007): 387–409. https://doi.org/10.1007/s11113-007-9036-7.

Esteve, Albert, and David S. Reher. "Trends in Living Arrangements around the World." *Population and Development Review* 50, no. 1 (March 2024): 211–32. https://doi.org/10.1111/padr.12603.

Evans, Gary W. "Child Development and the Physical Environment." *Annual Review of Psychology* 57, no. 1 (January 2006): 423–51. https://doi.org/10.1146/annurev.psych.57.102904.190057.

Eviction Lab. "National Estimates: Eviction in America." https://evictionlab.org/national-estimates/ (accessed September 24, 2020).

Faber, Jacob. "The Future of Segregation Studies: Questions, Challenges, and Opportunities." In *The Sociology of Housing: How Homes Shape Our Social Lives*, edited by Brian J. McCabe and Evan Rosen, 253–64. Chicago: University of Chicago Press, 2023.

Flanagan, Christine, and Mary Schwartz. "Rental Housing Market Condition Measures: A Comparison of US Metropolitan Areas from 2009 to 2011." *American Community Survey Briefs* (April 2014). US Census Bureau. https://www2.census.gov/library/publications /2013/acs/acsbr11-07.pdf.

Folbre, Nancy, and Julie A. Nelson. "For Love or Money—Or Both?" *Journal of Economic Perspectives* 14, no. 4 (October 1, 2000): 123–40.

Fomby, Paula, and Andrew J. Cherlin. "Family Instability and Child Well-Being." *American Sociological Review* 72, no. 2 (April 2007): 181–204. https://doi.org/10.1177/00031224 0707200203.

Fomby, Paula, and David S. Johnson. "Continuity and Change in US Children's Family Composition, 1968–2017." *Demography* 59, no. 2 (April 1, 2022): 731–60. https://doi.org/10.1215 /00703370-9783507.

Fong, Kelley. *Investigating Families: Motherhood in the Shadow of Child Protective Services*. Princeton, NJ: Princeton University Press, 2023.

Furstenberg, Frank F., Jr. "On a New Schedule: Transitions to Adulthood and Family Change." *The Future of Children* 20, no. 1 (Spring 2010): 67–87. https://doi.org/10.1353/foc.0.0038.

Furstenberg, Frank F., Jr., Sheela Kennedy, Vonnie C. McLoyd, Rubén G. Rumbaut, and Richard A. Settersten. "Growing Up Is Harder to Do." *Contexts* 3, no. 3 (August 1, 2004): 33–41.

Furstenberg, Frank F., Jr., and Christine Winquist Nord. "Parenting Apart: Patterns of Childrearing after Marital Disruption." *Journal of Marriage and Family* 47, no. 4 (November 1985): 893–904. https://doi.org/10.2307/352332.

Garnham, Juan Pablo, Carl Gershenson, and Matthew Desmond. "New Data Release Shows That 3.6 Million Eviction Cases Were Filed in the United States in 2018." Eviction Lab, July 11, 2022. https://evictionlab.org/new-eviction-data-2022/.

Garrett-Peters, Raymond, and Linda M. Burton. "Tenuous Ties: The Nature and Costs of Kin Support among Low-Income Rural Black Mothers." *Women, Gender, and Families of Color* 4, no. 1 (2016): 4–35.

Gee, Kevin A., and Minahil Asim. "Parenting While Food Insecure: Links between Adult Food Insecurity, Parenting Aggravation, and Children's Behaviors." *Journal of Family Issues* 40, no. 11 (August 2019): 1462–85. https://doi.org/10.1177/0192513X19842902.

Gennetian, Lisa A., Sharon Wolf, Heather D. Hill, and Pamela A. Morris. "Intrayear Household Income Dynamics and Adolescent School Behavior." *Demography* 52, no. 2 (March 4, 2015): 455–83. https://doi.org/10.1007/s13524-015-0370-9.

Gershoff, Elizabeth T., J. Lawrence Aber, C. Cybele Raver, and Mary Clare Lennon. "Income Is Not Enough: Incorporating Material Hardship into Models of Income Associations with Parenting and Child Development." *Child Development* 78, no. 1 (January/February 2007): 70–95. https://doi.org/10.1111/j.1467-8624.2007.00986.x.

Gerstel, Naomi, and Natalia Sarkisian. "Marriage: The Good, the Bad, and the Greedy." *Contexts* 5, no. 4 (November 2006): 16–21. https://doi.org/10.1525/ctx.2006.5.4.16.

Gibson-Davis, Christina M., Kathryn Edin, and Sara McLanahan. "High Hopes but Even Higher Expectations: The Retreat from Marriage among Low-Income Couples." *Journal of

Marriage and Family 67, no. 5 (December 2005): 1301–12. https://doi.org/10.1111/j.1741 -3737.2005.00218.x.

Giddens, Anthony. *The Transformation of Intimacy: Sexuality, Love, and Society in the Late Modern Age.* Newark, UK: Polity Press, 1992.

Glass, Jennifer, Matthew A. Andersson, and Robin W. Simon. "Parenthood and Happiness: Effects of Work-Family Reconciliation Policies in 22 OECD Countries." *American Journal of Sociology* 122, no. 3 (2016): 886–929.

Gordon, Rachel A., Lindsay P. Chase-Lansdale, and Jeanne Brooks-Gunn. "Extended Households and the Life Course of Young Mothers: Understanding the Associations Using a Sample of Mothers with Premature, Low Birth Weight Babies." *Child Development* 75, no. 4 (July 2004): 1013–38. https://doi.org/10.1111/j.1467-8624.2004.00723.x.

Gornick, Janet C., Laurie C. Maldonado, and Amanda Sheely. "Single-Parent Families and Public Policy in High-Income Countries: Introduction to the Volume." *Annals of the American Academy of Political and Social Science* 702, no. 1 (July 1, 2022): 8–18. https://doi.org/10.1177 /00027162221133250.

Guetzkow, Joshua. "Beyond Deservingness: Congressional Discourse on Poverty, 1964–1996." *Annals of the American Academy of Political and Social Science* 629, no. 1 (May 2010): 173–97. https://doi.org/10.1177/0002716209357404.

Gundersen, Craig, and James P. Ziliak. "Food Insecurity and Health Outcomes." *Health Affairs* 34, no. 11 (November 2015): 1830–39. https://doi.org/10.1377/hlthaff.2015.0645.

Hacker, Jacob S. *The Great Risk Shift: The Assault on American Jobs, Families, Health Care, and Retirement and How You Can Fight Back.* New York: Oxford University Press, 2006.

Hall, Matthew, and Kyle Crowder. "Extended-Family Resources and Racial Inequality in the Transition to Homeownership." *Social Science Research* 40, no. 6 (November 2011): 1534–46. https://doi.org/10.1016/j.ssresearch.2011.07.002.

Hall, Matthew, Kelly Musick, and Youngmin Yi. "Living Arrangements and Household Complexity among Undocumented Immigrants." *Population and Development Review* 45, no. 1 (March 2019): 81–101. https://doi.org/10.1111/padr.12227.

Halpern-Meekin, Sarah, Kathryn Edin, Laura Tach, and Jennifer Sykes. *It's Not Like I'm Poor: How Working Families Make Ends Meet in a Post-Welfare World.* Berkeley: University of California Press, 2015.

Hansen, Karen V. *Not-So-Nuclear Families: Class, Gender, and Networks of Care.* New Brunswick, NJ: Rutgers University Press, 2004.

Hao, Lingxin, and Mary C. Brinton. "Productive Activities and Support Systems of Single Mothers." *American Journal of Sociology* 102, no. 5 (March 1997): 1305–44. https://doi.org/10 .1086/231085.

Hardy, Bradley L. "Childhood Income Volatility and Adult Outcomes." *Demography* 51, no. 5 (October 4, 2014): 1641–65. https://doi.org/10.1007/s13524-014-0329-2.

Harkness, Joseph, and Sandra J. Newman. "Housing Affordability and Children's Well-Being: Evidence from the National Survey of America's Families." *Housing Policy Debate* 16, no. 2 (January 2005): 223–55. https://doi.org/10.1080/10511482.2005.9521542.

Harknett, Kristen S., and Caroline Sten Hartnett. "Who Lacks Support and Why? An Examination of Mothers' Personal Safety Nets." *Journal of Marriage and Family* 73, no. 4 (2011): 861–75. https://doi.org/10.1111/j.1741-3737.2011.00852.x.

Harvey, Hope. "Cumulative Effects of Doubling up in Childhood on Young Adult Outcomes." *Demography* 57, no. 2 (March 23, 2020): 501–28. https://doi.org/10.1007/s13524-020-00860-0.

———. "When Mothers Can't 'Pay the Cost to Be the Boss': Roles and Identity within Doubled-Up Households." *Social Problems* 69, no. 1 (2022): 261–81. https://doi.org/10.1093/socpro/spaa022.

Harvey, Hope, and Rachel Dunifon. "Why Mothers Double Up: The Role of Demographic, Economic, and Family Characteristics." *Journal of Marriage and Family* 85, no. 3 (2023): 845–68. https://doi.org/10.1111/jomf.12903.

Harvey, Hope, Rachel Dunifon, and Natasha Pilkauskas. "Under Whose Roof? Understanding the Living Arrangements of Children in Doubled-Up Households." *Demography* 58, no. 3 (2021): 821–46. https://doi.org/10.1215/00703370-9101102.

Harvey, Hope, Kelley Fong, Kathryn Edin, and Stefanie DeLuca. "Forever Homes and Temporary Stops: Housing Search Logics and Residential Selection." *Social Forces* 98, no. 4 (June 2019): 1498–1523. https://doi.org/10.1093/sf/soz110.

Harvey, Hope, and Kristin Perkins. "Shared Housing and Housing Instability." In *The Sociology of Housing: How Homes Shape Our Social Lives*, edited by Brian J. McCabe and Eva Rosen, 135–48. Chicago: University of Chicago Press, 2023.

Haurin, Donald R., Christopher E. Herbert, and Stuart S. Rosenthal. "Homeownership Gaps among Low-Income and Minority Households." *Cityscape* 9, no. 2 (2007): 5–51.

Haynie, Dana L., and Scott J. South. "Residential Mobility and Adolescent Violence." *Social Forces* 84, no. 1 (September 2005): 361–74. https://doi.org/10.1353/sof.2005.0104.

Head Start ECLKC. "The Importance of Schedules and Routines." US Department of Health and Human Services, Administration for Children and Families, Updated May 20, 2024. https://eclkc.ohs.acf.hhs.gov/about-us/article/importance-schedules-routines.

HealthCare.gov. "Count Income & Household Size: Who to Include in Your Household." https://www.healthcare.gov/income-and-household-information/household-size/ (accessed August 1, 2023).

Heflin, Colleen M., and John Iceland. "Poverty, Material Hardship, and Depression." *Social Science Quarterly* 90, no. 5 (December 2009): 1051–71. https://doi.org/10.1111/j.1540-6237.2009.00645.x.

Heflin, Colleen M., and Mary Pattillo. "Kin Effects on Black-White Account and Home Ownership." *Sociological Inquiry* 72, no. 2 (January 1, 2002): 220–39. https://doi.org/10.1111/1475-682X.00014.

———. "Poverty in the Family: Race, Siblings, and Socioeconomic Heterogeneity." *Social Science Research* 35, no. 4 (December 2006): 804–22. https://doi.org/10.1016/j.ssresearch.2004.09.002.

Henly, Julia R., Sandra K. Danziger, and Shira Offer. "The Contribution of Social Support to the Material Well-Being of Low-Income Families." *Journal of Marriage and Family* 67, no. 1 (February 2005): 122–40. https://doi.org/10.1111/j.0022-2445.2005.00010.x.

Hepburn, Peter, Renee Louis, and Matthew Desmond. "Racial and Gender Disparities among Evicted Americans." Eviction Lab, December 16, 2020. https://evictionlab.org/demographics-of-eviction/.

Hill, Heather D., Jennifer Romich, Marybeth J. Mattingly, Shomon Shamsuddin, and Hilary Wething. "An Introduction to Household Economic Instability and Social Policy." *Social Service Review* 91, no. 3 (September 2017): 371–89. https://doi.org/10.1086/694110.

Hochschild, Arlie Russell. *The Commercialization of Intimate Life: Notes from Home and Work.* Berkeley: University of California Press, 2003.

Hogan, Dennis P., Ling-Xin Hao, and William L. Parish. "Race, Kin Networks, and Assistance to Mother-Headed Families." *Social Forces* 68, no. 3 (March 1990): 797–812. https://doi.org/10.2307/2579354.

Hogendoorn, Bram, and Juho Härkönen. "Single Motherhood and Multigenerational Coresidence in Europe." *Population and Development Review* 49, no. 1 (2023): 105–33. https://doi.org/10.1111/padr.12540.

Huang, Ying, Colleen M. Heflin, and Asiya Validova. "Material Hardship, Perceived Stress, and Health in Early Adulthood." *Annals of Epidemiology* 53 (January 2021): 69–75.e3. https://doi.org/10.1016/j.annepidem.2020.08.017.

Hughes, Cayce C. "From the Long Arm of the State to Eyes on the Street: How Poor African American Mothers Navigate Surveillance in the Social Safety Net." *Journal of Contemporary Ethnography* 48, no. 3 (June 1, 2019): 339–76. https://doi.org/10.1177/0891241618784151.

Hyde, Allen, and Mary J. Fischer. "Latino Homeownership: Opportunities and Challenges in the Twenty-First Century." In *The Sociology of Housing: How Homes Shape Our Social Lives*, edited by Brian J. McCabe and Eva Rosen, 29–38. Chicago: University of Chicago Press, 2023.

Iceland, John. "Measuring Poverty with Different Units of Analysis." In *Handbook of Measurement Issues in Family Research*, edited by Sandra L. Hofferth and Lynne M. Casper, 221–33. New York: Routledge, 2013.

Institute for Research on Poverty. "How Is Poverty Measured?" University of Wisconsin-Madison. https://www.irp.wisc.edu/resources/how-is-poverty-measured/ (accessed October 12, 2021).

Internal Revenue Service (IRS). "Publication 501 (2023), Dependents, Standard Deduction, and Filing Information." 2023. https://www.irs.gov/publications/p501.

Ishizuka, Patrick. "The Economic Foundations of Cohabiting Couples' Union Transitions." *Demography* 55, no. 2 (April 2018): 535–57. https://doi.org/10.1007/s13524-018-0651-1.

Jarrett, Robin L. "Living Poor: Family Life among Single Parent, African-American Women." *Social Problems* 41, no. 1 (February 1, 1994): 30–49. https://doi.org/10.2307/3096840.

Jarrett, Robin L., and Linda M. Burton. "Dynamic Dimensions of Family Structure in Low-Income African American Families: Emergent Themes in Qualitative Research." *Journal of Comparative Family Studies* 30, no. 2 (1999): 177–87.

Joint Center for Housing Studies. "America's Rental Housing 2020." Harvard University, 2020. https://www.jchs.harvard.edu/americas-rental-housing-2020.

———. "America's Rental Housing 2024." Harvard University, 2024. https://www.jchs.harvard.edu/sites/default/files/reports/files/Harvard_JCHS_Americas_Rental_Housing_2024.pdf.

———. "Housing America's Older Adults 2023." Harvard University, 2023. https://www.jchs.harvard.edu/sites/default/files/reports/files/Harvard_JCHS_Housing_Americas_Older_Adults_2023.pdf.

———. "The State of the Nation's Housing 2017." Harvard University, 2017. https://jchs.harvard
.edu/sites/default/files/reports/files/harvard_jchs_state_of_the_nations_housing_2017
.pdf.

———. "The State of the Nation's Housing 2022." Harvard University, 2022. https://www.jchs
.harvard.edu/state-nations-housing-2022.

———. "The State of the Nation's Housing 2023." Harvard University, 2023. https://www.jchs
.harvard.edu/sites/default/files/reports/files/Harvard_JCHS_The_State_of_the
_Nations_Housing_2023.pdf.

———. "The State of the Nation's Housing 2024." Harvard University, 2024. https://www.jchs
.harvard.edu/state-nations-housing-2024.

Joughin, Charles. "Latest Economic Data Underscores the Need for Significant, Sustained Investment in Child Care and Early Learning." First Five Years Fund, December 17, 2021.
https://www.ffyf.org/latest-economic-data-underscores-the-need-for-significant-sustained
-investment-in-child-care-and-early-learning/.

Kalil, Ariel, Rebecca Ryan, and Elise Chor. "Time Investments in Children across Family Structures." *Annals of the American Academy of Political and Social Science* 654, no. 1 (July 1, 2014):
150–68. https://doi.org/10.1177/0002716214528276.

Kalleberg, Arne L. *Precarious Lives: Job Insecurity and Well-Being in Rich Democracies*. Newark,
UK: Polity Press, 2018.

———. "The Social Contract in an Era of Precarious Work." *Pathways* (Fall 2012): 3–6.
https://inequality.stanford.edu/sites/default/files/media/_media/pdf/pathways/fall_2012
/Pathways_Fall_2012%20_Kalleberg.pdf.

Kang, Jeehye, and Philip N. Cohen. "Household Extension and Employment among Asian
Immigrant Women in the United States." *Journal of Family Issues* 39, no. 1 (January 2018):
128–54. https://doi.org/10.1177/0192513X15606489.

Keene, Danya E., Penelope Schlesinger, Shannon Carter, Amila Kapetanovic, Alana Rosenberg,
and Kim M. Blankenship. "Filling the Gaps in an Inadequate Housing Safety Net: The
Experiences of Informal Housing Providers and Implications for Their Housing Security,
Health, and Well-Being." *Socius* 8 (January 1, 2022): 23780231221115283. https://doi.org/10
.1177/23780231221115283.

Kenney, Catherine. "Cohabiting Couple, Filing Jointly? Resource Pooling and US Poverty Policies." *Family Relations* 53, no. 2 (March 2004): 237–47. https://doi.org/10.1111/j.0022-2445
.2004.00014.x.

Khater, Sam, Doug McManus, and Kadiri Karamon. "Family Budget Burdens Squeezing Housing: Child Care Costs." FreddieMac, January 7, 2020. https://www.freddiemac.com/research
/insight/20200107-family-budget-burdens.

Kimbro, Rachel Tolbert, and Justin T. Denney. "Transitions into Food Insecurity Associated
with Behavioral Problems and Worse Overall Health among Children." *Health Affairs* 34,
no. 11 (November 2015): 1949–55. https://doi.org/10.1377/hlthaff.2015.0626.

Kochhar, Rakesh, and D'Vera Cohn. "Fighting Poverty in a Tough Economy, Americans Move
in with Their Relatives." Pew Research Center, October 3, 2011. https://www.pewresearch
.org/wp-content/uploads/sites/3/2011/10/Multigenerational-Households-Final1.pdf.

Korver-Glenn, Elizabeth. *Race Brokers: Housing Markets and Segregation in 21st Century Urban
America*. New York: Oxford University Press, 2021.

Krysan, Maria, and Kyle Crowder. *Cycles of Segregation: Social Processes and Residential Stratification*. New York: Russell Sage Foundation, 2017.

Kurwa, Rahim. "The New *Man in the House* Rules: How the Regulation of Housing Vouchers Turns Personal Bonds into Eviction Liabilities." *Housing Policy Debate* 30, no. 6 (August 3, 2020): 926–49. https://doi.org/10.1080/10511482.2020.1778056.

Lamont, Michèle. *The Dignity of Working Men: Morality and the Boundaries of Race, Class, and Immigration*. New York: Russell Sage Foundation, 2000.

Landale, Nancy S., Kevin J. A. Thomas, and Jennifer Van Hook. "The Living Arrangements of Children of Immigrants." *The Future of Children* 21, no. 1 (2011): 43–70.

Landivar, Liana Christin, William J. Scarborough, Caitlyn Collins, and Leah Ruppanner. "Maternal Employment Drops When Child Care Is Expensive and Hard to Find." *IRP Focus on Poverty* 39, no. 2 (January 2024): 3–7. https://www.irp.wisc.edu/wp/wp-content/uploads/2024/01/Focus-on-Poverty-39-2b.pdf.

Lee, Barrett A., Kimberly A. Tyler, and James D. Wright. "The New Homelessness Revisited." *Annual Review of Sociology* 36 (August 2010): 501–21. https://doi.org/10.1146/annurev-soc-070308-115940.

Leopold, Josh. "The Housing Needs of Rental Assistance Applicants." *Cityscape* 14, no. 2 (2012): 275–98.

Leopold, Thomas, and Jan Skopek. "The Demography of Grandparenthood: An International Profile." *Social Forces* 94, no. 2 (December 2015): 801–32. https://doi.org/10.1093/sf/sov066.

Leventhal, Tama, and Jeanne Brooks-Gunn. "The Neighborhoods They Live in: The Effects of Neighborhood Residence on Child and Adolescent Outcomes." *Psychological Bulletin* 126, no. 2 (2000): 309–37. https://doi.org/10.1037/0033-2909.126.2.309.

Leventhal, Tama, and Sandra Newman. "Housing and Child Development." *Children and Youth Services Review* ("Meeting Children's Basic Needs") 32, no. 9 (September 2010): 1165–74. https://doi.org/10.1016/j.childyouth.2010.03.008.

Lloro, Alicia, Ellen Merry, Jeff Larrimore, Jacob Lockwood, Zofsha Merchant, and Anna Tranfaglia. "Economic Well-Being of US Households in 2022." Board of Governors of the Federal Reserve System, May 2023. https://www.federalreserve.gov/publications/files/2022-report-economic-well-being-us-households-202305.pdf.

Macmillan, Ross, and Ronda Copher. "Families in the Life Course: Interdependency of Roles, Role Configurations, and Pathways." *Journal of Marriage and Family* 67, no. 4 (November 2005): 858–79. https://doi.org/10.1111/j.1741-3737.2005.00180.x.

Maldonado, Solangel. "Sharing a House but Not a Household: Extended Families and Exclusionary Zoning Forty Years after Moore." *Fordham Law Review* 85 (2017): 2641–53.

Manning, Wendy D., and Pamela J. Smock. "Measuring and Modeling Cohabitation: New Perspectives from Qualitative Data." *Journal of Marriage and Family* 67, no. 4 (November 2005): 989–1002.

Mazelis, Joan Maya. *Surviving Poverty: Creating Sustainable Ties among the Poor*. New York: New York University Press, 2017.

Mazelis, Joan Maya, and Laryssa Mykyta. "I Might Stay to Myself: Activation and Avoidance of Assistance from Kin." *Journal of Marriage and Family* 82, no. 5 (October 2020): 1479–94. https://doi.org/10.1111/jomf.12680.

McCabe, Brian J. *No Place Like Home: Wealth, Community, and the Politics of Homeownership.* New York: Oxford University Press, 2016.

McDonald, Katrina Bell, and Elizabeth M. Armstrong. "De-Romanticizing Black Intergenerational Support: The Questionable Expectations of Welfare Reform." *Journal of Marriage and Family* 63, no. 1 (2001): 213–23.

McLanahan, Sara. "Fragile Families and the Reproduction of Poverty." *Annals of the American Academy of Political and Social Science* 621, no. 1 (January 2009): 111–131.

McLanahan, Sara, and Gary D. Sandefur. *Growing Up with a Single Parent: What Hurts, What Helps.* Cambridge, MA: Harvard University Press, 1994.

McMahon, Martha. *Engendering Motherhood: Identity and Self-Transformation in Women's Lives.* New York: Guilford Press, 1995.

Menjívar, Cecilia. *Fragmented Ties: Salvadoran Immigrant Networks in America.* Berkeley: University of California Press, 2000.

Michelmore, Katherine M., and Natasha V. Pilkauskas. "The Earned Income Tax Credit, Family Complexity, and Children's Living Arrangements." *RSF: The Russell Sage Foundation Journal of the Social Sciences* 8, no. 5 (2022): 143–65.

Minkin, Rachel, Kim Parker, Juliana Menasce Horowitz, and Carolina Aragão. "Financial Help and Independence in Young Adulthood." Pew Research Center, January 25, 2024. https://www.pewresearch.org/social-trends/2024/01/25/financial-help-and-independence-in-young-adulthood/.

Mollborn, Stefanie, Paula Fomby, and Jeff A. Dennis. "Extended Household Transitions, Race/Ethnicity, and Early Childhood Cognitive Outcomes." *Social Science Research* 41, no. 5 (September 2012): 1152–65. https://doi.org/10.1016/j.ssresearch.2012.04.002.

Mollborn, Stefanie, Elizabeth Lawrence, and Elisabeth Dowling Root. "Residential Mobility across Early Childhood and Children's Kindergarten Readiness." *Demography* 55, no. 2 (April 1, 2018): 485–510. https://doi.org/10.1007/s13524-018-0652-0.

Mouw, Ted. "Sequences of Early Adult Transitions: How Variable Are They, and Does It Matter." In *On the Frontier of Adulthood: Theory, Research, and Public Policy*, edited by Richard A. Settersten Jr., Frank F. Furstenberg Jr., and Rubén G. Rumbaut, 256–91. Chicago: University of Chicago Press, 2005.

Mpondo-Dika, Ekédi. 2019. "Adversity, Ambivalence, and Mental Health: The Emotional Costs of Severe Deprivation." PhD diss., Harvard University, Cambridge, MA.

Mullainathan, Sendhil, and Eldar Shafir. *Scarcity: Why Having Too Little Means So Much.* New York: Times Books, 2013.

Mutchler, Jan E., and Lindsey A. Baker. "The Implications of Grandparent Coresidence for Economic Hardship among Children in Mother-Only Families." *Journal of Family Issues* 30, no. 11 (November 2009): 1576–97. https://doi.org/10.1177/0192513X09340527.

Mykyta, Larissa, and Suzanne Macartney. "Sharing a Household: Household Composition and Economic Well-Being: 2007–2010." *Current Population Report*, US Census Bureau, June 2012. https://www2.census.gov/library/publications/2012/demo/p60-242.pdf.

National Alliance to End Homelessness. "State of Homelessness: 2020 Edition." 2020. https://endhomelessness.org/wp-content/uploads/2022/09/StateOfHomelessness_2020.pdf.

National Center for Homeless Education. "Determining Eligibility for McKinney-Vento Rights and Services." 2021. https://nche.ed.gov/wp-content/uploads/2018/10/det_elig.pdf.

———. "The Educational Rights of Children and Youth Experiencing Homelessness: What Service Providers Need to Know." August 2018. https://nche.ed.gov/wp-content/uploads/2018/10/service_providers.pdf.

———. "Understanding Doubled-Up." https://nche.ed.gov/understanding-doubled-up/ (accessed October 4, 2019).

National Equity Atlas. "Housing Burden." https://nationalequityatlas.org/indicators/Housing_burden?breakdown=by-gender&rentown01=2 (accessed October 23, 2023).

National Low Income Housing Coalition. "The Gap: A Shortage of Affordable Homes, 2023." March 2023. https://nlihc.org/gap.

———. "Out of Reach: The High Cost of Housing." 2024. https://nlihc.org/sites/default/files/2024_OOR.pdf.

———. "Out of Reach: Texas." 2024. https://nlihc.org/oor/state/tx.

Nelson, Margaret K. "Single Mothers and Social Support: The Commitment to, and Retreat from, Reciprocity." *Qualitative Sociology* 23, no. 3 (2000): 291–317.

———. *The Social Economy of Single Motherhood: Raising Children in Rural America*. New York: Routledge, 2005.

Newman, Katherine S. *The Accordion Family: Boomerang Kids, Anxious Parents, and the Private Toll of Global Competition*. Boston: Beacon Press, 2012.

———. *No Shame in My Game: The Working Poor in the Inner City*. New York: Vintage Books, 1999.

Nock, Steven L. "A Comparison of Marriages and Cohabiting Relationships." *Journal of Family Issues* 16, no. 1 (January 1995): 53–76.

O'Brien, Rourke L. "Depleting Capital? Race, Wealth, and Informal Financial Assistance." *Social Forces* 91, no. 2 (December 2012): 375–96. https://doi.org/10.1093/sf/sos132.

Oliver, Melvin, and Thomas Shapiro. *Black Wealth/White Wealth: A New Perspective on Racial Inequality*, 2nd ed. New York: Routledge, 2006.

Oliveri, Rigel C. "Single-Family Zoning, Intimate Association, and the Right to Choose Household Companions." *Florida Law Review* 67, no. 4 (March 2016): article 8. https://scholarship.law.ufl.edu/cgi/viewcontent.cgi?httpsredir=1&article=1293&context=flr.

Olsen, Skylar. "Doubled-up for Dollars." Zillow, October 9, 2014. http://www.zillow.com/research/doubling-up-households-7947/.

Pager, Devah, and Hana Shepherd. "The Sociology of Discrimination: Racial Discrimination in Employment, Housing, Credit, and Consumer Markets." *Annual Review of Sociology* 34 (January 1, 2008): 181–209.

Parsons, Talcott. "The Social Structure of the Family." In *The Family: Its Function and Destiny*, edited by Ruth Nanda Anshen, 173–201. New York: Harper, 1949.

Pattillo, Mary. *Black Picket Fences: Privilege and Peril among the Black Middle Class*. Chicago: University of Chicago Press, 1999.

Pelletiere, Danilo. "Getting to the Heart of Housing's Fundamental Question: How Much Can a Family Afford? A Primer on Housing Affordability Standards in US Housing Policy." National Low Income Housing Coalition, 2008. http://www.ssrn.com/abstract=1132551.

Perkins, Kristin L. "Changes in Household Composition and Children's Educational Attainment." *Demography* 56, no. 2 (April 1, 2019): 525–48. https://doi.org//10.1007/s13524-018-0757-5.

———. "Household Complexity and Change among Children in the United States, 1984–2010." *Sociological Science* 4 (December 6, 2017): 701–24. https://doi.org/10.15195/v4.a29.

———. "Household Instability and Girls' Teen Childbearing." *Demography* 60, no. 6 (December 2023): 1767–89. https://www.jstor.org/stable/48770218.

Pilkauskas, Natasha V. "Three-Generation Family Households: Differences by Family Structure at Birth." *Journal of Marriage and Family* 74, no. 5 (October 2012): 931–43. https://doi.org/10.1111/j.1741-3737.2012.01008.x.

Pilkauskas, Natasha V., Mariana Amorim, and Rachel E. Dunifon. "Historical Trends in Children Living in Multigenerational Households in the United States: 1870–2018." *Demography* 57, no. 6 (October 1, 2020): 2269–96. https://doi.org/10.1007/s13524-020-00920-5.

Pilkauskas, Natasha V., and Christina Cross. "Beyond the Nuclear Family: Trends in Children Living in Shared Households." *Demography* 55, no. 6 (2018): 2283–97. https://doi.org/10.1007/s13524-018-0719-y.

Pilkauskas, Natasha V., Irwin Garfinkel, and Sara S. McLanahan. "The Prevalence and Economic Value of Doubling Up." *Demography* 51, no. 5 (October 2014): 1667–76.

Pilkauskas, Natasha V., and Melissa L. Martinson. "Three-Generation Family Households in Early Childhood: Comparisons between the United States, the United Kingdom, and Australia." *Demographic Research* 30 (2014): 1639–52.

Pilkauskas, Natasha, and Katherine Michelmore. "The Effect of the Earned Income Tax Credit on Housing and Living Arrangements." *Demography* 56, no. 4 (2019): 1303–26.

Pittman, LaShawnDa L. *Grandmothering While Black: A Twenty-First-Century Story of Love, Coercion, and Survival.* Berkeley: University of California Press, 2023.

Portes, Alejandro, and Julia Sensenbrenner. "Embeddedness and Immigration: Notes on the Social Determinants of Economic Action." *American Journal of Sociology* 98, no. 6 (1993): 1320–50.

Prager, Sarah. "When the Forms Don't Fit Your Family." *New York Times*, September 1, 2020. https://www.nytimes.com/2020/09/01/parenting/lgbtq-family-paperwork.html.

Pribesh, Shana, and Douglas B. Downey. "Why Are Residential and School Moves Associated with Poor School Performance?" *Demography* 36, no. 4 (November 1, 1999): 521–34. https://doi.org/10.2307/2648088.

Raley, R. Kelly, Inbar Weiss, Robert Reynolds, and Shannon E. Cavanagh. "Estimating Children's Household Instability between Birth and Age 18 Using Longitudinal Household Roster Data." *Demography* 56, no. 5 (August 12, 2019): 1957–73. https://doi.org/10.1007/s13524-019-00806-1.

Randles, Jennifer M. "Partnering and Parenting in Poverty: A Qualitative Analysis of a Relationship Skills Program for Low-Income, Unmarried Families." *Journal of Policy Analysis and Management* 33, no. 2 (March 2014): 385–412. https://doi.org/10.1002/pam.21742.

———. *Proposing Prosperity? Marriage Education Policy and Inequality in America.* New York: Columbia University Press, 2016.

Ratliff, Erika, and Kristin S. Seefeldt. "There's No Room, Not Even for a Dog: How Doubling Up Affects Those with Housing." Paper presented at the Martin School of Public Policy and Administration Seminar, University of Kentucky, February 26, 2021.

Reher, David S. "The Aftermath of the Demographic Transition in the Developed World: In-
terpreting Enduring Disparities in Reproductive Behavior." *Population and Development
Review* 47, no. 2 (2021): 475–503. https://doi.org/10.1111/padr.12266.

Reid, Megan. "Social Policy, 'Deservingness,' and Sociotemporal Marginalization: Katrina Sur-
vivors and FEMA." *Sociological Forum* 28, no. 4 (2013): 742–63.

Rendall, Michael S., Margaret M. Weden, and Joey Brown. "Family and Household Sources of
Poverty for Black, Hispanic, and White Newborns." *Journal of Marriage and Family* 84, no. 1
(2022): 330–46. https://doi.org/10.1111/jomf.12781.

Reyes, Adriana M. "Mitigating Poverty through the Formation of Extended Family Households: Race and Ethnic Differences." *Social Problems* 67, no. 4 (November 2020): 782–99.
https://doi.org/10.1093/socpro/spz046.

Richard, Molly K., Julie Dworkin, Katherine Grace Rule, Suniya Farooqui, Zachary Glenden-
ing, and Sam Carlson. "Quantifying Doubled-Up Homelessness: Presenting a New Measure
Using US Census Microdata." *Housing Policy Debate* 34, no. 1 (January 17, 2022): 3–24.
https://doi.org/10.1080/10511482.2021.1981976.

Roschelle, Anne R. *No More Kin: Exploring Race, Class, and Gender in Family Networks.* Thousand Oaks, CA: SAGE Publications, 1997.

Rosen, Eva. *The Voucher Promise: "Section 8" and the Fate of an American Neighborhood.* Princeton, NJ: Princeton University Press, 2020.

Rosen, Eva, and Philip M. E. Garboden. "Landlord Paternalism: Housing the Poor with a Velvet
Glove." *Social Problems* 69, no. 2 (May 2020): 470–91. https://doi.org/10.1093/socpro/spaa037.

Rosen, Eva, Philip M. E. Garboden, and Jennifer E. Cossyleon. "Racial Discrimination in Housing:
How Landlords Use Algorithms and Home Visits to Screen Tenants." *American Sociological
Review* 86, no. 5 (2021): 00031224211029618. https://doi.org/10.1177/00031224211029618.

Ross, Martha, and Nicole Bateman. "Meet the Low-Wage Workforce." Brookings, Metropolitan
Policy Program, November 2019. https://www.brookings.edu/wp-content/uploads/2019
/11/201911_Brookings-Metro_low-wage-workforce_Ross-Bateman.pdf.

Rothstein, Richard. *The Color of Law: A Forgotten History of How Our Government Segregated
America.* New York: Liveright Publishing, 2017.

Rucks-Ahidiana, Zawadi. "Housing as Capital: US Policy, Homeownership, and the Racial
Wealth Gap." In *The Sociology of Housing: How Homes Shape Our Social Lives*, edited by
Brian J. McCabe and Eva Rosen, 15–28. Chicago: University of Chicago Press, 2023.

Ruggles, Steven. "The Origins of African-American Family Structure." *American Sociological
Review* 59, no. 1 (February 1994): 136–51. https://doi.org/10.2307/2096137.

———. "The Transformation of American Family Structure." *American Historical Review* 99,
no. 1 (1994): 103–28. https://doi.org/10.2307/2166164.

Ryan, Rebecca M., Ariel Kalil, and Lindsey Leininger. "Low-Income Mothers' Private Safety
Nets and Children's Socioemotional Well-Being." *Journal of Marriage and Family* 71, no. 2
(May 2009): 278–97. https://doi.org/10.1111/j.1741-3737.2008.00599.x.

Sampson, Robert J. *Great American City: Chicago and the Enduring Neighborhood Effect.* Chicago: University of Chicago Press, 2012.

Sampson, Robert J., Jeffrey D. Morenoff, and Thomas Gannon-Rowley. "Assessing 'Neighborhood Effects': Social Processes and New Directions in Research." *Annual Review of Sociology*
28 (August 2002): 443–78.

Sarkisian, Natalia, Mariana Gerena, and Naomi Gerstel. "Extended Family Integration among Euro and Mexican Americans: Ethnicity, Gender, and Class." *Journal of Marriage and Family* 69, no. 1 (February 2007): 40–54. https://doi.org/10.1111/j.1741-3737.2006.00342.x.

Sarkisian, Natalia, and Naomi Gerstel. "Kin Support among Blacks and Whites: Race and Family Organization." *American Sociological Review* 69, no. 6 (December 2004): 812–37. https://doi.org/10.1177/000312240406900604.

———. *Nuclear Family Values, Extended Family Lives: The Power of Race, Class, and Gender*. New York: Routledge, 2012.

Sassler, Sharon, Desiree Ciambrone, and Gaelan Benway. "Are They Really Mama's Boys/Daddy's Girls? The Negotiation of Adulthood upon Returning to the Parental Home." *Sociological Forum* 23, no. 4 (December 2008): 670–98.

Sassler, Sharon, and Amanda Miller. *Cohabitation Nation: Gender, Class, and the Remaking of Relationships*. Berkeley: University of California Press, 2017.

Schneider, Daniel. "Wealth and the Marital Divide." *American Journal of Sociology* 117, no. 2 (September 2011): 627–67. https://doi.org/10.1086/661594.

Schneider, Daniel, and Kristen Harknett. "Paid Family and Medical Leave in the US Service Sector." Research brief, Harvard University, June 2021. https://shift.hks.harvard.edu/wp-content/uploads/2021/06/PMFL_Brief_6.09.21.pdf.

Scommegna, Paola. "Family Caregiving." *Today's Research on Aging* (Population Reference Bureau) 33 (February 2016). https://www.prb.org/wp-content/uploads/2016/02/TodaysResearchAging33.pdf.

Seefeldt, Kristin S. *Abandoned Families: Social Isolation in the Twenty-First Century*. New York: Russell Sage Foundation, 2016.

Seefeldt, Kristin S., and Heather Sandstrom. "When There Is No Welfare: The Income Packaging Strategies of Mothers without Earnings or Cash Assistance Following an Economic Downturn." *RSF: The Russell Sage Foundation Journal of the Social Sciences* 1, no. 1 (November 2015): 139–58. https://doi.org/10.7758/RSF.2015.1.1.08.

Seltzer, Judith A., Charles Q. Lau, and Suzanne M. Bianchi. "Doubling Up When Times Are Tough: A Study of Obligations to Share a Home in Response to Economic Hardship." *Social Science Research* 41, no. 5 (September 2012): 1307–19. https://doi.org/10.1016/j.ssresearch.2012.05.008.

Settersten, Richard, and Barbara E. Ray. *Not Quite Adults: Why 20-Somethings Are Choosing a Slower Path to Adulthood, and Why It's Good for Everyone*. New York: Bantam Books, 2010.

Shanahan, Michael J. "Pathways to Adulthood in Changing Societies: Variability and Mechanisms in Life Course Perspective." *Annual Review of Sociology* 26 (August 2000): 667–92.

Sharkey, Patrick, and Jacob W. Faber. "Where, When, Why, and for Whom Do Residential Contexts Matter? Moving Away from the Dichotomous Understanding of Neighborhood Effects." *Annual Review of Sociology* 40, no. 1 (July 2014): 559–79. https://doi.org/10.1146/annurev-soc-071913-043350.

Sharp, Gregory, Ellen Whitehead, and Matthew Hall. "Tapped Out? Racial Disparities in Extrahousehold Kin Resources and the Loss of Homeownership." *Demography* 57, no. 5 (October 1, 2020): 1903–28. https://doi.org/10.1007/s13524-020-00913-4.

Sherman, Jennifer. "Surviving the Great Recession: Growing Need and the Stigmatized Safety Net." *Social Problems* 60, no. 4 (November 1, 2013): 409–32.

————. *Those Who Work, Those Who Don't: Poverty, Morality, and Family in Rural America.* Minneapolis: University of Minnesota Press, 2009.

Short, Kathleen, and Timothy Smeeding. "Consumer Units, Households, and Sharing: A View from the Survey of Income and Program Participation (SIPP)." Presented at the University of Michigan National Poverty Center conference "Mixed Methods Research on Economic Conditions, Public Policy, and Family and Child Well-Being." Ann Arbor, June 26–28, 2005. http://www.npc.umich.edu/news/events/mixedmethods_agenda/smeedingshortfinal.pdf.

Silva, Jennifer M. *Coming Up Short: Working-Class Adulthood in an Age of Uncertainty.* New York: Oxford University Press, 2013.

Skobba, Kimberly, and Edward G. Goetz. "Doubling Up and the Erosion of Social Capital among Very Low Income Households." *International Journal of Housing Policy* 15, no. 2 (April 3, 2015): 127–47. https://doi.org/10.1080/14616718.2014.961753.

————. "Mobility Decisions of Very Low-Income Households." *Cityscape* 15, no. 2 (2013): 155–71.

Small, Mario Luis, David J. Harding, and Michèle Lamont. "Reconsidering Culture and Poverty." *Annals* 629 (May 2010): 6–27.

Smith, Sandra Susan. "'Don't Put My Name on It': Social Capital Activation and Job-Finding Assistance among the Black Urban Poor." *American Journal of Sociology* 111, no. 1 (2005): 1–57.

————. *Lone Pursuit: Distrust and Defensive Individualism among the Black Poor.* New York: Russell Sage Foundation, 2007.

Social Security Administration. "SSI Spotlight on Living Arrangements." 2024. https://www.ssa.gov/ssi/spotlights/spot-living-arrangements.htm.

Soss, Joe. "Making Clients and Citizens: Welfare Policy as a Source of Status, Belief, and Action." In *Deserving and Entitled: Social Constructions and Public Policy*, edited by Anne L. Schneider and Helen M. Ingram, 291–328. Albany: State University of New York Press, 2004.

Spitze, Glenna, and Russell Ward. "Household Labor in Intergenerational Households." *Journal of Marriage and Family* 57, no. 2 (May 1995): 355–61. https://doi.org/10.2307/353689.

St. Louis Federal Reserve Bank. "Comparing Unemployment Rates by Race: The Great Recession vs. COVID-19." The FRED Blog, May 23, 2022. https://fredblog.stlouisfed.org/2022/05/comparing-unemployment-rates-by-race-the-great-recession-vs-covid-19/.

Stack, Carol B. *All Our Kin: Strategies for Survival in a Black Community.* New York: Harper & Row, 1974.

Stack, Carol B., and Linda M. Burton. "Kinscripts." *Journal of Comparative Family Studies* 24, no. 2 (July 1, 1993): 157–70.

Steensland, Brian. "Cultural Categories and the American Welfare State: The Case of Guaranteed Income Policy." *American Journal of Sociology* 111, no. 5 (March 2006): 1273–1326. https://doi.org/10.1086/499508.

Stets, Jan E. "The Social Psychology of the Moral Identity." In *Handbook of the Sociology of Morality*, edited by Steven Hitlin and Stephen Vaisey, 385–409. New York: Springer New York, 2010.

Swenson, Kendall, and Kimberly Burgess Simms. "Increases in Out-of-Pocket Child Care Costs: 1995 to 2016." US Department of Health and Human Services, Office of the Assistant Secretary for Planning and Evaluation, May 2021. https://aspe.hhs.gov/sites/default/files/migrated_legacy_files//200606/increases-in-out-of-pocket-child-care-costs.pdf.

Tach, Laura, and Kathryn Edin. "The Social Safety Net after Welfare Reform: Recent Developments and Consequences for Household Dynamics." *Annual Review of Sociology* 43, no. 1 (2017): 541–61. https://doi.org/10.1146/annurev-soc-060116-053300.

Taylor, Keeanga-Yamahtta. *Race for Profit: How Banks and the Real Estate Industry Undermined Black Homeownership.* Chapel Hill: University of North Carolina Press, 2019.

Treas, Judith. "Money in the Bank: Transaction Costs and the Economic Organization of Marriage." *American Sociological Review* 58, no. 5 (1993): 723–34.

Uehara, Edwina. "Dual Exchange Theory, Social Networks, and Informal Social Support." *American Journal of Sociology* 96, no. 3 (November 1, 1990): 521–57.

Unger, Donald G., and Marcia Cooley. "Partner and Grandmother Contact in Black and White Teen Parent Families." *Journal of Adolescent Health* 13, no. 7 (November 1992): 546–52.

Urban Institute. "Category Descriptions: Treatment of Additional Adults in Household." The Welfare Rules Database, 2024. https://wrd.urban.org/getting-started/policy-categories/category-descriptions#Treatment_of_additional_adults_in_household.

US Census Bureau. "Cuyahoga County Quick Facts." 2014. https://www.census.gov/quickfacts/fact/table/cuyahogacountyohio,clevelandcityohio,US/PST045222 (accessed August 18, 2024).

———. "Dallas County Quick Facts." 2014. https://www.census.gov/quickfacts/fact/table/dallascountytexas,TX/PST045223 (accessed August 18, 2024).

———. "Historical Living Arrangements of Children." November 2022. https://www.census.gov/data/tables/time-series/demo/families/children.html.

US Department of Health and Human Services. "Frequently Asked Questions Related to the Poverty Guidelines and Poverty." Assistant Secretary for Planning and Evaluation. https://aspe.hhs.gov/topics/poverty-economic-mobility/poverty-guidelines/frequently-asked-questions-related-to-poverty-guidelines-poverty (accessed August 28, 2023).

US Department of Housing and Urban Development. "Use of Shared Housing in the Housing Choice Voucher (HCV) Program." PIH notice 2021-05. January 15, 2021. https://www.hud.gov/sites/dfiles/OCHCO/documents/2021-05pihn.pdf.

US Department of Labor. "State Minimum Wage Laws." Wage and Hour Division, September 30, 2023. http://www.dol.gov/agencies/whd/minimum-wage/state.

US Department of the Treasury. "The Economics of Child Care Supply in the United States." September 2021. https://home.treasury.gov/system/files/136/The-Economics-of-Childcare-Supply-09-14-final.pdf.

US Department of Agriculture. "Child Nutrition Programs: Income Eligibility Guidelines (2023–2024)." Food and Nutrition Service, February 9, 2023. https://www.fns.usda.gov/cn/fr-020923.

———. "SNAP Eligibility." Food and Nutrition Service, 2021. https://www.fns.usda.gov/snap/recipient/eligibility.

US Government Accountability Office. "Child Care: Subsidy Eligibility and Use in Fiscal Year 2019 and State Program Changes during the Pandemic." GAO-23-106073, March 29, 2023. https://www.gao.gov/products/gao-23-106073.

Vacha, Edward F., and Marguerite V. Marin. "Doubling Up: Low Income Households Sheltering the Hidden Homeless." *Journal of Sociology and Social Welfare* 20 no. 3 (September 1993): 25.

Van Hook, Jennifer, and Jennifer E. Glick. "Immigration and Living Arrangements: Moving beyond Economic Need versus Acculturation." *Demography* 44, no. 2 (May 1, 2007): 225–49. https://doi.org/10.1353/dem.2007.0019.

Wakschlag, Lauren S., P. Lindsay Chase-Lansdale, and Jeanne Brooks-Gunn. "Not Just 'Ghosts in the Nursery': Contemporaneous Intergenerational Relationships and Parenting in Young African-American Families." *Child Development* 67, no. 5 (October 1, 1996): 2131–47.

Waters, Michael. "Where Living with Friends Is Still Technically Illegal." *Atlantic*, May 23, 2023.

Watkins-Hayes, Celeste, and Elyse Kovalsky. "The Discourse of Deservingness: Morality and the Dilemmas of Poverty Relief in Debate and Practice." In *The Oxford Handbook of the Social Science of Poverty*, edited by David Brady and Linda M. Burton, 193–220. Oxford: Oxford University Press, 2016.

Weiss, Elayne. "Housing Access for People with Criminal Records." In *National Low Income Housing Coalition: 2019 Advocate's Guide*, 2019, 6–27–6–33. https://nlihc.org/sites/default/files/AG-2019/06-07_Housing-Access-Criminal-Records.pdf.

Welsh, Whitney, and Linda M. Burton. "Home, Heart, and Being Latina: Housing and Intimate Relationship Power among Low-Income Mexican Mothers." *Sociology of Race and Ethnicity* 2, no. 3 (July 1, 2016): 307–22.

Western, Bruce, Deirdre Bloome, Benjamin Sosnaud, and Laura Tach. "Economic Insecurity and Social Stratification." *Annual Review of Sociology* 38, no. 1 (2012): 341–59. https://doi.org/10.1146/annurev-soc-071811-145434.

Western, Bruce, Deirdre Bloome, Benjamin Sosnaud, and Laura M. Tach. "Trends in Income Insecurity among US Children, 1984–2010." *Demography* 53 (April 2016): 419–47. https://doi.org/10.1007/s13524-016-0463-0.

Westrick-Payne, Krista K., and Corrine E. Wiborg. "Children's Family Structure, 2021." Family Profile 26. Bowling Green State University, National Center for Family and Marriage Research, 2021. https://doi.org/10.25035/ncfmr/fp-21-26.

Wherry, Frederick F., Kristin S. Seefeldt, and Anthony S. Alvarez. "To Lend or Not to Lend to Friends and Kin: Awkwardness, Obfuscation, and Negative Reciprocity." *Social Forces* 98, no. 2 (December 2019): 753–93. https://doi.org/10.1093/sf/soy127.

Whitehead, Ellen. "Paying for Their Stay: Race, Coresiding Arrangements, and Rent Payments among Fragile Families." *Journal of Family Issues* 39, no. 17 (December 2018): 4041–65. https://doi.org/10.1177/0192513X18804287.

Whitney, Peyton. "More than 42 Million US Households Were Cost Burdened in 2022." Joint Center for Housing Studies at Harvard University, January 19, 2024. https://www.jchs.harvard.edu/blog/more-42-million-us-households-were-cost-burdened-2022.

Wu, Lawrence L., and Brian C. Martinson. "Family Structure and the Risk of a Premarital Birth." *American Sociological Review* 58, no. 2 (April 1993): 210–32. https://doi.org/10.2307/2095967.

INDEX

Eduardo (friend of Carlos), 125–26
educational attainment, 8–9; household instability inversely linked to, 174
elder care, 138
energy costs, 4
Erica (girlfriend of Eduardo), 125–26
Eva (guest), 21, 120–23, 194–97, 210–11
eviction, 3, 86; appeals of, 78, 164; of host, 108; informal, 40, 197; records of, 28, 109, 119, 159, 171
Ezra (son of Lauren), 45–46, 48

family complexity, 9, 12
Federal Emergency Management Agency (FEMA), 12, 231n63
food insecurity, 105, 161
food stamps (Supplemental Nutrition Assistance Program, SNAP), 1, 84, 87, 96, 98, 102–3, 105, 122, 156, 162; eligibility for, 103, 167, 209, 210; insufficiency of, 103; pooling of, 84, 95, 102–3, 162; sale of, 108, 116
foster parenting, 144, 207, 243n18
"functional families," 248n35

Gabby (guest), 19–20, 31–34, 42–43
Gail (host and guest), 53–57, 60, 98
Garfinkel, Irwin, 96
gender: cultural expectations and, 55, 59–60, 115, 121–25, 131, 150; household authority and, 74–76; housework and, 121, 242n10; housing conditions and, 177; in labor market, 3, 198; men's vs. women's coresidence and, 125; poverty risk and, 3
Gerstel, Naomi, 10
gig economy, 2
Gilbert (father of Jennifer), 187, 188
Gram (mother of Annalise's stepfather), 139–41, 143, 145, 147
grandparents, 8, 11, 16, 46, 134–35, 199–200, 204
Granny (grandmother of TaKayla), 69–72, 74, 112–13
Great Recession, 93

guests, 27–44; age of, 59–60; crises motivating, 39–42; income of, 106; in-kind support from, 98–99; natal home of, 36–39; rental payments from, 52–56, 62, 77, 97–98, 99, 101–3, 129; voluntary, 31–36

Hansen, Karen, 10, 109
Head Start, 13, 209
Hochschild, Arlie, 105–6
homelessness, 20, 116, 199, 229–30n41, 232–33n2, 244–45n10; doubling up likened to, 28, 29
homeownership, 32
hosts, 45–65; cost of being, 60–61; income of, 106; self-worth of, 204
household complexity, 13–15
housework, 106
Housing Choice Voucher Program, 86, 184
How Parents House Kids (HPHK), 15–16, 17, 19, 217–18, 222
Hurricane Katrina (2005), 12

immigrants, 19
incarceration, 1, 51, 116, 133, 146, 157
income pooling, 93
incomplete institutionalization, 14, 201, 209
indebtedness, 33
in-kind support, from guests, 98–99
instability, of households, 14–15; children damaged by, 160; as economic instability, 161–64; hosts' feelings of, 167–70; household space and, 235n15; positive outcomes of, 178–79, 186; programmatic stability vs., 208–9; as residential instability, 164–66; subjective feeling of, 166–67, 208; types of, 159; unexpected, 183, 185
Internal Revenue Service (IRS), 13, 209
Isa (guest), 1, 6, 7, 13, 132–39, 143, 151; child-rearing by, 21; religious beliefs of, 137, 139; residential independence idealized by, 150

Jasmine (friend of Ron), 61, 62–63, 86
JC (host), 20, 51–53, 57–58, 60